An exciting portrait of how the Buddha and meditators since his time have gone back into raw nature to try to understand themselves and humanity's place in the world.
Jack Kornfield, guiding teacher of the Spirit Rock Meditation Center and author of many books on meditation.

An astonishing fusion of interpretation and inspiration distilled over a lifetime of study of both natural history and the Buddhist dharma.
Wade Davis, *National Geographic* Explorer in Residence, and author of *Into the Silence, One River,* and *The Serpent and the Rainbow*.

As Buddhist meditation becomes ever more widely practiced today, it is vital to recognize its intimate connection to the natural world. In returning us to the sources of the tradition, Charles Fisher's timely book affirms how mindfulness is inseparable from a heightened awareness of the sublime and fragile environment of which we are inextricably tied through every breath we take.
Stephen Batchelor, author of *Confession of a Buddhist Atheist*.

"... nature is fundamentally unreliable, mostly uncomfortable. Nature is too cold, too hot, too windy. It opens us to what is. That is the Dharma. We work with that." This is just one of many kernels of wisdom Charlie Fisher reveals for us in his astonishing distillation of Buddhism's fundamental connection to the natural world. For those who care about the environment, this book is an important reminder of the need for frequent, contemplative reconnection with nature in order to best protect it.

Jon Miceler, Eastern Himalayas and Mainland Asia Programs World Wildlife Fund

---

Meditation in the Wild: Buddhism's Origin in the Heart of Nature follows up on Fisher's earlier *Dismantling Discontent: Buddha's Way Through Darwin's World*, which showed how Buddhism didn't come out of nowhere but was a measured response to restore a natural animal being in a world that had been truncated—phenomenologically bulldozed—in the wake of encroaching civilization. *Meditation in the Wild* backs up and extends that most credible thesis, but here he zeros in on centuries of Buddhist adepts, forest monks and mountain meditators whose varied practices illuminate the historical roots and natural context of the practice that Alan Watts called the no-religion religion. Studded with poetry, historical details, and level-headed analysis, Fisher again proves a most credible guide to the modern relevance of an ancient tradition.

Dorion Sagan, science writer, author of *Notes from the Holocene*.

Intriguing and insightful, *Meditation in the Wild* hits a sweet spot between Buddhism and the environment. Charlie Fisher asserts that Buddhist practice must be understood in the context of closeness with wild nature—the context in which Buddha himself attained enlightenment. As a professor and a scholar, Charlie has clearly broken new ground. Through a detailed exploration of the writings and stories of past Buddhist masters, he reveals the details of how wild nature aided their quest for enlightenment. As a man (and longtime meditator) who has himself lived close to the wilderness much of his life, Charlie's authentic connection to the wild shines through on every page, especially as he describes his close encounters with bears and wolves. The teaching tools of the wild are sometimes harsh: fear, cold, hunger, loneliness. Yet from them the sages learned to let go of ego, cease grasping, and find their place in the natural world. It's a lesson all humanity must take to heart.

Tim Ward, author of *What the Buddha Never Taught*: a "behind the robes" account of life in a Thai forest monastery.

Meditation in the Wild:

Buddhism's Origin in
the Heart of Nature

Meditation in the Wild:

Buddhism's Origin in
the Heart of Nature

Charles S. Fisher Ph.D.

**CHANGE
MAKERS
BOOKS**

Winchester, UK
Washington, USA

First published by Changemakers Books, 2013
Changemakers Books is an imprint of John Hunt Publishing Ltd., Laurel House, Station Approach,
Alresford, Hants, SO24 9JH, UK
office1@jhpbooks.net
www.johnhuntpublishing.com
www.changemakers-books.com

For distributor details and how to order please visit the 'Ordering' section on our website.

Text copyright: Charles S. Fisher 2013

ISBN: 978 1 78099 692 9

A CIP catalogue record for this book is available from the British Library.

Design: Stuart Davies

Printed and bound by CPI Group (UK) Ltd, Croydon, CR0 4YY

We operate a distinctive and ethical publishing philosophy in all
areas of our business, from our global network of authors to
production and worldwide distribution.

CONTENTS

To
My colleague and friend
Maurice Stein
Who played
Shih-te to my Han-shan
In the University

Foreword

I first met Charlie Fisher in the spring of 1976 in a plant taxonomy class at Harvard College. I was one of a dozen undergraduates. He was an older man, very warm and friendly, with a sparkle in his eye and a manner that was immediately engaging. He had a naturalist's love of plants and was auditing the course just for fun. From his dress he might have been a carpenter or mechanic, a gardener, or indeed a forest monk. He described himself simply as a teacher.

Charlie loved the New England woods, and I especially enjoyed his company on our field trips, as he spotted and identified birds on the wing, turned over rocks and rotting logs with the delight of a child, or peered into the calyx of a blossom held to the light in his calloused hand.

Toward the end of the semester Charlie asked me about my summer plans. I was in fact on my way to work as a park ranger on Haida Gwaii, a remote archipelago off the northwest coast of British Columbia then known as the Queen Charlotte Islands. I mentioned only that I was heading home to Canada to a place he most likely had never heard about.

Not only did Charlie know the islands, he confessed that he had a prized and much coveted graduate student living there doing her dissertation research. It was only then, several months after we had met, that I learned that Charlie, having received a doctorate in mathematics from UC Berkeley, was a tenured professor of sociology at Brandeis, with academic interests that ranged across the widest possible sweep of intellectual curiosity and ambition. Such modesty was irresistible.

Over the years Charlie became many things to me—friend, brother, confessor, mentor, guide, confident, savior, counselor, and so much more. I have never known a wiser or more constant friend, or a more inspired teacher. And I watched with great compassion and interest as this son of a Chicago stockyard merchant who made his trade in the wholesale distribution of animal entrails turned his vision and heart to the pursuit of a spiritual path that took him from the remote reaches of India to dharma communities scattered from Boston to Santa Fe, Seattle to Carmel.

Charlie chose always to live a simple life of intention and care, trading his wizardly ability as an electrician and mechanic for time and teachings at retreat centers where such practical skills were rare and much in demand. He was the ultimate houseguest. Both literally and metaphorically, in every situation and encounter, he always gave far more than he took.

The great beneficiaries of Charlie's spiritual travels and devotional practice were his students at Brandeis, where he taught meditation for 20 or more years. His was an unusual academic career, for he had little interest in conventional research, and no ability whatsoever to put his own needs as a scholar above those of his students. In his wisdom he always understood that the student is as important as the mentor in the lineage of knowledge.

My only concern over the years was a fear that this extraordinary repository of knowledge, this wonderful man who seemed to know everything about everything, would slip into the Bardo without having left a tangible record of his insights and intuitions, this astonishing fusion of interpretation and inspiration distilled over a lifetime of study of both natural history and the Buddhist dharma.

Happily, with his retirement from the university Charlie unexpectedly launched the download so many of us had been fervently anticipating. In his first book, *Dismantling Discontent*, he traced the manner by which the contemplative path of Buddhist practice arose as a treatment or antidote to the existential discontent, always part of the human condition, that became ever more acute and magnified with the rise of agriculture and ultimately industrial civilization. Viewing the Neolithic revolution of but 12,000 years ago, when the poetry of the shaman became the prose of the priesthood, and humanity succumbed to the cult of the seed, through the lens of Darwinian evolution, Charlie revealed how the practical techniques of Buddhism are more applicable than ever in our modern world. His new book, *Meditation in the Wild*, is in a certain sense a companion of *Dismantling Discontent*.

Meditation in the Wild is magical, luminous, accessible, and revelatory in a manner unlike anything he has previously written. A product of a dozen years of research, the book leaves little doubt that the potential of the Buddhist path is as relevant today as it was at the inception of the Dharma 2,500 years ago. Charlie reveals the very source of the Buddha's inspiration and knowledge, the fountain from which Shakyamuni drank, the wild and untamed forests where all of life, every sentient creature, is and will always be engaged in the primal struggle of existence.

Why the Buddhist lens you may ask? What is it about this science of the mind, this baroque and wordless evocation of the divine that deserves and commands our attention?

The essence of the Buddhist path is distilled in the Four Noble Truths. All life is suffering. By this the Buddha did not mean that all life was negation, but only that terrible things happen. Evil was not exceptional but part of the existing order of things, a consequence of human actions or karma. The cause of suffering was ignorance. By ignorance the Buddha did not mean stupidity. He meant the tendency of human beings to cling to the cruel illusion of their own permanence and centrality, their isolation and separation from the stream of universal existence. The third of the Noble Truths was the revelation that ignorance could be overcome, and the fourth and most essential was the delineation of a contemplative practice that, if followed, promised an end to suffering and a true liberation and transformation of the human heart. The goal was not to escape the world but to escape being enslaved by it. The purpose of practice was not the elimination of self but the annihilation of ignorance and the unmasking of the true Buddha nature, which like a buried jewel shines bright within every human being waiting to be revealed. The Buddha's transmission, in short, offered nothing less than a road map to a clear understanding of existence.

The Buddhists speak not of sin and judgment, of good and evil, but only of ignorance and suffering, with all emphasis being on compassion. To take refuge in the Buddha demands no act of blind faith and certainly implies no mandate to go out and persuade the rest of the world to think as you think. At its core, as Charlie always taught, Buddhism is simply a wisdom philosophy, a set of contemplative practices, a spiritual path informed by 2,500 years of empirical observation and deduction that, if followed, offers the possibility of a transformation of the human heart. It may be hard to understand what all of this means, but the struggles of wild meditators, as Charlie illustrates, are examples.

Wild meditators lived in a context where things we spend most of our lives pretending do not exist were ever-present. We dwell in a whirlwind of activity, racing against time, defining success by measures of the material world, wealth and achievements, credentials of one sort or another. For the Buddha this is the essence of ignorance. He reminds us that all life grows old and that all possessions decay. Every moment is precious and we all have a choice, to continue on the spinning carousel of delusion or to step off. The Buddha offered an alternative that is not dogma but a path requiring much effort. With each breath the pilgrim moves that much closer to his or her goal, which is not a place but a state of mind; not a destination but a way of living.

In the *Diamond Sutra*, the Buddha cautions that the world is fleeting, like a candle in the wind, a phantom, a dream, the light of stars fading with the dawn. It is upon this insight that Mahayanists measure their past and chart their future. This leaves us to ask how we possibly allow so much sorrow to sweep through the world, like the wrath of China in Tibet, the rain of death from drones, or killing in the name of religion.

This is something that Charlie Fisher understands in the very fiber of his being. Meditation taught by the Buddha is a physician's tool kit addressing our discontent. Charlie is drawn to practice because of its fundamental honesty. Meditation does not need to proselytize. The fruit it bears will be found in its doing. What's more, Buddhism does not claim any monopoly on the truth. Meditation aims to be a science of the mind that transforms individuals and gives a clearer view of the human condition. It states very directly that the goal is not to convert people but to contribute to their wellbeing. Meditation is but a guidebook describing a pathway to wisdom and non-harming. A meditator, Charlie often says, seeks simply to understand. All life is part of nature and faces nature's challenges. Meditation is an effort to penetrate everything that hides this. It is a process of purification, not of original sin but of the multiple layers that conceal reality from us.

The goal is not to escape the world, but to avoid being enslaved by it. The world is not bad; the problem is the way we perceive it and the manner in which these perceptions trap us in the vicious cycle of the world of existences. Our sense of a form or object as being desirable or undesirable does not reside in the object but in the way we perceive it. As a Zen master famously wrote: "To her lover a beautiful woman is a delight; to an ascetic a distraction; to a wolf a good meal."

Buddhism does not neglect the material needs of humanity. It simply suggests that satisfying external needs is not enough. To neglect internal development in favor of material development can have harmful consequences, because it is from the external world that come intolerance and aggression, war, the insatiable thirst to possess, the pursuit of power, and selfishness. To seek happiness through worldly pursuits is as hopeless as casting fishing nets into a dry riverbed.

Yet the Buddha offered a solution, a technique of understanding. And it was this that led Charlie to spend a good measure of his final years writing these astonishing books. Every science, Charlie once told me, has its own instruments. Without a telescope you can't see the craters of the moon. Without contemplative practice, you can't see the nature of mind. The meditative process allows a hermit to see how the mind operates, and find a calm relationship to it. Charlie likes the forest monk Ajaan Cha's characterization of the mind as a still forest pool. When the mind is not focused, the water remains murky. Focus the mind and the pool and its visitors can be seen. The goal is inner simplicity and awareness, freedom not of thoughts but of the harm that mindless thinking can initiate. It is neither submission nor resignation.

Bending toward peace is the ultimate proof of the efficacy of the science of the mind that is meditation. Like a mountain the wind cannot shake, a meditator achieves an inner equanimity that is neither apathy nor indifference but rather clarity of action which may range from sitting quietly on a mountain top to raising a family to engaging in political struggle.

Meditators in the wild, whose lives Charlie traces, endeavored to find meaning and inner peace away from the distractions which society so abundantly offers. How their endeavors contrast to our existence can give us insight into the challenges we face.

Wade Davis
Explorer in Residence
National Geographic Society
www.daviswade.com

Preface

In the summer of 2010 I headed 2,500 miles northward toward Telegraph Creek in the coastal mountains of northwestern British Columbia. I usually spend a month or two there at my brother's homestead. I travel in my old Dodge van with a bed in the back. I had been on the road for eight days when I arrived at my friend Wade Davis' summer place, an old fishing lodge on Ealue Lake (pronounced Eya-luweh by the local First Nations, meaning sky fish) in the Skeena Mountains about five hours southeast of my brother's place. I got there a few days in advance of Wade and his family. I wanted to spend that time sitting quietly. As my van came to a stop near the lake, I noticed a bird pecking away in the fire pit. Surprised, it flew up into the nearby spruce, then settled again among the ashes. I knew right away it was a bird I had never seen. Grabbing my binoculars I saw for the first time a white-winged crossbill, an interruptive species whose flocks grace a lucky northerner who chances to see them. It flew off, and I proceeded to set up camp. During the day I sat meditating on Wade's dock, looking out at the lake. Over the years my meditation has gotten simpler and simpler. I just sit and listen and feel the changes in wind and weather. While sitting I realized that there was fluttering behind me, so I turned to watch a family of crossbills doing their odd behavior of jumping down to a cave-like opening at the base of a tree and rummaging in the litter there. There was mom, dad, and several fledglings. Since crossbills, as their name indicates, have crossed bills, which allow them to specialize in extracting seeds from evergreen cones, I found their behavior intriguing. I assumed they were hunting for insects, which is often the food they feed their young. It was peaceful sitting on the dock, silently watching the sun cross the sky, listening to the sounds of nature, and simply being with exotic creatures like a crossbill. After a few days so spent I thought I would take a walk over to a nearby abandoned campground. I headed out to the road, down it a short way, and then onto the rutted entrance of the old campground. My mind was at rest, so I was very alert. The brush along the entrance was quite thick. A couple of hundred feet in I stopped short, noticing a large bear at the edge of the roadway. It saw me at exactly the same time I saw it but grunted in surprise. It was a beautiful gold color with dark head and extended muzzle. I thought at once, "grizzly," but wasn't sure. I am very familiar with black bear behavior, but my encounters with grizzlies have been few. It clearly didn't care for my presence and backed away into the dense brush, peeking out at me. My curiosity got the better of my discretion. I looked at it through my binoculars, wanting to see if it had a hump, which would have confirmed it was a grizzly. So I scraped my foot on the ground. Its curiosity also overcame its fear. It returned to the edge of the road but then defied my understanding of correct behavior and kept advancing toward me. Instantly my calm vanished, and I could feel my heart beating. I slowly walked backward toward the road then retreated back to Wade's place. A beeline between the campground and the lodge was a mere hundred feet of tall grass, and when I returned to sitting on the dock I faced inland in the direction the bear would have come. My sitting had changed.

This sort of experience was central to the practice of many forest monks in the millennia after the Buddha. They left the civilized world to face life and death in the wilds. Their sojourns became the stuff of myth, canonized by their monastery brethren. The reality of their experiences was somewhat different. This reality can be excavated from the stories told about them but also from journals, poetry, and art they left behind. It is a scanty history, much of which can be inferred by comparing it to live experiences. In the past 20 to 30 years nature has become popular. It is a diverse kind of popularity. There is armchair enjoyment of movies about birds and penguins, with truly breathtaking shots (but these are also a construct of technology). Bird watching has become the most popular hobby in the United States. Although often done without much physical effort, it has gotten people out of doors and encouraged them to pay attention to nature. There is also a newfound enjoyment of physical effort, which can range from mountain biking to skiing glaciers to hikes in the mountains with the latest camping equipment or what is now called extreme sport, such as rocketing down a class five river in a tiny, rolling, one-person kayak. Each of these is a kind of reconnection to nature. Preceding these activities were the spiritual nature poets of our day. They not only create paeans of nature but offer nature as a solace for our worldly troubles. Their sentiments are offered both as therapy and as inspiration for understanding our place in a larger world. All of these modern activities intersect with what forest monks were trying to achieve, but removing themselves from society with little to protect them was crucial to the monks' lives. This made them different. While they could not escape the neurochemicals, like endorphins and cortisol, that life in the wild elicited, they sought to conquer them or die trying. Without discounting our lives and sentiments it is interesting to examine this difference. It will give us new insights into the world where we live and the struggles we have.

After my encounter with the bear my meditation changed. While sitting on the dock looking landward my alertness increased. It took a while for my heart to stop beating so distinctly. That night my sleep was filled with inchoate fear, so I got up and sat for some time and watched as the fear melted away. Emotions are such curious things. The bear had violated my understanding of distance. Later, when I heard stories of others' encounters with this bear, my sense that its behavior was odd was confirmed. It also occurred to me that it found me strange too. I made the mistake of staring at it with binoculars. It couldn't see my eyes, crucial to identifying me as a human. It must have thought me like C-3PO and wanted to investigate.

In 1977 I was on sabbatical from the University and going

through a personal crisis. I sat crossed-legged for a month-long meditation retreat at the Insight Meditation Society in Barre, Massachusetts. I had never meditated before. After that retreat I balanced my teaching with a month or two of retreats a year and time spent in the garden growing vegetables. A few years after my initial retreat I had the opportunity to sit with Ajaan Cha, a revered forest monk, during his one visit to the United States. Ajaan Cha strongly influenced me, although at the time I had no understanding of forest practice or its principles.

In the years that followed, during the course of my sojourns in various rural and wilderness places, I found myself meditating more and more out of doors. My life seemed to be drawing closer to nature. Meditating in the woods or on mountains deepened my sense of belonging in the wilds. As my experiences grew, I began to bring what I learned into my classrooms. Ironically, I had to teach mostly by metaphor, since the reality of life out of doors was alien to my urban and suburban students.

The effort to convey a clear understanding of this kind of meditation sent me into the library to find what I could about the forest tradition that Ajaan Cha represented. While doing this research and talking with those few people who had contact with actual forest practice I began to realize I had been meditating in the spirit of Ajaan Cha, who spent days wandering in the jungles of Southeast Asia. I came to see that I had much rapport with Chinese recluses and Zen Hermits, about whom I had known little. If I had to claim a lineage of teachers, I would undoubtedly claim them. This book and its companion on natural history and meditation, *Dismantling Discontent: Buddha's Way Through Darwin's World*, represent explorations of the unexpected extent to which nature informs Buddhist practice. Buddhism, I argue, is indissociable from the realization that nature is the mind's greatest teacher. Just as Renaissance scientists found they had to study nature directly, and not depend too much on ancient texts, so the Buddhist contemplator can return to nature. Ironically, they will need to clear the mind of both society's delusions and of confusing and sometimes misleading texts preserved by monastic traditions far removed from Buddhism's wild sources. My research was both exciting and frustrating. I found tantalizing anecdotes about the forest traditions, but knew from my own experience that there was much more to these wild ones than had been preserved in books. Because most civilized monks and scholars who preserved or translated the tales of forest monks had little experience with either forest practice or nature, I had to read between the lines. To do so I drew on my own practice and familiarity with nature. Even as I was originally writing this I was aware of the quarter-inch-long wolf spider crawling up the power cord of my computer. She leapt back and forth between cord and computer in a fruitless search for an insect on which to pounce. Would a forest monk leave this spider alone, knowing that it might starve in my house so lacking in its prey? Or should I carry the wolf spider outside and let it take its chances there? In the past I have meditated out of doors, sitting silently next to a spider web for days and days until its creator died. Although it may seem ludicrous, I would argue such experiences are profoundly valuable, providing lessons I have yet to fully assimilate. Then there was the time when I was pre-walking a field trip for First Nation youngsters in a dark, woody swamp. As I and my guide approached the edge of the swamp we were greeted by three wolf pups expecting their mother, who was off hunting. As my guide fumbled in his rain gear for his bear spray, the pups retreated into the bush. His instinct was self-preservation. The little gray wolf wagged its tail like a happy puppy, but a black one had eyes that burned with a wildness that riveted my attention as it backed away. I simply wanted to sit with these beasts of the woods as a forest monk might have, harmlessly sharing both the familiar and the wild, forsaking self-defense in order to learn the meaning of life and death.

One of the purposes in writing this book and its companion

on natural history and meditation, *Dismantling Discontent: Buddha's Way Through Darwin's World*, is to speak to meditators about the traditions that some only vaguely understand. Like my students, most meditators are only dimly aware of how nature operates and how much some of what they practice was developed in environments much closer to nature than we now have available to us. How did the recluses and forest monks pioneer the practice of meditation in the wilds? This question seems more than pertinent for people now so interested in Buddhism, nature, and how the two interrelate. I emphasize that because of how we live and what we believe: We have many illusions about nature, and meditation is often presented without the context in which it developed. The forest monks are perhaps the best example of seekers who know how to see and express the silence that is inherent in the flow of a nature completely indifferent to human aspirations. By stepping out of the illusions created by civilization, they were able to observe how nature teaches Buddha's lessons.

My goal is for readers to gain an appreciation of the forest tradition. You may try sitting quietly out of doors wherever you can find a bit of silence to experience firsthand, your mind embedded in the ever-changing natural context. I firmly believe that tasting a bit of forest practice can change how one understands our world. This, in turn, may help in enabling us to live in it with more love and less harming. Meditating on nature may permit us to achieve *something like* oneness with nature, both nature within and the nature around us, with which we have tended to lose contact over the course of civilization.

A Note on Citations: Although this is a book with scholarly elements, in the interest of narrative flow, I have collectively footnoted chains of quotes; interested readers will find complete references in the Bibliography and Further Reading. Also, I have continued to use earlier conventions of transliteration of Asian words and names.

Acknowledgements

I am sort of a traveler in the wilderness, so should have sought more assistance along the way than I did. Nonetheless, a number of people have helped me. They include Dorion Sagan who rode herd on earlier versions of my manuscript; Lynn Margulis, who, despite her questions about religious matters, was encouraging; Jack Kornfield, whose teacher Ajaan Cha was the paradigm of a forest monk; Maury Stein, whose abiding faith in my abilities keeps me going; Wade Davis, with whom I share a love of nature, history, and writing; Tim Ward, whose experiences in a Thai monastery and interest in nature were background to an enthusiastic reading of my manuscript; and Sangeet Duchane for her editorial skill.

Permissions

I wish to acknowledge and thank the following authors, literary heirs, and publishing companies for granting me permission to reproduce translations of the poems of recluses, hermits, and forest monks. Extensive attempts have been made to locate the rights for all translations. Some translators, literary heirs, or publishers have not responded, could not be found, or have not made themselves known.

#23 (18 lines) from *The Way According to Lao Tzu* © W. Bynner, © renewed 1972 by Dorothy Chauvenet and Paul Horgan. Reprinted by permission of HarperCollins Publisher.

Basho, M. (1966). *The Narrow Road to the Deep North* (N. Yuasa, Trans.). By permission of Penguin UK.

Basho, M. (1986). *Back Roads to Far Towns* (Trans., C. Corman). Fredonia, NY: White Pine Press. By permission of White Pine Press.

Cold Mountain excerpts from *The Collected Poems of Cold Mountain* © 2000 by Red Pine, both reprinted with the permission of The Permission Company, Inc. on behalf of Copper Canyon Press, coppercanyonpress.org

Copyright © 1978 by Robert Aitken from *A Zen Wave*. Reprinted by permission of Counterpoint.

Excerpts from "Chinese-style Poems" and "Dogen's Teaching"" from "Introduction" from *Moon In A Dewdrop: Writings of Zen Master Dogen*, edited by Kazuaki Tanahashi. Copyright © 1985 by the San Francisco Zen Center. Reprinted by permission of North Point Press, a division of Farrar, Straus and Giroux, LLC.

Feng-kan. (1984). *From Temple Walls, the Collected Poems of Big Shield and Pickup* (Red Pine, Trans.). Port Townsend, WA: Empty Bowl. By permission of Bill Porter (aka Red Pine) ©.

Han Shan (1969). *Cold Mountain* (G. Snyder, Trans.). San Francisco: Four Seasons © 2009 by Gary Snyder from *Riprap and*

Cold Mountain Poems. Reprinted by permission of Counterpoint Press

Hori, I. (1968). *Folk Religion in Japan*. By permission of the University of Chicago Press.

Ikkyu. (1986). *Ikkyu and the Crazy Cloud Anthology* (Arntzen, S., Trans.). Tokyo: University of Tokyo. By Permission of Prof. Arntzen ©.

Issa, *The Dumpling Field*. Copyright © 1991 L. Stryk. This material is used by permission of Ohio University Press, www.ohioswallow.com

Poem reprinted from *The First Buddhist Women: Translations and Commentary on the Therigatha* (1991) by Susan Murcott with permission of Parallax Press, Berkeley, California, www.parallax.org

Poems from *Basho and his Interpreters, Selected Hokku with Commentary* by Makoto Ueda. Copyright © by the Board of Trustees of the Leland Stanford Jr. University. All rights reserved. Used with the Permission of Stanford University Press, www.sup.org

Poems of a Mountain Home by Burton Watson. Copyright © 1991 Columbia University Press. Reprinted with permission of the publisher.

Pollack, D. (1985). *Zen Poems of the Five Mountains*. New York: Crossroad. By permission of Professor Pollack ©.

Rational Zen: The Mind of Dogen Zenji, translated and edited by Thomas Cleary, ©1992 by Thomas Cleary. Reprinted by arrangement with Shambhala Publications Inc., Boston, MA, www.shambhala.com

Ryokan, *The Zen Poems of Ryokan* © 1981 by Princeton University Press. Reprinted by permission of Princeton University Press.

Seaton, J. P. & Maloney, D. (Eds.). (1994). *A Drifting Boat*. Fredonia, NY: White Pine Press. By permission of White Pine Press.

Stevens, J. (1993). *Three Zen Masters*. Tokyo: Kodansha by permission of the author.

T'ao Ch'ien excerpts from "Back Home Again Chant," from *Selected Poems of T'ao Chien* © 1993 by David Hinton.

The Zen Works of Stonehouse. Copyright © 1999 by Red Pine (Bill Porter). Reprinted by permission of Counterpoint.

Tu Fu (1988). *Facing the Snow* (S. Hamill, Trans). Fredonia, NY: White Pine Press. By permission of White Pine Press.

Unpublished poem translated by J. Seaton and J. Sanford quoted in LaFleur, W., 1988. *Buddhism.* Permission granted by the translators.

Chapter I

Wilderness as Teacher

And all is seared with trade; bleared, smeared with toil;
And wears man's smudge; and shares man's smell: the soil
Is bare now, nor can foot feel, being shod.
Gerard Manley Hopkins

It is difficult for us to imagine what life was like for the Buddha 2,500 years ago in the forests of India, but we can try. Equipped with a begging bowl, a rough-woven insect net, and cotton robes made from rags, the Buddha sat quietly or walked peacefully in a landscape where poisonous snakes abounded, dangerous animals roamed, and insects were unavoidable. As the Buddha wandered he sought an end to the suffering that so often plagues humans. For the Buddha, the forests helped reveal the character of human discontent. The wilds challenged his humanity and gave him insight into how human suffering can be overcome.

Every week or so I drive a few miles to a meditation retreat on several thousand acres of land, a few miles from the Pacific Ocean in northern California. When it is not too rainy or cold I sit for hours out of doors. Sometimes, as my mind quiets down and I become aware of my surroundings, I hear different birds singing. A song sparrow defines its territory in the masses of periwinkle spreading next to the lawn, or I watch a black phoebe fledgling noisily begging its parent for food. High up in the trees, acorn woodpeckers may chatter at each other. An anise swallowtail butterfly with a piece missing from its wing sweeps by. When the other sounds of nature subside, I sometimes hear exotic fallow deer (from Europe) and axis deer (from India), who graze among the cows, talking to each other with little whimpering sounds. And during rutting season, alpha bucks gather harems and patrol them trumpeting warnings to potential interlopers. Their calls suggest the sounds of the barking deer forest monks mention. Even in this setting, which bears the stamp of human domestication, I am impressed by how much nature proceeds without any concern for my individual desires or the industry that provides for my needs. I could sit quietly season after season, and unless they were kept at bay by mowing and brush cutting, the trees would fill the pasture in, the buildings would crumble, different birds would come and feed butterflies to their young, and the number of deer would decline as the forests regrew and coyotes and mountain lions became emboldened.

In contrast to sounds of nature are the penetrating sounds of society. Behind the bird songs is the ever-present hum of cars and airplanes. The ringing bell of a large machine penetrates the silence. The retreat center's tractor can be heard; so can a vacuum cleaner in the building. I am, after all, meditating in a religious institution, which, although it offers a bit of quiet, is part of our sprawling human civilization. In my earlier work, *Dismantling Discontent: Buddha's Way Through Darwin's World*, I argued that the essence of Buddhist meditation practice can be traced to the radical changes from a foraging to an agricultural society. This move to a sedentary life from one of day-to-day survival in nature was, I argued, crucial in exacerbating the conditions that lead to discontent. In addition, during the centuries since Buddha the material progress of civilization has brought along with it an increase in the sources of our discontent, specifically, chronic medical conditions, extended old age, a drawn out "conversation with death," and ever more seductive ways of living in our heads. In *Dismantling Discontent* I advanced the thesis that Buddha's practices were designed to address precisely the sort of discontent magnified first by agricultural and then industrial civilization, and I tried to show that Buddhist meditation, insofar as it is effective, is as pertinent and potent now as it was in

Buddha's times, or more so. These ideas are further illustrated in the experiences of forest monks who turned their backs on civilization's amplification of discontent to investigate it in the wilds, where discontent originally evolved as a part of our animal nature.

While the Buddha did go forth into the forests, he came from a civilization already in the process of taming the wild. Upon achieving a new understanding of human nature, he returned to his civilized world and taught. Most of his followers, and the religions which they supported, were creatures of society. And yet the Buddha of the wilds stands in contrast to much of the Buddhist religion and institutions that claim him as their founder.

This contradiction is one that I will address and, ultimately, dissolve. While Buddhism as we know it today has been thoroughly (and sometimes surreptitiously) civilized, it is less well-known that the Buddha inspired a tradition of forest meditators. These meditators sought an understanding of their humanity by returning to the wilds. Of course, what we know of them comes down through historical reports, adulterated, as it were, by civilization. Thus, we must make a leap of faith in attempting to retrieve from Buddhist texts the experience of early Buddhists meditating in the wild. The effort is well worth making, as it can instruct us on ways to re-place ourselves in nature, both in mind and body.

The wilderness-oriented followers of Buddha included renunciants in ancient India, the Buddhist recluses of China who struggled with their strident civilization, eccentric Zen hermits living in the Japanese mountains, and early twentieth-century forest monks in Southeast Asia, who returned to the jungles just as their societies began to emerge into the modern world. Although the story of the Buddha's sojourn in the forests, like the story of Jesus' in the desert, is an important Buddhist tale, and a few other forest monks achieved notoriety, the tradition of forest practice has not received its public due. Playing a shadowy role, it was praised but seldom undertaken. We will look at what the forest tradition has to offer and why it has remained a mere icon. To understand its marginality we must appreciate the historical marginalization of nature itself. Because technology so permeates our existence and promises to cure our physical and emotional ailments, we have lost sight of nature and its potential to teach to us the meaning of our existence. In contrast to most modern city dwellers, suburbanites, and even farmers, the Buddha and his forest followers attended deeply to the nonhuman, and more-than-human, lessons of nature.

I live in Marin County, north across Golden Gate Bridge from San Francisco. Marin is one of the wealthiest counties in the United States. Its wealth has allowed it to preserve much of its beautiful landscape. Still, its multilane highways are congested with oversized cars driven by cell phone-toting drivers whose spacious homes are well endowed with computers, large televisions, kitchen machinery, and stereos.

In the post-modern world, of which Marin is an extreme example, daily life is filled with conveniences. The human body seems only accidental to survival. When people exercise, they often use machines, and nature is experienced through enhanced media or out of a car window. Our contact with the earth is mediated by ergonomically designed running shoes and Spandex clothes. When we experience the out of doors, it is from groomed trails, a mountain bike, or with high-tech camping equipment. An increasing amount of the work people do uses few of the capabilities designed into our bodies. The life humans led for 100,000 years of hunting and gathering, several thousand years of agricultural civilization, and even a few hundred years of early industry has little meaning. No longer do we know what it is like to forage in a world of hot and cold, a world where physical survival was often in question.

Modern civilization confers conveniences upon its citizens

that would have been inconceivable several hundred years ago. We live, on average, almost *three times as long* as past humans. Infections, once the scourge of the very young and the reason most people never reached old age, are now held at bay. The amount of raw physical power which is available to an average person today matches only what royalty of past civilizations could command. We speak of horsepower with little understanding what it means. A 160-horsepower car is equivalent to a team of horses much larger than was ever assembled to harvest grain on the Great Plains in the days just before the gasoline engine became available. A picture of 50 horses pulling a giant harvester in 1900 is impressive, but step on the gas, and those horses are put to shame. Watch a high-rise office building go up in a couple of months and imagine the years and lives that it took to build a pyramid. From electric can openers to leaf blowers and riding mowers, from jet planes to email to surround sound, from vaccination to antibiotics to knee replacements, we live in a world where pristine nature has been greatly supplemented and the limitations of our ancestral environments have been radically exceeded.

But are we human beings in general better off now in how we feel about ourselves or how we behave toward others? Material progress does not translate directly into greater self-content or kindliness. One still wonders how a people as prosperous, intelligent, and civilized as the Germans could do what they did under the Nazis. And the questions linger as to how Americans could have dropped so many millions of tons of bombs on the peasants of Southeast Asia, or the Yugoslavs, after years of living and working together, could turn on each other with barbaric ferocity. Although poverty may contribute to violence, its opposite, material prosperity, does not ensure humane treatment of others. Ajaan Cha, a well-known forest monk, observed that when a society obtains electric lights, the inner lights of its inhabitants become dim.

Nor is individual happiness a necessary byproduct of material abundance. Many studies indicate that wealth does not confer happiness. A myriad of social statistics identify the post-World War II period with the breakdown of families and increases in psychiatric problems, social isolation, depression, and problems of self-esteem. In many ways, consumption has replaced traditional relationships. Children come home to watch television or play on computers for many hours of their waking day. Paid childcare has replaced kin, and Smartphones are preferred to the live interaction of traditional human play. Because of physical inactivity and convenience foods, obesity has become epidemic, leading to diabetes and other diseases. Behavior modification drugs are given to millions of children and adults with attention deficit disorder and depression. Rising rates of hearing disability among young adults is directly linked to the use of personal stereos that assault the ears and remove the listener into a private world. Cell phone users seem unconscious of how they disrupt public spaces or endanger others.

Although the enumeration of such facts can be interpreted as a criticism of modernity, they are simply current versions of problems that may be no worse than those of past societies. There is research which shows that the traditional family never matched our romantic ideas of it. In agricultural societies, for example, there was incest and child labor, and though extended families may have been tighter units, there was psychological abuse. Anthropology has presented evidence that hunter-gatherer societies were rife with personal violence and not immune to psychological problems. It is an open question whether post-industrial society has progressed socially.

Nonetheless, one thing is clear: We are much more cut off from nature than our predecessors. Indeed, it is difficult for us to see the extent to which we have become so isolated. Lucy, our *Australopithecus* ancestor, walking the savanna of Africa with her mate (as is so humanly displayed in a diorama in the Museum of

Natural History in New York) is a complete stranger to our contemporary sentiments.[1] We feel the common link when looking at her reconstructed body and environment, but we have little idea what it might have been like to rest silently in nature, acting out the demands of survival and procreation. Lucy possessed all the responses of fear, anger, aggression, desire, love, nurturance, and sharing that we possess. But she likely experienced them without the worry, anxiety, fantasy, and obsessive anger that so occupy us. She lived without thought as we know it. She also lived her life immersed in nature. It was where she had to find her food, connect to her mate, bear young, and defend herself against predators and the elements. And though her social connection to other members of her group would have given her some power of abstraction, it is likely that she experienced minimal mental and material separation. Life may well have been presented to her with an immediacy of which we can barely imagine. But was Lucy happy or not? This is impossible to say. It is clear that she did not experience road rage or issues of self-esteem. Those are problems ushered in with language and reinforced by the lifestyle civilization affords. They are also problems which spiritual seekers have sought to address. From shamans in hunter-gatherer societies to the holy persons of great religions, people have been offered remedies for unhappiness and an end to human violence. These have included promises of paradise or reincarnation to be achieved through ritual, prayer, sacrifice, or meditation. Such solutions were very much a product of the societies in which they arose.

In my previous book, looking through a lens of Darwinian evolution, I showed how Buddha's techniques are more applicable than ever in our modern world. In this book, I want to focus more directly on the untamed forests as the source of the knowledge Buddha acquired, and how his practice there was enhanced by those who followed and imitated him.

Buddhism was the first world religion. It arose in India as

agricultural civilization was beginning to consolidate and spread. With armies and merchants, Buddhism was carried into Central Asia, South Asia, Southeast Asia, and the Far East. During its first half century it was embraced by millions of people in many different forms. Like Judaism, Christianity, Hinduism, and Islam, the Buddhist religion came to terms with the rulers, priests, military, and peasantry of different cultures. Buddhism became very much a part of the societies into which it diffused. But there were also parts of Buddhism which could not so easily be assimilated. One reason for this, I propose, is the birth of Buddhism in the wilds from which civilizations were becoming progressively alienated.

Buddhism was born in the forests of India when those forests still covered much of the landscape. The Buddha found his original revelation while practicing as a forest monk. He brought something from his time in the forests back into the society he had left. He developed an understanding of nature which would become part of the remedy he proposed for the problem of human discontent. In his own search he turned his back on the conveniences of his society in order to look anew at what it means to be human. Without necessarily knowing it he chose wild nature—the evolutionary context in which humans arose— as the place to do this. He turned to the setting in which Lucy lived in order to understand how to cure problems his humanity and his civilization had created. He explored the character of human discontent in wild nature where life and death were ever present. He went to a place in the human mind where there is understanding without words.

Some of the other world religions have enjoined strategies similar to that developed in Buddha's return to the forests. Five hundred years into Chinese civilization the Taoists looked backward to nature as a remedy for the stress they experienced while running the growing Chinese state. The Jews began as a wandering pastoral people and spawned sects who withdrew into the hills and caves, away from the Jewish theocracy that eventually developed. Jesus went off into the desert as part of his own search. His example inspired a lineage of desert fathers, and Hinduism grew out of an ancient tradition of forest Brahmans, of which Buddha might qualify as an example. Heirs of these forest Brahmans, joining with devotional sects, existed in Buddhist India until invading Muslims destroyed Buddhism and composite Hinduism emerged as the predominant religion. An original picture of peoples tied to the earth can be found in many of the world religions. Whether they grew from reclusive ancients, forest wanderers, sheep herders, nomadic desert dwellers, or peasant farmers, religions drew morals from these simpler beginnings and applied them to the more civilized social settings where they ruled.

In our modern world, we search around for models of how to live. We know that there is something "out of balance." Life is too complex, stress almost omnipresent. There is just too much to do in order to make a living and run a family. People carry tiny computers to communicate and keep track of their complicated lives. They are reminded of family events and check on the weather; family and weather used to be the organizing principles of daily life but now are obscured by technology. There are an overwhelming number of choices for food, transportation, housing, and entertainment. Consuming is sometimes all-consuming. A video store contains 5,000 to 10,000 choices, and Walmart may stock 100,000 items. Then there is the problem of health, both physical and mental, and the survival of the disabled and elderly. In the midst of all this simpler times seem to offer an escape from the problems of the modern world. Such yearning creates the interest in writing and movies about nature, and this yearning is a bona fide emotion with connections to the heart of Buddhism.

In my earlier book on the origins of human discontent, I offered a way of understanding how our discontent came into existence and what part of our biological makeup it is.[2] In that book both natural history and meditation are presented as tools for understanding our civilized predicament. By seeing humans as part of wild nature out of which we arose and by examining how nature continues to penetrate our technically sophisticated world, we can begin to understand why we stubbornly embrace the trends of technological society that sustain us, even as they increase our discontent.

Although the Buddha could not have imagined automobiles, the Internet, virtual reality, or jet planes, he had great insight into the sources of human discontent which his own society engendered. His childhood as the royal prince, Siddhartha, was endowed with all the luxury his civilization could afford. Born in the sixth century BCE, Siddhartha's agricultural clan provided him with food in abundance, a primitive palace, and all the pleasures and crafts that military security, artisans, servants, slaves, and concubines could offer. Knowing nothing of movies, frozen gourmet dinners, or microwaves, Siddhartha was regaled by storytellers, enchanted by dancers, and offered any delicacy his kingdom could obtain. Wandering from this pleasure palace, he chanced upon disease, old age, death, and a mendicant who he was told had taken the path of renunciation in order to overcome human suffering. The inevitability of disease, old age, and death so disturbed Siddhartha that he forsook his home and went forth into the forests to find relief through self-abnegation. He realized that his palace protected no one from the inexorable processes of nature. For all his bounty was worth (and the more it gave pleasure, the more one might suffer its absence), everything that Prince Siddhartha held dear would not last.

In the forests Siddhartha observed that the human mind created the illusion of permanence. People lived as if pleasure would continue and pain was avoidable. Because of this attitude people could not handle the disappointment that came when nature caught up with them. For Siddhartha, grasping pleasure and denying pain was at the heart of human discontent. Society, with its creature comforts and entertainment, helped sustain the illusion.

Siddhartha chose to withdraw from society's illusions and immerse himself in the wilds. Only there, he felt, could he see through his suffering. In the forest Siddhartha encountered life and death in the raw, unmediated by social connections and the distractions of civilization. After following a number of teachers to no avail, Siddhartha settled under a Bodhi tree, vowing not to move until he either died or found surcease. While he was rooted to that tree undiluted nature presented itself to him and he saw through his own illusions. He observed how the human mind grasps hold of desire and pushes away objects which are unpleasant. In seeing this clearly and letting go of it, Siddhartha gained freedom. He became "awakened" or enlightened. He was henceforth a Buddha, an "awakened one": one who sees clearly.

The method which emerged from his struggles was meditation, and for the next 50 years of his life he taught many ways of doing meditation. He offered techniques to observe how body and mind worked. Meditation became a method for exploring discontent, and the Buddha, sitting cross-legged in nature, was iconic to Buddhists over the next 2,500 years.

As Jesus suffering on the cross became the key symbol of Christianity, so the Buddha wandering the forests and sitting under the Bodhi tree has been central to Buddhism. Yet while the idea of returning to the wilds became a basic part of Buddhist tradition, the actual practice was rarely done. Buddhism, like the other world religions, held its charismatic leader up as a model but domesticated religious practice to fit within the bosom of the societies which sponsored it. In the millennia-long history of Buddhism there were as few forest monks as there were desert fathers in Christianity. World religions have been religions of civil societies—of royalty, soldiers, merchants, and peasants. The practices civil societies encouraged included prayer, ritual, and meditation, practices that fit nicely into the dominant civil order. So, while honor was paid to charismatic founders and their anti-social behavior, for followers religious practice was largely confined to homes, churches, and monasteries, or within the context of governments and armies. It was all well and good for saints to wrestle with gods, demons, or ultimate meaning on mountain tops, in darks woods, and barren deserts. But ordinary believers, as well as the priests and monks ministering to them, were expected to have their religious experiences in more domesticated settings. Obscured as it may be by keepers of religious tradition, the friction between wild roots and domestication stands out in Buddhism, because Siddhartha's formative experiences *away* from civilization were canonized and later monks tried to imitate his efforts.

Looking back over the 2,500-year history of Buddhism we can find a narrow thread of practitioners who took seriously the Buddha's recommendation to forsake society. The individuals and movements that embraced life in the wilderness were few and far between. For those of us wishing to learn from Buddha's forays and those he inspired, it is not always easy to separate truth from legend. So many myths have been spun around charismatic forest practitioners that it is difficult to know what they really did and experienced. Nonetheless, some records have been left by individuals and lineages who did meditate in wild places. It is to these crucial sources that I turn.

The traditions for which I have been able to find sufficient evidence fall into four main groups: the Buddha and some immediate followers, Chinese recluses, Japanese Zen hermits, and the forest monks of Southeast Asia. Influenced by the example which the Buddha set, some monks wandered through the forests of ancient India and South Asia. They attempted to carry on forest practice with the authenticity of Buddha. Their practice was abetted by the fact that agricultural land had not yet swallowed up most of the wilderness. Monks and nuns who lived as neighbors to wildlands could easily access nature and use it as a setting for their practice.

The second group we explore consisted of the recluses of China. When Buddhism reached China about the time of Jesus, it found the most developed civilization in the world. The Chinese had dynastic chronicles going back 1,000 years or more. Chinese agriculture and crafts supported a widespread, prosperous civilization, in contrast to which Rome appeared backward and the rest of the world, well, primitive. In China the Mahayana Buddhist concept of Buddha-nature encountered the Taoist ideal of living "naturally" (as opposed to conforming to the social mores of the orderly Confucian state). Combining Mahayana and Taoism, some Chinese Buddhists founded a tradition of recluses who withdrew from society to meditate and contemplate life. These recluses left poems and paintings.

A third group of wild meditators was made up of the Zen hermits of Japan. Haiku poets, Japanese landscape painters, and contemporary Americans who studied Zen, tea ceremony, gardening, and poetry in Japan give us a sense of an underlying rapport between Zen and nature. There is much in this picture that is accurate, but there are also complexities which are less apparent. When Buddhism arrived in Japan in the sixth century the Japanese were arguably much closer to nature than the Chinese (whose civilization was much older). Living at the transition between hunting-gathering and agriculture the Japanese retained a connection to nature through the realities of their daily lives, the harshness of their landscape, and Shintoism, which had roots in nature deities. As the Japanese became more civilized, both by imitating their dominant Chinese neighbors and reacting against them, some Buddhist meditators emulated the Chinese recluses. As they were both materially and sentimentally closer to nature than the Chinese, I will argue that it was easier for the Japanese recluses to be in tune with the raw, wild sources of Buddhism, but that they also fell prey to some of the same romantic posturing that was more pronounced in Chinese practice. The final group we will investigate is made up of the forest monks of Southeast Asia. Beginning with two monks in the late nineteenth century, a tradition of forest renunciation developed. Surrounded by the jungles of Northeast Thailand, monks, reared in a world of slash-and-burn farmers, read recently translated commentaries that inspired them to emulate the Buddha. Living in a landscape similar to the Buddha's time and dedicating themselves to meditation, the monks went forth into the forests. It seemed as if the texts had been scribed with their very situation in mind, which in a sense they had. One monk, Ajaan Mun, was such a charismatic practitioner that he inspired many others, until he became the informal head of a movement of several hundred monks wandering the forests from Laos and Cambodia across Thailand to Burma. Thus, from the last part of the nineteenth century until overwhelmed by the modern world in 1969, a living forest tradition flourished in Southeast Asia—one which bore similarities to that of Buddha's day.

To understand forest practitioners I will call upon natural history, geography, and anthropology. India, China, Japan, and Southeast Asia possess specific sets of flora, fauna, geomorphology, climate, agriculture, material economy, and natural resources that contribute to the histories of the humans living there. In each country the relationship between people and their environments changed. The peoples of these regions, now named for their nation-states, went from being hunter-gatherers to early agriculturists and herders and finally builders of civilizations. Their specific relationship to nature influenced their Buddhism and the forest practice they undertook. My claim that geography and natural history influenced Buddhism and practice in these Asian countries continues the ideas I developed in *Dismantling Discontent: Buddha's Way Through Darwin's World* of the crucial role of nature in understanding Buddha's message about civilization's discontents.

In the scholarly disciplines of environmental history and anthropology, human culture is seen to be influenced by the settings in which it occurs. The contrast between the historical cultures we are considering and the outlook of North Americans is an important ingredient in our understanding of meditation in the wilds. Our relationship to nature is a crucial part of how we act on a daily basis, our popular culture, our beliefs about life, and the way we think about nature. Although our culture will influence any picture we draw of the past, by understanding how earlier cultures related to nature we can gain insight into how our own views are limited.

In the spirit of environmental history and anthropology, I will begin each chapter with a sketch of the geographical and material setting of renunciants, as well as a depiction of the kind of society from which they withdrew. Then I will present the particular history of the forest meditators, along with how they related to the established Buddhism of their time. Of particular interest are the forest meditators' relationships to the wilds in which they immersed themselves. The recluses, hermits, and forest monks wanted to examine their humanity as it unfolded in unmediated nature. What elements of nature they were aware of and what sense they made of what they experienced helps us understand what nature really meant to them. The forest monks were neither natural historians nor hunter-gatherers. This influenced what they saw and how they understood it. Unlike our anthropoid ancestor Lucy, many of them opted out of certain survival tasks. Some forswore gathering. Others took solemn pledges not to harm any sentient being. Some lived almost like farmers. In one way or another all put themselves at the mercy of nature. We will look at the renunciants' view of wilderness and how their means of living there affected their understanding of nature and the meaning of life.

From these traditions of meditation in nature we get a sense of how limited the world we live in is and how utterly transformed our relationship to nature has become. A technological containment of nature supplies our comfort and pleasure, but it also blinds us. These wild meditators exemplify a way of seeing through the illusions of technological society. Our alienation may find ease by looking at this ancient tradition of living intimately with nature—a tradition that Siddhartha initiated while wrestling with civilization's inroads into pre-agricultural India. Forest meditators inspire us today. Stepping out of our world for a time will make us less sanguine about living in it as we have. If nature is healing, as many claim, then looking closely at forest practitioners' contact with it may help in our struggles.

Chapter 2

A Hand on the Earth: The Elders and Nature

Buddhism is a complex religion. Contemporary Western understanding of it derives largely from popularized meditation
techniques, as well as the public image of charismatic Buddhist
leaders, such as the Dalai Lama and Thich Nhat Hanh, a
Vietnamese Zen master who became famous for his opposition
to the Vietnam War and his books of poetry. For many years
Tibetan monks, driven from their homeland by the Chinese,
drew the attention of only a few Westerners who made their way
to India or Nepal. Since then, for Westerners, Tibetan Buddhism
has come to represent the Buddhist outlook on life. In the early
1990s the Dalai Lama launched a media campaign against the
Chinese occupation of Tibet. He promoted Tibetan Buddhism
and culture to the world, using it as a lever to force China to
compromise politically and grant Tibet a degree of autonomy.
Tibetan Buddhism has been the subject of movies, drawn
celebrities and film stars such as Richard Gere under its spell,
and become the premier global symbol of Buddhist practice,
happiness, and non-violence. In fact, Tibetan Buddhists
represent only a tiny minority of this 2,500-year-old religion with
adherents in 10 other Buddhist countries besides Tibet.

Similarly, popular Buddhist meditation techniques represent
a small fraction of the kinds of ways Buddhism has been
practiced throughout its history. In the West more than a half a
dozen forms of Zen are taught. They range from devotional
Chinese and Japanese chanting through Thich Nhat Hanh's
Vietnamese Zen, focused on forgiveness and non-harming, to
rigorous Korean and Japanese Zen, with their respective earthy
and highly stylized sitting practices. Of the meditation traditions

of South and Southeast Asia, Theravada Buddhism or the "Doctrine of the Elders" was brought to the West in the form of Vipassana or Insight Meditation. As a technique Vipassana is often presented with few of its original Buddhist trappings, which included village monasticism penetrating many aspects of peasant life, devotional practices, magic, and the veneration of relics. Separated from its Asian settings, Vipassana has been accessible to those Westerners not drawn to the Buddhist cultures with which other meditation techniques have been packaged.

A rough-order approximation of our distance from Buddhism can be gained by being mindful of those Buddhist images most current in the West. These include images such as the Dalai Lama sitting on a throne surrounded by pictures of wrathful deities and monks with long trumpets. He is laughing and may be speaking about complex Tibetan ideas but connecting them with great charm to the ordinary acts of life or the Chinese who are suffocating Tibetan Buddhism. There are also pictures of Caucasian monks and nuns with shaved heads in black robes synchronously chanting, ritually eating from bowls, or sitting totally still in cross-legged meditation facing the wall of an austere Japanese style Zen temple; or people in ordinary dress sitting quietly on cushions or chairs in a large meditation hall being addressed by someone who seems not too different from a friendly psychotherapist or minister.

Each of these forms of Buddhist practice has Asian roots of which most contemporary Western adherents have only the vaguest understanding. And each of the Asian traditions is itself part of a complex of competing sects that arch back to the time of the Buddha in ancient India. Theravada asserts a lineal purity derived directly from the Buddha; this is acknowledged by some Buddhist sects but contested by others. In what follows, we will touch on some of these disputes, but we will not enter them in any great detail. We wish to concentrate upon what is held in common by all the Buddhist traditions: the belief that the Buddha achieved enlightenment and that by using methods either presented by the Buddha or developed by later Buddhist saints, ordinary people can replicate the Buddha's accomplishment. Although there are some variations, the main elements of the story of the Buddha's life are believed by all of the Buddhist traditions. We mentioned in Chapter 1 that Siddhartha became distraught when he encountered the reality that humans were subject to the laws of nature. The realization that birth inevitably leads to disease or old age and death was upsetting. His abandonment of the comforts of society and his search for ways to still his troubled heart became models for the Buddhism that was built upon his endeavors. In this book we will examine two sometimes conflicting roads taken by his followers: dwelling in monasteries or temples versus actual retreat into the wilds. Most became monastics residing in monasteries built for them by the Buddhist societies in which they lived. A few tried to literally follow the Buddha's example. They withdrew to the forests to replicate his struggles and successes. Before we look at the differences between social monasticism and returning to the wilds, we need to present something about meditation, so that a reader unfamiliar with it can get some sense of what it is that the Buddha discovered, practiced, and recommended others do to address their discontent.

The sutra, or Buddhist sacred text containing the sayings of the Buddha, entitled *The Foundations of Mindfulness* has been called the heart of Buddhist meditation.[1] In this sutra the Buddha instructs meditators to pay attention to their bodies and their minds. The classical way to do so is to sit quietly under a tree and pay attention to the feel of one's breath as it enters and leaves one's body. After you are able to do that with some regularity, the Buddha suggests that you begin to observe bodily sensation. When a meditator gains this sense of bodily processes, the Buddha then suggests he or she attend to the tendency one has to draw toward things which are pleasant and push away those that are not, then the comings and goings of thought and emotions, and, finally, our being as a whole. Observation is to be done dispassionately, looking at how changeable our existence is. Sometimes our bodies have pain and our mind twists one way or another to wish it away. Sometimes thoughts are overwhelming. Sometimes there is sloth. Sometimes life is wonderful, and we think it will always be that way. And sometimes everything is very still. In whatever state existence is presented, the Buddha recommends that the meditator rests in a clear seeing of what is there and observes how each state of being comes and goes.

For the Buddha discontent with life will evaporate when we see deeply within our being that all of existence is temporary: The things we cling to will not last and we pull away from things that are unpleasant. Although he did not put it this way the Buddha was instructing his followers to examine how much they were objects of the natural world. Humans, like the rest of nature, will come and go regardless of how much one might like it to be otherwise. For the Buddha a disciplined mind observing the impermanence of existence will overcome discontent.

Meditators can also notice how much their minds themselves are an artifice in a world of change and so not cling to the claims of identity that the mind always makes. "I am a great meditator," has no more solidity than "father," "mother," "doctor," "lawyer," or psychological identities such as "I am depressed" or "I am the champ!" Without identification one might still be a good mother, and it is possible to be depressed without clinging to that identity. But although we can try to apply the Buddha's ideas in the world of work and family, the Buddha emphasized monastic renunciation. Most of what he said about meditation was within that context. Monasticism implied renouncing society for nature and, ultimately, renouncing nature itself for the greater truth of impermanence in a world of finite human duration.

The first of the Buddha's realizations is called the doctrine of impermanence: Change is inevitable. The second is the idea of no-self: Any answer to the question "Who am I?" is inadequate. The Buddha claims that a close examination of the images of the selves we hold dear will show that they lack substance. Far from being highly conceptual the Buddha's evidence for the assertion of no-self was simple and practical: The way to see that it is true is to continually examine identities whenever they are present. With concentrated attention "father" doesn't quite fit changing situations, and the way the mind holds on to the image of "father" feels stale.

The third of the Buddha's discoveries is that humans who act from their everyday minds eventually experience discontent. As long as we cling to our pleasures and try to avoid pain, there is suffering. The only way out of this dilemma is to observe our minds and bodies. By taking a seat under the Bodhi tree, Siddhartha was able to see through life's illusions and embrace the reality.

All Buddhist traditions accept this story as the core of their religion. As we will see, they added to it and introduced different ways of meditating. They also existed in very different cultural and theological contexts. Meditators who wanted to imitate the Buddha's immersion in nature had to deal with both culture and theology. For most of Buddhist history, the story of the Buddha's sojourn in nature was held in great reverence. Nonetheless, practitioners who may have wished to do the same found their way blocked by ideologies and monastic institutions. The Buddhist meditators who returned to nature represent only a fraction of those who have meditated over the centuries. Yet those who successfully made their escape show us something about the societies they lived in and how far we ourselves have drifted from the wilds which, evolutionarily, gave us existence.

Long before Siddhartha individuals withdrew from society and plunged into the forests, seeking solitude and transcendence. Over the 2,500 years since Buddha, both lone meditators and whole sects have gone to the woods or mountains to find peace. We begin with the setting in which the Buddha lived, then move to the Buddha's sojourn in the forests and his use of nature in meditation. Finally, we will look, with an eye to our own situation, at the forest practices of his followers and how civilized Buddhism regarded those practices.

Where the Buddha is thought to have lived 2,500 years ago lies in the plains of the Ganges River below the foothills of the Himalayas in India, just south of the current Indian-Nepalese border. The modern Indian states of Bihar and Uttar Pradesh cover most of the region. The climate ranges from temperate to subtropical. During the dry season temperatures can be well over 100°F. In the winter mountain temperatures go down to freezing. For four months of the summer, monsoon winds bring an average of 50 inches of rain. Swollen rivers flood the alluvial plains, carrying silt from the Himalayas and enriching the land. The Gangetic plains are the most fertile area of India. They once teemed with wildlife and a diverse flora.

In aboriginal times there were dense forests. Some locales were almost jungle. In others there were impenetrable canebrakes of bamboo. A large number of dangerous, predatory animals thrived. They included man-eating tigers, leopards, wild elephants, rhinoceroses, wild water buffalo, crocodiles, and snakes. Modern India is still plagued by poisonous snakes. There are 200,000 to 300,000 snakebites a year that result in 20,000 deaths. Dangerous snakes include cobras, kriats, and vipers.[2] Since *Homo sapiens* spread from Africa over 100,000 years ago, humans have been living as foragers on the Indian subcontinent. Starting about 10,000 years ago, Neolithic herders and agriculturists began to filter into this world of Paleolithic hunter-gatherers.

The roots of agriculture and animal husbandry in India are not clear. Perhaps rice was first domesticated in India. There is, in any case, evidence of rice's domestication on the subcontinent between 7,000 and 5,000 years ago. About 4000 BCE lentils and other pulses (edible legumes) were brought to India from the northwest. An archeological site on the northeastern edge of the area of the earliest Buddhist influence, located today in Uttar Pradesh on a tributary of the Ganges, revealed that by 600 BCE all the crops of classical ancient India had become well established. Before 1500 BCE there is evidence of double cropping of rice and barley but no surplus of food. This meant that farmers had plenty to eat but still not enough to support a more complex society. Between 1200 and 600 BCE, however, improvements in agriculture began to create surpluses. From 600 BCE on rice accounts for 98% of the cereal produced and a new highly nutritious pulse, urad, is introduced. Rice is special among grains in that improvements to irrigation systems and additional labor from growing populations produce higher yields from a given area.[3] Rice and human beings lived a kind of symbiosis. Populations of both organisms spread, laying the foundations for Eastern civilization.

From 2000 to 1500 BCE the Neolithic inhabitants of the Ganges plains and Himalayan foothills were already choosing only the high quality woods from among the large variety of native trees growing nearby. They also imported a pine from the far away Khyber Pass to be used for incense. Only one local tree was used for building. Other lumber was transported 200 kilometers or more. From 600 BCE on cedar and cypress were brought from the Himalayas. Dating from as early as 2000 to 1500 BCE hoards of copper have been found by archeologists.[4] The copper was used for tools and ornaments. In the 500 years before 500 BCE production of grains and the use of animals increased to the point that castes with rulers, soldiers, and priests could all live off of the surplus provided by peasant farmers. Little iron was used before the time of the Buddha, but iron plowshares along with the introduction of the farming technique of transplanting rice may have increased production significantly. Banana plantations and mango groves began to appear. Sugar had already been established.[5]

Around the sixth century settlements seem to have become town-like. There are differing opinions about the cities mentioned in the Buddhist sutras. Some scholars take them to have been towns, while others oversized villages.[6] Before the earliest date suggested for the Buddha's birth they were little more than collections of houses. Nonetheless, these proto-urban centers may have provided urban functions for the surrounding countryside. At the very least these ancient local centers of trade and governance would have supported specialized craftpersons.

About the middle of the second millennium Indo-Aryans, speaking Sanskrit, rode south and east from Russia and Iran. As they reached India they changed their lifestyle from being cattle-raiding nomads, cowboys on horseback, to being agriculturists who grew barley and used cattle as draft animals. As they settled in to the subcontinent they interbred with the natives, whose cultures and languages they absorbed and replaced. The Aryans brought with them a complex Brahmanism that included the Vedic myths and rituals out of which Brahmanical Hinduism was eventually born. The Brahmans were a hereditary caste who could recite the Vedas and were entitled to carry out the rituals they dictated.

The belief systems of hunter-gatherers differed greatly from those who lived off of domesticated plants and animals.[7] While both hunter-gatherers and domesticators felt that rituals and words had power in the world, hunter-gatherers communicated directly as beings who shared the same world with animal totems and spirits; agriculturists, by contrast, petitioned the gods of the elements—rain and sun gods, the goddess of the harvest, and so forth—who were seen as distant and omnipotent. At the whim of the sky and earth gods, the grain on which farmers depended thrived or was lost. If monsoon rains were late or overabundant, farming societies starved. How different this was, how much more precarious than the hunter-gatherers for whom periods of deprivation and moving to areas where resources were more abundant were a normal part of life. The animal totems of hunter-gatherers were intimate and personal. Their live counterparts were often encountered and engaged in conversation. Although agriculturists usually had domestic deities governing the household (which were akin to totems), the gods of the elements on whom their existence depended were more like the elements themselves—distant and awesome. Greek polytheism and Hebrew monotheism are closer to agricultural than hunter-gatherer belief systems.

Early Vedic Brahmans bridge the boundary between hunter-gatherer shamanism and agro-pastoral religion. The origin of the word Brahman means "to quiver." It may derive from ritual trances entered by Brahmans or by the use of a substance called *soma*—perhaps the common, moderately poisonous psychedelic mushroom, Fly Agaric (*Amanita muscaria*).[8] Some people can tolerate its toxins and eat it in relatively large amounts; others cannot, but feel psychoactive effects if they drink the urine of someone who has eaten this white-flecked, yellow or red mushroom.[9] Siberian shamans drank the urine of others or of reindeer who had eaten *muscaria*. Another's digestive system filtered out the poisons of the mushroom. Whether the Brahmanical practice of drinking small amounts of their own urine dates back to Aryan invaders of India, and whether ancient Brahmans consumed *muscaria*, is not clear. There is popular literature claiming the "apple" in the Old Testament is really a mistranslation of the word for this mushroom which, like many fungi, grows in association with certain trees.[10] In the *Vedas* soma and fire featured in ritual sacrifices of horses and cattle, sometimes involving many animals.

Brahmans were a diverse social class within their agricultural societies. Some were landowners whose spiritual activity centered around efforts to ritually maintain their purity. Others were more like casual ceremonial leaders than shamans or priests per se.[11] They functioned somewhere between the two. When magic was needed a forest Brahman was sought; when a marriage ceremony was required a village Brahman would suffice. The *Vedas* on which Brahmans drew were a collection of hymns dating from 1500 to 500 BCE composed in an older form of Sanskrit. By the sixth century BCE they were intelligible only to Brahmans specially trained to recite and interpret them. This ability, along with ritual purity, was the badge of Brahmans' spiritual authority. In the *Brahamanas*, sacred hymns of the later Vedas, there are descriptions of human sacrifice, but no one knows if such sacrifices actually took place. And part of the *Brahamanas*, called the *Aranyakas* or forest books, contains descriptions of esoteric rituals involving ceremonies, fire, and animal sacrifice, which were to be done only in the forests. As we will see, the *Aranyakas'* claim that forests were places of special power contributed to the atmosphere which led to the Buddha's retreat there.

As Brahmanism spread through northern India it interacted with local spiritual practices. *Samanas*, or recluses, had their origins among the darker skinned Dravidian peoples who populated India before the Aryans arrived. The *Samanas* appear to have been wandering teachers whose teachings may have been idiosyncratic, rather than part of a systematic belief system. Like the "quivering" from which Brahmans got their name, some *Samanas* used asceticism, self-mortification, or practices similar to yoga, fasting, and the suppression of sexual urges to create *tapas* or heat, which was reputed to confer special powers, such as fortune-telling or healing. Among the Brahmans were Vedic fire worshippers, who lived in forest huts and came to villages occasionally for provisions. Some Brahmans were unkempt, unwashed, and wild looking, sporting long hair, and soiled yellowish clothes.[12] Other *Samanas* wandered naked, surviving on wild edibles. The sometimes unsavory *Samanas* included vagabonds, astrologers, magicians, seekers, and philosophers.

The sixth and fifth centuries BCE were a time of spiritual change in central India. Brahmanism went from elaborate fire sacrifices to more subtle, internally directed rituals.

The famous *Upanishads* were compiled about 600 BCE as appendices to the *Aranyakas*. Even though they contain horse and soma sacrifices the *Upanishads* sometimes criticize ritual and expand a theme begun in the *Brahamanas* of directing attention to the meanings behind the rituals.[13] Sacrifices originated as a method to appease the gods. Some scholars see a gradual shift in the *Vedic* literature from overt actions to interior contemplation of the meaning of self and the development of power via inner ritual. This set the stage for meditation.[14]

As Brahmanism developed in the later *Vedas*, the *Aranyakas*, and the *Upanishads* existential meanings were incorporated into esoteric rituals, and meditation on symbols gradually began to take the place of sacrifice. Rituals in the earlier *Vedas* focused on success and prosperity. By the time of the *Upanishads* there was a turning inward in order to escape the endless cycle of reincarnation. Forms that this search took included asceticism, yoga, and meditation practices examining the inner nature of being. By the sixth century in India, there were many organized and individual beliefs about spirit and practice. No one viewpoint was dominant, although Brahmanism was clearly present.

Brahmanism plays such an important role as a background for early Buddhism because it is the only pre-Buddhist religion we know much about. Only one other religion contemporary with Buddhism, Jainism, has survived. Records of other beliefs, except those preserved in the texts of these current religions, are lost. Scholars debate how much Buddhism owes to Brahmanism. Some feel that the Buddha was reacting to Brahmanical beliefs. Others think there is insufficient evidence for this. Interesting discussions of how Buddhism may have related to Brahmanism are found in sources listed in the Bibliography and Further Reading.[15] Most people repeat the cliché that Buddhism grew out of Hinduism, but Hinduism is really a much later synthesis of Brahmanism and devotional beliefs in the gods of the Ramayana and the Mahabharata. It emerged in the first millennium of the Common Era.

Siddhartha Gotama was born into this pre-Hindu milieu. There are disagreements over the dates of his birth and life. He may have lived sometime between the middle of the sixth and fourth centuries BCE, that is, sometime between 580 and 370 BCE.[16] There are extensive religious histories of his life, his meditation practices, and the monastic community which followed him. But like founders of other great religions there is no contemporary non-religious evidence of his actual existence. We will draw only those parts of religious texts which are relevant to the role that nature played in the Buddha's and his followers' meditation practices.

Before we look into the situation of meditation at the time of the Buddha we need to examine some problems of historiography, that is, how the history of Buddhism we now possess was constructed. To begin, we have no evidence of writing for the Buddha's time and place. In fact, there are no surviving examples of writing from before the third century BCE.[17] There may have been some kind of account keeping. The Buddha's native language, Magadha, left no trace. The Buddhist sutras were not written down until hundreds of years after the Buddha. Religious tradition claims that these were passed down, uncorrupted, from the time of Buddha's death by monks who memorized parts of extensive narratives. There is much scholarly debate about what can be accurately known from Buddha's time. Because religious beliefs hang on the outcome of these concerns, the discussion is not dispassionate. My own predilection runs toward scientific skepticism. If there is no good independent evidence for a given conclusion then religious belief is fine, as long as we understand it to be just that, religious belief!

Even evidence for Brahmanism, which is thought to be much

more ancient, comes from *Vedic*, orally transmitted texts, rather than from archeology. Some competent authorities claim that even Brahmanical practices of the Buddha's time are uncertain.[18] As one Buddhist scholar puts it, "it has come to be widely agreed that nothing definitive can be known about the Buddha himself and the Buddhism he founded."[19] Prior to the rule of the emperor Asoka over wide areas of India in the third century BCE there is no independent evidence of the Buddha. From Asoka's time on, however, there is plenty of evidence of Buddhism.[20]

Much of the information we will use comes from the sutras and other Buddhist texts that were preserved by groups of monks. As we will see, the monks had distinct interests in what version of reality was put forward. In the sutras, there is no simple narrative of Buddha's life. Pieces of biographical information are spread throughout. Early Buddhists seemed less interested in the Buddha as an individual than as an entity of many manifestations. Not until the second century BCE was the first life of the Buddha assembled, and a more complete version was composed in the second century CE.[21]

Although the Buddha's world was a changing one, looking at it 2,500 years later, there is a tendency to see more change than the people living then actually experienced. By the Buddha's time surplus grain supported agricultural monarchies. Standing armies arose, as did long-distance trade and conflicts over sources of iron. For several hundred years prior to the Buddha people had settled along trade routes as agriculture expanded. Traders began to use accurately weighed, blank silver coins. Eliminating the need for item-by-item barter, the coins allowed commercial relationships to become more complex and fluid. Trading routes may have stretched from Central Asia to Burma. Transportation involved huge caravans of hundreds of oxen-pulled, leather-rimmed, wheeled carts traveling along rough paths. Articles traded included horses, cloth, metal, salt, and bamboo. Sandalwood was used instead of soap, which had not yet been invented. As Amerindians thought sixteenth-century European visitors stank, so must the remaining hunter-gatherers of the Buddha's time been offended by their more civilized invaders.

Because metal ore deposits lay within the jungles, miners, who were part of the agricultural civilization, needed to have friendly relations with the hunter-gatherers living there. As D. Kosambi, an authority on the material life of ancient India, characterized it:

> Beyond Gaya came the primeval forest through which hardy explorers passed to locate copper and iron ores in the hills to the south-east, the richest such deposits in India. The ore was mined and reduced on the spot, the metal brought back to be traded in the central Gangetic basin... This was Magadha's great source of power, for the state used the metal systematically to clear land and to bring it under the plow... The virgin forest which covered the greater portion of the land was infested with a thin population of food-gathering savages who still used stone axes... and would be increasingly dangerous to trade caravans as time went on. Even on the two main trade routes, this primeval forest separated the (more civilized peoples) by long distances through which the convoys had to pass with care, generally under heavy escort.[22]

So preoccupied were the people of the time with farming, trade, and politics that they no longer had any sense of what the transition from hunting-gathering lifestyle to that of a settled agricultural civilization had been like. In this they were no different from the Sumerians, the Chinese dynasties, or the Mayans. Early civilizations regarded hunter-gatherers as primitive and uncivilized, in short, barbarians.

According to the sutras Siddhartha Gotama was born into a royal family among a possibly non-Aryan people, the Sakyas, who governed by counsel rather than kingly authority. As one Buddhist scholar reconstructs it, young Siddhartha heard songs celebrating the forest, and longed to see it.[23] At age 29 he chanced upon what are called "the four signs": disease, old age, death, and meditation. Startled, he renounced his princely privileges to seek an end to suffering by adopting the life of a recluse, a *samana*. While the Buddha was sitting and meditating a wandering ascetic came by and told him of the life of forest renunciation. And so Siddhartha went deeper into the forest, begging for his food and seeking teachers. For six years he tried the prescriptions of different teachers. Some of them may have been various kinds of Brahmans, while others taught self-proclaimed truths. The first two he encountered had large followings. They could not answer his questions, so he continued his search. After wandering for some time Siddhartha settled in a forest near a large village where he could beg for alms. There he engaged in rigorous ascetic practices, including trying to cut off his thoughts, restricting his breathing, and fasting.[24]

Thich Nhat Hanh gives a modern rendition of Siddhartha's search.[25] Finding no solution in extreme asceticism, he finally settled under a tree where he was fed and given cut grass on which to sleep. There he meditated until he reached enlightenment. For the next 50 years he taught and founded a community of nuns and monks.

Although the Buddha rejected extreme asceticism for what he called "the middle way," trees and the forest retained an important role in meditation. His "awakening" took place under a wild fig tree. As the story goes, Siddhartha's final struggle was with the spirit named Mara, who represents doubt. Mara questioned Siddhartha's right to be sitting there on the earth trying to overcome suffering. In a gesture immortalized in Buddhist art Siddhartha put his hand on the earth and vanquished doubt by asserting that the earth was inanimate and, as such, it would stand as unbiased witness to the authenticity of his endeavor.[26] By invoking the authority of the earth the last stumbling block to enlightenment was swept away. Although the sutra personifies doubt it is understood that Siddhartha vanquished his own doubt by fully recognizing that nature was indeed indifferent to the hopes and despairs of humans. With this realization his attachment to greed, fear, and delusion fell away, and he became a Buddha, the awakened one, the one who sees reality clearly.

Subsequent Buddhists have given many different interpretations to his gesture. A fundamental assumption I make here is that the Buddha insisted humans can understand their inner workings only by dispassionately observing themselves as part of nature. If we can look at how our reactions fit into the larger context of nature we can see how desire and aversion trigger our discontent. The Buddha suggested that by understanding the natural roots of desire and aversion these forces will begin to weaken, taking discontent with them.

Although the Buddha did not spend much time in the wilds after he began to teach, trees and forests continued to play an important role in his teachings. He often described meditation as taking place alone in the nature: "Here a [monk], gone to the forest or to the root of a tree or to an empty hut, sits down, having folded his legs crosswise, sets himself erect, established in mindfulness in front of him."[27]

Before we explore the early Buddhists' relationship with nature we need to say some more about the elements which made up early Buddhist practice. The most important ones the Buddha proposed can be broken down into two main elements. One, *samadhi*, has been translated variously as concentration, serenity, and one-pointedness. However it is translated, *samadhi* boils down to the ability to hold one's attention on a given object or be present without distraction. Most readers will have observed the phenomenon of becoming so involved with a computer that time and bodily feelings seem to vanish. In this case your mind becomes so engaged in responding to the simulations of the computer that all else vanishes. The Buddha felt that meditation required such concentration, but, and this is key, *without stimulation*. Sitting still, paying attention to the subtlest of changes in the sensations of your breath as it flows in and out of your body is the prerequisite for developing the kind of close attention necessary if you hope to be able to observe the intricate workings of your mind and body.

While concentrating on the computer seems as easy as rolling off a log, achieving Buddha's one-pointedness is more difficult than it seems. Many contemporary teachers and books present techniques for developing concentration and warn meditators of potential stumbling blocks. People who try meditation learn how many years it sometimes takes to gather their attention. As mentioned, the Buddha began with breath and then extended the realm of attention to the body, mind, emotions, and being as a whole. Only after *samadhi* becomes sufficiently sharp can a meditator appreciate the full subtlety and components of life.

Theravada Buddhism or the Doctrine of the Elders used *Vipassana* or "insight meditation." This describes the second element of meditation. With calm, stable observation we can observe how desire leads to attachment and attachment leads to discontent. Insight is the "Aha—if I do that then I will again be unhappy with the outcome." Insight has the potential to lead to wisdom. "If I don't pursue the attachment which comes from desire, if I am not so reactive to misfortune, then I can live more in peace." So, wisdom is the fruit of insight. It can express itself in one's personal life but also with respect to others. Seeing clearly how one's attachment affects others has the potential to open one's life to ways of foregoing actions likely to hurt others. This awakening to the ways of non-harming can be a result of meditation. Buddha claimed successful meditation would lead to personal peace, and his enlightenment stands as a model of how to end discontent and initiate a life of non-harming.

The Buddha summarized the process of meditation and its implications in his "Four Noble Truths." These assert that the discontent that plagues humans can be ended by meditation. Buddha's famous "Eightfold Path" is an outline of the necessary moral behaviors and meditation perspectives needed to end suffering. Less well-known is Buddha's causal chain that links sensation to attachment and suffering. This causal chain is known as the "Twelve Factors of Dependent Origination." The factors include: body and mind, the senses, contact, feeling, craving, clinging, and karma. Such factors are part of the sequence by which our connection to the world becomes transformed into states of being that lead to discontent. Karma refers to the untoward consequences of worldly actions that arise from the confusion or suffering of the actor. Because the Buddha believed in rebirth, unclear actions may not only cause harm to oneself and others in this life but also affect people in their lives to come.

The Four Noble Truths, the Eightfold Path, and Dependent Origination are important signposts on the map of Buddhist meditation. We will consider parts of this map more closely when it helps to illuminate forest meditation and its history in different Buddhist cultures.

Two other elements of the Buddha's worldview also need be considered. They concern how a meditator should conduct him- or herself, as well as the role of the meditator in the larger social world. The answers to both these quests, the ethical and the sociopolitical, again, are thought to find their ideal expression in the life of the Buddha. Although at the time of the Buddha Brahmans regarded celibacy as holy, they also held that house-holding was a crucial, if only intermediary, stage in the fulfillment of a spiritual life. When family responsibilities were done, a Brahman was supposed to embark on a life of spiritual quest. For the Buddha renunciation was starker: It implied leaving home and giving up its benefits and its attachments. Siddhartha "went forth," abandoning his child and doting parents. (His wife had died. Later his family embraced his teachings.) Leaving home was not an absolute requirement, but monasticism was strongly encouraged. Most of the Buddha's instructions were directed toward monastics, and followers who chose that path were honored. The vow of monasticism began with five precepts: to refrain from killing, from taking what is not offered, from harmful speech, from sexual misconduct, and from intoxicants. As Buddhism developed, the number of monastic precepts increased to several hundred. One crucial vow that may strike the modern reader as strange was to not engage in productive work. Such work might distract one from meditation, have harmful consequences, and expose the seeker to the seductions of the material world. Monks and nuns were thus obliged to beg for their food.

Having renounced the worldly setting where desires and aversion are so often stimulated, a monk or nun's task became to root out craving at its source: the point at which the mind responds to sensations. It is here that the Buddha claimed his path was a "middle way." Through his own experience Siddhartha discovered that neither extreme asceticism nor the life of the household provided peace. Neither bodily torture nor living an ordinary life stilled one's mind and ended discontent. Buddha's solution was, therefore, a balanced asceticism. The middle way meant moderate abstentions, living by the precepts and meditating, not absolute renunciation.

The sutras are filled with different meditation techniques the Buddha recommended. An essential ingredient of them all is to still the body so that one can then still the mind. Sitting under a tree, away from distractions, was encouraged. Theoretically, renunciation and meditation do not require any special setting. In the tradition that followed the Buddha most practice was done in monasteries. We will look at some of the ways this monasticism influenced practice.

While there were many different contexts in which

meditation has been done, our primary goal here is to look at its special ties to the setting from which it arose, wild nature, and to see how meditation reconnected to the wilds as Buddhism developed historically. In Christianity monks who remained in monasteries were known as cenobites (from the Greek, "to live in community"), while those, like the desert fathers, who took to the wilds were called eremites (from the Greek, "to live alone"). We are interested in eremites, but their lives and what we know of them were deeply affected by their cenobitic brethren.

Having reached enlightenment at age 35 the Buddha, dressed in the saffron robes of a renunciant, shaved his head, and wandered around like Brahmans and other *samanas*. He preached a doctrine of meditation and a middle way. As he traveled from the villages to the cities of the time, he gathered followers. To them he elaborated a system of meditation and created rules for a monastic community. We will first look at the role nature played in this, then more at the physical and socio-economic world in which he taught. Finally, we will look at those parts of his ideas and the community he formed, which mitigated against meditation in its original, natural setting.

Following their itinerant teacher, the Buddha's students began practicing the path he laid out. They sat themselves down to meditate on the edge of towns where they went once each day to beg for their food. It is likely that there were monastics who lived in community and others who chose the woods.[28] In one sutra it says that the forest provides an ideal setting for perfection of one's inner being: it "arrest[ed] the decay of the monk."[29] There a renunciant could find solitude beyond the temptations of town. One of the Buddha's major disciples, Mahakasyapa, was a champion of forest life, and another senior monk would only take students willing to do forest practice.

Although theoretically an ideal place in which to meditate, the forests could be difficult. Unless meditators had suitable personalities, if there was little to distract unbridled imagination would lead them astray. Such a person would be unable to appreciate the solitude: "the wilderness would whirl away his mind." The Buddha thought forest practice inappropriate for one student, pointing out "the hopelessness of forest-life for one who fails to gain tranquility of mind."[30] What was necessary was not perfection of spirit but strong and renewing spiritual aspirations. By ignoring hardships one monk overcame terrible cramps he got while in the forest.

Some authors think that the earliest dated sutras were eremitic. In these sutras you find, "let not two of you go the same way... So long as the [monks] delight in the forest-seats, so long they may be expected not to decline but to prosper." And, "The man who wears dirty raiments, who is emaciated and covered with veins, who lives alone in the forest, and meditates, him I call [god-like]."[31] At one point the Buddha sets down four conditions for monks: begging (as we just saw), the wearing of clothes made from discarded rags, dwelling under trees, and the prohibition of medicines other than cow's urine. These are rules we would associate with the life of an eremite.

Descriptions of nature are most prominent in those sutras scholars think are the oldest. In the *"Rhinoceros" Sutra* the solitary life is extolled. Nature is a model for the renunciant: "Alone as wild things... free to range the woodlands...browse at pleasure where they will, the sage seeks liberty;" and, "Copy the bamboo shoot which grows up straight and free."[32] The eremite is urged to emulate "a deer which is not tied up [but] goes wherever it wishes in the forest for pasture."[33] Life in the woods has challenges and rewards. "It is better to live alone... with few wishes, like an elephant or a boa in the forest."[34] "Cold and heat, hunger [and] thirst, wind and heat [of the sun], gadflies and snakes... having endured all these, one should wander solitary as a rhinoceros horn."[35] Buddhists regarded rhinos as loners, and dangerous when roused. Their single horn was a symbol of self-reliance.

The conditions of raw nature become a teacher. "Not giving up seclusion [and] meditation, constantly [living in accordance with the doctrine in the world of phenomena], understanding the peril [which is] in existence, one should wander solitary as a rhinoceros horn." "Not trembling, as a lion [does not tremble] at sounds, not caught up [with others] as the wind [is not caught up] in a net, not defiled [by passion], as a lotus [is not defiled] by Water."[36] In the wilds danger and fear are constant companions. There are no supports from society to mask these harsh realities. The meditator faces disease, old age, and death, without protection.

In the forests, violence is a part of daily existence. Hunter-gatherers know this intimately. They recognize that life feeds on life. They often honor the animals they hunt and realize that, like their prey, they will eventually succumb to nature's forces. Forest renunciants, however, had a different compact with the wilds. Monks and nuns were prohibited from taking life or from doing work to sustain themselves, because worldly work increases the risks of initiating harmful karma. The active face of these prohibitions is the adoption of the stance of non-harming or *ahimsa*. Non-harming is crucial for stepping out of the flow of karma, but non-harming also has practical implications. It is a kind of passive protection. Since renunciants were not allowed to engage in violence, they could only surrender or flee. But flight would undermine the very reason for going into the forest. If one wants to meditate where raw nature teaches, then running away in self-defense defeats the original purpose. So, unlike hunter-gatherers attuned to self-preservation or villagers who feared the wilds, forest monks and nuns were challenged to surrender to natural dangers.

The sutras stress this surrendering. In the *Rhinoceros Sutra* renunciants are urged to lay "aside violence in respect to all beings, not harming even one of them... Cultivating at the right time loving-kindness, equanimity, [pity], release, and sympathetic joy, [unimpeded by the whole world], one should wander solitary as a rhinoceros horn."[37] And, "Hurt naught that lives."[38] The Buddha ascribed the death of a monk from a snake's bite to lack of loving kindness "toward the four royal families of snakes." Loving kindness and sympathetic joy are active steps beyond simply non-harming. Not only do renunciants avoid harmful karma, they also embrace what is dangerous in nature. Later we will see how Buddhist attitudes toward nature include "pity" for wild beings.

The Buddha prescribed a protective mantra to be recited by eremites when they encounter wild animals:

> Kindness from me to the footless ones; kindness from me to the two-footed ones, kindness from me to the four-footed ones; kindness from me to the many-footed ones.
> Let not the footless ones harm me...
> Limitless is the Buddha, limitless is the [Dharma or truth], limitless is the [Community of Monks and Nuns or Sangha].
> Limited are the creatures that creep: snakes scorpions, centipedes, spiders, lizards, and mice.
> I have made protection. I have made a charm. Let living beings retreat.[39]

Finally, even though renunciants were encouraged to emulate the solitary rhinoceros horn, the prohibition against companionship is not absolute. "If one can obtain a zealous companion, an associate of good disposition, [who is] resolute, overcoming all [dangers] one should wander with him, with elated mind, mindful."[40] But the relationship is only to aid liberation. Traveling partners must avoid attachment: "One should not wish [for the presence of] a son, let alone a companion."[41] So while the forest practitioner might find support in another of their kind, the search ultimately depends on individual persistence and courage. Nature is a model for this endeavor: "Alone! Dwell far aloof... as after spring and kill, the strong-fanged king of beasts seeks out a distant lair."[42] In one sutra there is a description of ascetic practices often associated with forest dwelling, referred to as "following the practice of elephants."[43]

Some of the struggles of Buddha's early followers were preserved as *The Sayings* [or Poems] *of the Elder Monks and Nuns.* These sayings represent some of the earliest surviving Buddhist texts, passed on by recitation. Biographies appear with them by the fifth century CE, some 900 years after they were first composed. The Elder Nuns and Monks may have been the original forest practitioners. They may even have preceded the Buddha, although, as their poems now stand, they reflect later Buddhist influence. In her study of the Elder Nuns, Susan Murcott believes, "The true source was the oral tradition, the body of inherited folklore that consisted of legends of antiquity probably based on a kernel of historical fact."[44]

Both men and women wandered the forest in search of a deeper reality. In *The Sayings* ordination was less elaborate than it later became in monasteries. Either under the supervision of an ordained monastic or after a self-administered vow, seekers would cut off their hair and go off into the forests to meditate beneath trees. They wore rags and begged, as the Buddha instructed. "Forests are delightful where [ordinary] people find no delight. [Only] those rid of desire will delight there." "I have dwelt in woods, caves, in solitary lodgings, in places frequented by beasts of prey."[45] The Elders obtained food where they could without preference for what they ate.

The Sayings presented solitude as a path: "Alone in a forest like a tree rejected in a wood."[46] Solitude supported meditation and mitigated against desire and sloth. When threatened with attack by a criminal, one elder Nun describes the situation as simply another impediment to practice and vows not to succumb. As in the *Rhinoceros Sutra*, aloneness is sometimes balanced by the company of other renunciants. But they keep a deeper silence as a crucial ingredient of practice. "In two rainy seasons I uttered only one word."[47] The forest is an ever demanding teacher: "Tormented by gnats and mosquitoes in the forest, in the great wood... one should endure there mindful." There are other difficulties like disease, lack of food, wild beasts, loneliness, weather, vagabonds, and disapproval.

And yet the rewards can be unparalleled: "[T]he pain springing from seclusion is better than the happiness from sensual pleasures." "The sounds of the forest are welcome because they awaken the sleeper to meditation." "When in the sky the thunder cloud rumble[s], full of torrent of rains all around, and the [eremite]... has gone into the cave meditates, he does not find greater contentment than this."[48]

The Sayings exemplify forest practice:

Sopaka: Just as a woman would be good toward her beloved only son, so should one be good to all living creatures everywhere.

Vimala: The earth is sprinkled, the wind blows, lightning flashes in the sky. My thoughts are quieted, my mind is well concentrated.

Godhika: The Sky Deva rains melodiously; my small hut is roofed, pleasant, draught-free and my mind is concentrated. Son rain, Sky Deva, if you wish.

Usabha: The trees on the mountain-tops have shot up, well watered by the fresh rain-cloud on high. More and more it produces excellence for Usabha, who desires solitude and possesses forest-sentiment.

Vanavaccha: With clear water and wide crags, haunted by monkeys and deer, covered with oozing moss, those rocks delight me.

Mahanama: You are found wanting by the mountain with its many shrubs and trees—.

Vakkali: Brought low by colic, dwelling in the grove, in the wood, where there is restricted food supply, where it is harsh, how will you fare, [monk]?... Developing the applications of mindfulness... I shall dwell in the grove.

Talaputa: [with mind tamed] In the cave and on the mountain crest, frequented and plunged into by wild boars and antelopes, or on a naturally pleasant space, or in a grove sprinkled with fresh water by rain, having gone to your cave house you will rejoice there. Birds with beautiful blue necks, with beautiful crests... will delight you as you meditate in the wood... I shall lie among the mountains like a tree. It will be soft for me like cotton... But I shall be master.[49]

These renunciants engaged nature with still, concentrated minds.

Because *The Sayings* may derive from an oral tradition not written until centuries later, an oral tradition, moreover, translated through two religious languages, there is much freedom in how they are rendered. A further complication is that the translators probably had no experience of the forest practice they described. Modern urban scholars added elements of their cultures' attitudes toward nature, as we will see their village-dwelling cenobitic predecessors did elsewhere. So, in reality, we have only hints of the Elders' original forest practice.

One of the first Western women scholars to translate Buddhist texts was Caroline Rhys-Davids. During World War II, she rendered some of the nuns' poems with great flare. With women then working and serving in the military, her translations justifiably tilted away from the bias of previous Western male translators and their monastic predecessors.

Who doth not love to see on either bank
Clustered rose-apple trees in fair array
Behind the great cave of my hermitage,
Or hear the soft croak of the frogs, well rid
Of their undying mortal foes proclaim

> *'Not from mountain-stream is't time today*
> *To flit. Safe is the Ajakarani [River].*
> *She brings us luck. Here is it good to be.'*[50]

And:

> *Thou who foredone with cramping pains*
> *Dwell'st in the jungle, in the woods,*
> *Thy range confined in hardship dire—*
> *How wilt thou fare?*

> *With bliss and rapture's flooding wave*
> *This mortal frame will I suffuse.*
> *Though hard and rough I will endure,*
> *Yet I will in the jungle dwell.*[51]

After a nun was raped and women were forbidden to wander by themselves, Elder nuns still sought solace in nature.

> *Though I be suffering and weak, and all*
> *My youthful spring be gone, yet have I come,*
> *Leaning upon my staff, and climb aloft*
> *The mountain peak. My cloak thrown off,*
> *...*
> *There on the mountain where no crowd can come*
> *... never doubt*
> *That thou shalt surely win to the beyond.*[52]

Romantic nature frames Buddhist struggle.

> *I'll seat me on the mountain top, the while*
> *The wind blows cool and fragrant on my brow*
> *And burst the baffling mists of ignorance.*
> *Then on the flower-carpet of the wood,*

Anon in the cool cavern of the cliff,
Blest in the bliss of liberty I'll take
Mine ease on thee, old Fastness of the Crag.[53]

These lines are reminiscent of the poet William Wordsworth's striding across the English countryside, yet, although Mrs. Rhys-Davids translations have been criticized, her assertion that *The Sayings'* origins lay close to nature seems accurate.

We have seen that some of the Buddha's followers took to the woods from a society which was thoroughly agricultural. That society was surrounded by wildlands inhabited by dangerous animals and tribals who still lived by hunting and gathering. Although the Buddha's contemporaries had completely forgotten their own hunter-gathering past, they had contact with people still living that way. *The Vedas*, which preceded the Buddha, portrayed society as pastoral and tribal. By the later *Brahamanas* society had become royal. By the Buddha's time foraging lifestyles had been eliminated in quasi-urban settings, although as in the modern world, some foragers had contact with farmers.[54]

Most of the Buddha's followers seem to have been merchants and wealthy agriculturists. As they traveled with the Buddha from town to town, and occasionally to a proto-city, they experienced the hardships and danger of travel at that period. The early Buddhists stopped at *gamas*. *Gamas* were groups of people of various kinds, although the exact meaning of the word is not entirely clear. The *gamas* included market towns, army posts, or dispersed settlements of three or four houses in forests, woodlands, hills, and mountainous areas of the Ganges Valley. Because the Buddha's followers were required to beg daily for their food, they could not stray far from farms or *gamas*. When local farmers complained about damage to their monsoon-soaked fields by monks walking through them, the Buddha required monks to go on retreat during the four months of the rainy season. For the rains retreats monks built huts in the mountains within reach of a *gama*. They destroyed their huts when the retreat was over and again traveled. Other renunciants, such as the Vedic fire worshippers who lived in forest huts, scavenged for food or came to town for provisions. Because of marauders, locals *gamas* were often deserted. In their travels, monks sometimes stayed in temporary cattle camps or with caravans. Caravan camps lasting four months or longer were also called *gamas*. Because the forests were so dangerous, the refuge provided by a *gama* was welcome.[55] Caravans may have had as many as a thousand members. During the rainy season travel was often impossible, so caravans stopped along the way.

As the ways of hunting and gathering had become strange to the farmers and merchants of the Ganges Plains, so too were their lives utterly different from ours. Despite the towns, proto-cities, and royal patronage, the early Buddhist community spent most of its time out of doors dealing with weather, insects, and primitive food. They traveled with little more than robes, sandals, begging bowl, umbrella, and mosquito net. The Buddha often stayed near towns in groves or leftover pieces of jungle which had not yet succumbed to clearing or agriculture. Many of the urban places he visited had names derived from nature. Kajangala means "a place once forested." The Sakya capital, the Buddha's hometown, may have been named after wild monkeys living in the forests there. Lumbinivana, the birthplace of Siddhartha, means "the forest of Lumbini." Other towns transliterate as "stump of a tree," "a place that had to be cleared of reeds to be settled," and "bamboo forest."

Early Buddhists were part of an expanding civilization. They lived the life of that society. The metaphors of the sutras are derived mainly from agriculture and trade. References to raw nature are few, and there is no mention of the foragers who lived in the surrounding forests. So, while the sutras extol the virtues of going off into the woods, the woods that most monks and nuns resorted to were the relatively benign groves near towns, not the primal jungles in which tribals still lived. Monks and nuns traveled as merchants and farmers did, in protected groups, avoiding as much as possible the hazards of weather, wild animals, bandits, and tribals.

Only a few of the Buddhist community sought refuge in the wilds, begging food as required, but also sometimes living off the land. At the Buddha's time towns were located at distances from each other. The surrounding countryside was still virgin forest from which many *samanas* sustained themselves. As Mrs. Rhys-Davids notes, "Some followers of the Sakyan... dwelt in forests, there to subsist on fruit and roots and to dress in bark and antelope hides. For this reason it has been suggested that the emerging Buddhist movement, in common with the whole tradition of wandering renunciants, constituted a return to the old ways of food gathering, aboriginal forest dwellers."[56] *Samanas* signified their different beliefs by what they wore. The Buddhists shaved their heads, an act which was offensive to Brahmans, who sported dreadlocks. One elder nun switched allegiances:

> *I used to worship fire,*
> *the moon, the sun,*
> *and the gods.*
> *I bathed at fjords,*
> *took many vows,*
> *I shaved half my head,*
> *slept on the ground,*
> *and did not eat after dark.*[57]

At what point ascetics became members of nascent religions such as Buddhism we don't know. They lived in an expanding agricultural and extractive world which, over the next thousand years, cut down more and more of the wildlands and beat back or assimilated their inhabitants. The forest monks' more domesticated brethren, the town-dwelling cenobites, were part of civilization's encroachment upon the wilds. Beginning before Buddha and accelerating through the Asokan Empire in the third century BCE, agricultural civilization expanded its exploitative relationship with the forests. During the earlier Vedic period, some of the forests in the Ganges Plains were cleared for cultivation, and lumber was harvested for buildings, chariots, carts, and agricultural tools. In the *Rg-Veda* the forests are *Aranyani*, the mother goddess, "who takes care of wild life and ensures the availability of food to man."[58] The *Aranya Sanskriti* or the culture of forest ashrams was thought to be the highest human achievement. In the last phase of life one was supposed to retire to the forests to meditate. All life was regarded as sacred and to be worshipped as deities. The forests of the later Hindu *Mahabharata* and *Ramayana* are full of lions, tigers, and elephants. The *Ramayana* begins with the author, Valmiki, observing a tribal killing the male of a pair of copulating swans for food. Since the swans were symbolic of gods, and in the act of mating, the commentary suggests the Brahman's disapproval of the tribal's uncivilized behavior.[59] Although forests were sacred in the *Vedas*, by the time of the *Ramayana* Agni, the fire god, gets Krishna and Arjuna to agree to his burning the Khandavi forest with all its inhabitants. The forest is set ablaze and Krishna and Arjuna drive all creatures trying to escape back into the flames. The land is cleared so that Arjuna's agro-pastoral clan can build its capital.

"Brahmans, who presided over fire sacrifices... served as pioneers, establishing their outposts in forests and initiating rituals which consumed large quantities of wood and animal fat. Thus provoked, the native food gatherers, termed demons... would attempt to disrupt the holocaust to retain control over their territories." Soldiers were summoned to "[kill] wild animals with complete abandon."[60] Although extensive forests survived into the Buddha's era, early sutras mention the burning of forests. The Buddhists had a strong affiliation to the four trees which played a role in the Buddha's life. Other disciples also had prominent trees associated with their realizations. All of these were shade giving and called "Bodhi" (i.e., Buddha) trees. Some scholars feel the Buddhists and the Jains (another contemporaneous sect) had a conservationist attitude about forests. Nonetheless, the growing societies incorporating Buddhism continued to clear land. Indeed—and ironically considering Buddhism's original stress on the wilds—Buddhists regarded the making of farms, parks, groves, wells, dikes, and bridges as meritorious acts leading to a better rebirth. So, while there were both sentimental and sacred feelings about trees, the Buddha and most of his followers consented to and even praised the expansion of civilization at the expense of the wild.

The changing shape of the landscape is illustrated in the *Jataka Tales*, which include stories of the Buddha's past incarnations. They were composed hundreds of years after the earliest sutras. They have been dated by scholars using both linguistic analysis and their descriptions of social and material life. The villages of the *Jataka Tales* had from 30 to 1,000 families, a sacred grove of uncut forest surrounded by cleared fields, pastures, and then primeval forest. In the woodlands people collected firewood and debris for fertilizer. Roads and caravan routes through the forests were farther away from villages than in the earlier era because more of the countryside had been developed, but it was still difficult to pass, as well as dangerous because of wild animals. This was the world in the era after the Buddha. The economy grew from the egalitarian Sakyas to the Mauryan Empire of Asoka that conquered much of India.

The kingdoms of Magadha that preceded Asoka were made up of colonizers, and the growth of those kingdoms depended upon destruction of the wilderness. Chandra Gupta, Maurya's defeated predecessor, cut trees for revenue. He established a royal forestry department whose duties included such things as increasing productivity, setting prices, and commercially collecting trade items, such as native medicinal plants, poisonous snakes, and spiders. Gupta erected and ran factories to make things from forest raw materials. Because of the importance of elephants in warfare, his conqueror, Asoka, and later Mauryan kings set aside special forest preserves. Among these were elephant forests, where the elephants were allowed to roam because elephants will not breed in captivity. Elephant forests were guarded and people were employed to care for the elephants and capture and domesticate their offspring. They sought those "possessed of auspicious characteristics and good character."[61] Elephant forests tended to be thorny and open, probably because they had already been cut and were regrowing. It was illegal in Maurya to kill elephants. Tribals who did so were punished, which further impacted their free-roaming lifestyles. Yet, despite the fact that the forests were receding, they still influenced civilization. During the Mauryan Empire, risk to cattle included being "devoured by tigers, bitten by snakes or dragged into water by crocodiles."[62] Besides elephant preserves, forests were put aside for public gatherings, for Brahmans' rituals, and as hunting grounds for noblemen. And for entertainment, the rulers maintained reserves near cities in which defanged and declawed wild animals roamed. As civilization grew, forests declined.

Asoka is famous for his alleged humane management of his empire. Surviving proclamations urged conservation and just punishment. These may have been influenced by Buddhism, but not exclusively so.[63] Asoka planted fruit orchards for shade and for the common people. He instituted game laws and set up wildlife sanctuaries. He forbade the killing of certain species and may have proscribed meat eating, but the rules appear to have been inconsistent. Asoka forbade the burning of chaff so as not to kill insects and outlawed the malevolent burning of forests. Yet Asoka developed and pacified the countryside. "Asoka maintained intimate contact with tribal people, who were exhorted to observe [Buddhist morality]." But he also intended "that tribal... people would take to the habits of a settled... peasant society, and develop respect for... monks, priests and officers who would help enforce... authority... Asoka claimed that hunters and fishermen had given up killing and practiced dharma. This means that food gatherers were persuaded to take to a sedentary agricultural life."[64] In spite of his pacifistic proclamations Asoka conquered and forcefully maintained an empire that spread over large parts of the Indian subcontinent. To improve travel he ordered rest houses built every nine miles.

The puzzle of Asoka's exact relationship to Buddhism may not be solvable with the historical evidence we now have. One model of what happened during Asoka's reign can be found in the legalization of Christianity under Constantine. His acceptance of Christians who were making troubles in the Roman Empire was more a political strategy than a religious conviction. During his lifetime he took part in distinctly unchristian, traditional Roman religious ceremonies.[65] Similarly Asoka's Buddhist-like public utterances may have merely been acknowledgement of the presence of Buddhists and Jains in his empire. Such acknowledgement, like Constantine's granting tax-free status to Christian churches, may have given impetus to the growth of Buddhism. As a result, during the thousand years after Asoka's regime Buddhism became the major religion in India, with royal sponsorship and temples and shrines being built. The wealthy founded great monasteries and universities. Missionaries were sent to the countries with which India traded. Buddhism became the first major, worldwide religion.

In this period the Silk Road, an avenue of trade crossing Central Asia dating back before the Buddha, was extended from China to Syria. Great markets arose in northwest India in the third century BCE, maybe earlier. Buddhist merchants led large caravans on arduous journeys. Dust was a constant enemy. At rivers with no fords rudimentary bridges or rafts were constructed. Jungles harbored naked savage tribes armed with poison arrows, but they dared not attack a large caravan. Brigands lurked in the forests. Guides admonished travelers not to eat unfamiliar plants when experiencing privation and not to stray because there were wild animals and quicksand. "Desert crossings were the most feared of all."[66] They traveled by night because of hot sun and sand. A "land pilot" would guide them by the stars. Travelers reported attacks by demons. Sea voyages were even more dangerous. By the time of Christ, the monsoon currents were understood and there was regular commerce between Rome and China. Along some of these routes Buddhism spread.

These developments affected forest practice. Society was expanding. The wildlands as places to tame the mind and body were vanishing, although still present on the edges of civilization. To understand what happened to the tradition of eremites, the hermits off alone in a nature increasingly under attack by spreading civilization, we return to historiography and the development of monastery Buddhism.

The sutras feature two distinct styles of meditation practice. One is to practice in the wilds. But, as the Buddha pointed out, this was not for everyone. Only a few of the Buddha's disciples were eremites. The second style became that of monastery or village Buddhism. It was adopted by monks and nuns who lived within society. They walked from town to town or settled near villages and did their practice in huts or under trees but were not ascetics wandering in the jungles. These were the cenobites. From the time of the Buddha onward, the overwhelming majority of monastics were indeed cenobites, and Buddhism became largely a religion of monasteries and village monks. This drift away from nature toward the village fit well within developing Indian society. The forests were places of danger and fear and needed to be subdued.

Although Buddhism is rationalistic, particularly with respect to meditation and theological debates, nonetheless it incorporated some of the shamanism that existed in the forests of India. This shamanism may be evident in the mystical powers attributed to the Buddha. The Buddha supposedly could travel through the realms of Buddhist cosmology, read minds, foretell the future, and see people's karma. Although many Buddhist sects have focused on these powers, and these miracles may have drawn millions of people to Buddhism (as also happened in Christianity), the rationalistic component represented by meditation often regarded the Buddha's alleged supernormal powers as secondary, sometimes even stumbling blocks upon the road to understanding the core teachings. We will thus not belabor these shamanistic components as some scholars have. We need only note here that such miraculous powers have often been associated with forest renunciation in general, for example the belief that forest Brahmans could ensure prosperity with Vedic rituals. There are sutras (we will look at later) which picture the lives of some disciples as mystical forest masters. In one text Mahakasyapa emerges from his forest dwelling place with long hair, beard, and coarse robe. And Upagupta, a Sanskrit, Asokan saint with direct lineage to Mahakasyapa, also had long hair and became a miraculous forest teacher.

Different kinds of Buddhas are mentioned in Buddhist literature. One is the Buddha himself. Others are Buddhas taught by a Buddha. Finally, there are *Pratyekabuddhas*, solitary Buddhas who had no teacher and did not themselves teach. In some traditions they cannot exist when fully enlightened Buddhas, such as Shakyamuni Buddha, the Buddha of the Sakyas, are present. The idea of a *Pratyekabuddha* probably predates the Buddha, which lends some credence to the association of *Pratyekabuddhas* with early forest practice.[67] Some *Pratyekabuddhas* are said to have dwelled in caves in the Himalayas. They plastered the walls and dyed their clothes. When come upon in the woods, they were likely to be found meditating under trees for such long periods of time that the interloper would be unable to wait until they emerged from meditation. They often remained silent even when begging. Their meditation sometimes involved such extreme concentration that they could not be called out of it. They were reputed to have lured monks away from their more comfortable existence in royal parks. The *Pratyekabuddha's* wisdom is "not sown, not strewn, not explained, not taught, not made known, not established, not unveiled, not explained in detail, and not made manifest or shown."[68] In short, the *Pratyekabuddhas* were unsocial, possibly antisocial, and potentially dangerous to established Buddhism. Here is further evidence of the isolation building between Buddhism's civilized uses and its birth in the forests.

Monasteries were established after the Buddha's death. They developed where monks resided in clearings near towns or in the pleasure-grounds of the gentry. It is surmised that they progressed from separate huts to verandah-covered multiple units and finally complex monasteries. The first references to monasteries comes at end of the second century CE from the Greeks who occupied northwest India, the limit of Alexander the Great's eastern conquests. In contrast, earlier Greek writings give evidence of the eremitical ideal.

In the sutra, *The Kindred Sayings of Kassapa*, the Buddha bemoans the passing of the forest way of life and criticizes those who depart from it.[69] Nonetheless, there is good evidence that at least one monk who insisted upon forest discipline, Devadatta, was either drummed out of the Buddhist community after the Buddha died or was written out of the sutras by the later scholars. Devadatta, who apparently founded an order that may have lasted till the sixth century CE, is vilified in later texts for splitting the community. One of the few rules mandating excommunication was the making of schisms.[70] Monastic scholars disapproved of Devadatta and may have denounced forest practice in general by association with him. Forest renunciants, after all, were not under the control of monasteries and, therefore, were suspect. Because of the charisma of forest monks in early twentieth-century Thailand the Buddhist establishment had to deal with this issue. Although the eremitic tradition continued after the Buddha it was not preeminent. Even though the edicts of the Asokan era set aside forests for Brahmans, there is no similar mention of refuges for Buddhist eremites! From such clues we can conclude that the marginalization of Buddhism's roots in the wilds began early on.

But what becomes of nature in a Buddhism increasingly dominated by monasteries and scholar monks? Part of the answer is illustrated in a *Jataka Tale* that dates from at least the second century BCE. *The Perfect Generosity of Prince Vessantara* is an anti-Brahman story that teaches generosity. It is supposed to be about the Buddha's two previous incarnations before he was born as Siddhartha.[71] In the story townspeople ostracize Vessantara for giving away all his possessions, including his children. When his neighbors finally expel him for giving away the elephants that bring rain, he imagines the Himalayas as a "terrible forest, infested with fierce wild beasts." To which his wife responds that the children will be, "sweetly chattering... sitting among bushes of the forest" with garlands in a lovely hermitage. Around them will be wild blossoms, and the land will be crowded with beasts of prey on every side, deer and dancing fawns, cries of the owl and beasts of prey with dancing peacocks in the winter. "The earth green and covered with cochineal beetles [which are thought to be particularly friendly and beautiful]." The forests bloom in the winter with lotus and tree flowers. On hearing of her son's banishment, Vessantara's mother laments in a voice like the jackal howl, the owl shriek, the bird whose chicks are killed, and the ruddy goose whose pond has dried. And his father tells his son's wife all the horrors that await in the forest: "Many bugs and insects, mosquitoes and bees. They would hurt you, it would be unpleasant for you." There are also goat-swallowing snakes with no poison, bears that climb trees after their victims, sharp-horned buffalo, and frightful monkeys. "Even at midday when the birds are settled down, the great jungle is full of noise."

Vessantara and his wife live seven months of exile in the mountain forest where the wife collects fruits and berries. Their hermitage is endowed with fruit-bearing trees, rice, and other delightful things. The Brahman to whom Vessantara gave his children goes to the jungle to return them and is terrified. An ascetic he meets on the way assures him that he can gather lots of food and "there are few gadflies and mosquitoes and creepy-crawlies[,] and I meet with no harm in the forest with wild beasts." The Brahman is portrayed as seamy, with matted hair and dressed in animal skin. The idyllic nature of surroundings as provided by the gods is retold to the Brahman by the ascetic. At one point, he lists 99 plants and animals. These have been identified from historical lists of plants and animals of India, where the original names are correlated with later Sanskrit renditions of them, although some of the creatures mentioned are fanciful. When they all meet up, Vessantara's wife is wearing an ascetic's antelope skin and her hair too is matted like the Brahman's.

What is interesting for us is not the story or even the moral—that generosity pays—but rather the picture of nature which emerges. It is mixed. Part of it is realistic: The wilds are a place of discomfort and danger and woe to a civilized person who wanders there. But part of it is fanciful: The wife sees the wilds as a place of peace and bounty, but it is only that way because the gods want to reward Vessantara, a past incarnation of the Buddha. So they domesticate the wild. This is how civilization solves the problem of the forests. It is the cenobites' view of the wilds, only livable if turned into a Garden of Eden, as opposed to the forest renunciants whose idea is not to escape the wilds but to live with the dangers and discomforts as teachers. Since the monastic reciters, who orally transmitted the story, and the scribes, who finally wrote it down, knew the names of many of the 99 plants and animals, they or their society must have had some interaction with the wilds, if only by hunting or extracting the forest's wealth. They may even have had contact with forest monks.

The Perfect Generosity of Prince Vessantara represents the increasing alienation of society from nature and the cenobitic view of the forests. Buddhist practice by the time of the sutra has become adulterated to include citified elements. This is in essence a compromise with the civilization, which, I argue, elicited and made dire the need for the Buddha's remedy in the first place. The implication that, even among meditators, nature is to be tamed is completed in the great codification of Theravada Buddhist practice called the *Visudhimagga* or *Path of Purification*. It was written in the fifth century CE in Sri Lanka. We know nothing of forest practice in the 400 to 500 years in between the two works. Before we can understand the role of the *Visuddhimagga* we need to take a little digression into Buddhist historiography.

Prior to the first century BCE, when the Buddhist sutras were written down for the first time in Sri Lanka, their content was orally transmitted by scholar monks who were specially trained to memorize different parts of the tradition. Writing was widespread by the time of Asoka, but religious works were not written down. I asked a meditation monk of a modern forest lineage, who is also a scholar, why such important religious work was not written. He looked down his nose and said, with a touch of disdain, that they regarded writing as something accountants did, not worthy of holy words. His response carried what may have been the feeling 2,000 years ago. Whatever the reason, if the sutras are even as old as Asoka's reign they were transmitted orally for at least 150 years, and maybe up to 350 years, and not written down.

Two factors may have affected their later preservation. The

first is language. The Buddha's native language may or may not have been a form of Sanskrit. His teachings, on the other hand, may have been in Magadha, an old-Sanskrit-derived common language of the era. In the years after Asoka one of the religious languages of Buddhist monasteries was religious Sanskrit, which had been formalized from Brahman or maybe Buddhist sources, so that, after hundreds of years, it could be understood. Pali, another scholarly language similar to Sanskrit, was derived from Magadha.[72] The two former may have existed side by side. Common languages were replaced by scholarly ones because the former changed too much over time. How religious works were kept constant over centuries through oral recitation was illustrated to me in a description of contemporary Vedic reciters who use various techniques, such as group recitation or teacher and student saying every other line.[73] Among the Lamas of Tibet there are contests in which monks check each other. Whether or not such methods, spanning languages and centuries, kept the verses pure is open to question. Some scholars think not. "So much of the material attributed to [the Buddha] in those scriptures is so obviously inauthentic that we can suspect almost everything. In fact, it seems impossible to establish what the Buddha really taught. We can only know what early Buddhists believed he taught."[74] "[A]ccording to the Sri Lankan tradition, the texts were transmitted orally for some 400 years, and this leads to doubts as to the reliability of even the earlier strata of the Pali canon."[75]

A second factor affecting preservation of religious texts has to do with religious sectarianism. It has been suggested that the guilds of reciters were possessive of their texts and did not want to lose their authority if the texts were committed to writing. One sect embraced writing to make their version permanent and even burned those of competing groups.[76] What appears in the *Visuddhimagga* and the first-century Sri Lankan Pali Canon is just one sect's version of the tradition. From the time of the First

Council of monks, just after the Buddha's death, disagreement arose not only about the meaning of the Buddha's sayings but at what point in history revelation stops. Just as Jewish scribes and scholars codified the Old Testament hundreds of years after its inception, including some material and leaving out other, there were different codifications of the sutras. The two main schools that survive today are Theravada and Mahayana. Theravada or "the Doctrine of the Elders" would freeze Buddhism in the Pali Canon that contains little revelation after the Buddha's death and no emphasis on the saints who became enlightened after the Buddha. Mahayana, on the other hand, recognizes many post-Buddha Buddhas who add new dimensions to doctrine. Mahayana is the source of Zen, Tibetan Buddhism, and other forms of Chinese and Japanese Buddhism.

A point of dispute between these schools was the role of the *Abhidamma*, or the sacred text concerning Buddhist psychology. Mahayanists objected to the way they felt *Abhidamma* experts made certain categories of meditation observation concrete. For them later Buddhas revealed the essential emptiness of every-thing, including the *Abhidamma*'s basic categories. There were also other schools with complex doctrinal differences. When the Chinese traveler Fa-hsien visited India in the fifth century CE, he found members of different schools living comfortably together in the same monasteries and in the great Buddhist university, Nalanda. They all observed the same monastic rules and coexisted without sectarian struggles. Differences seemed acceptable within the same community, not grounds for religious rivalry. The sacred texts that survive today include the Pali Canon of the Theravadans, which claims antiquity and historical accuracy but which has materials from obviously different periods; the Mahayana sutras with earlier and avowedly later materials; and fragments of sutras found in Central Asia from the large Buddhist communities that thrived there in the first 700 to 900 years of the first millennium CE. There is also a non-

Mahayana Sanskrit Canon, which exists only in Chinese translation.[77] Its essence is the same as the Pali Canon, but the details differ. We probably cannot determine which, if any, of these texts is historically accurate. It seems as though sometime in the first century BCE, some of the sacred works that had been orally transmitted and others, maybe from folkloric traditions, got written down. Each religious community holds for the truth of its own. As the Buddhist scholar Paul Williams puts it, "We are dealing with centuries of doctrinal change combined with geographic dispersal over a subcontinent. It is easy to forget that while we can write in a few words about changes which took, say, two hundred years, this is nevertheless to render artificially definite what was in reality a gradual shift not experienced, not lived through, by any one person. A series of gradual changes, almost imperceptible changes, from the perspective of the scholar who stands back and observes centuries in one glance, can indicate a massive change which no monk or layperson ever actually experienced."[78]

The emerging dominance of monastery life is associated with a shift in the relative importance of meditation. A forest renunciant goes to the forest because that setting is conducive to deepening meditation. With the need to preserve the sutras and the rules of monasticism and to convey the religion to patrons and potential converts Buddhists needed people who could maintain the tradition. There were almost 50 years of the Buddha's sayings. The jungle was hardly the place for a monk to memorize sutras or teach them to others. Most forest monks of early twentieth-century Thailand had only sketchy knowledge of the sutras. So, a long-standing distinction emerged in Buddhism between the scholar monk and the meditation monk. Meditation monks might reside in monastery or jungle, but scholar monks were rarely, if ever, found in the forests. Scholar monks fit well with royal patronage. As Buddhism formalized into religion the states that sponsored it also contributed to the preservation of its texts and saw to it that these texts were spread throughout their domains. Associated with this emphasis on scholarship was the idea that one could become enlightened through intellectual analysis alone. This, in effect, eliminates the need for forest practice. One scholar claims that Theravada is the only sect which holds the view that analysis would suffice.[79] The shift toward cenobitic Buddhism was enforced by the monastic code: "[I]t accepts in principle the major forms of the earlier wandering ideal but then adds so many exceptions that it emasculates the ideal. [With its regulations it] makes the wandering life no longer possible."[80]

In the earliest Greek description of Buddhism, one contemporaneous scholar sees the move toward monasteries as the shifting from an asceticism of lifestyle to an asceticism of attitude, that is, non-attachment which can be practiced in a monastery.[81] With this also came a shift from meditation to the vocation of texts and scholarship. To memorize very lengthy sutras monks had to be trained from a young age. This led to the recruiting of children into monasteries. Some have thought that the shaved head, which had been meant to differentiate Buddhists from their dread-locked Brahman competitors, became, for the children, a symbol of submission. Between the vocations of scholarship and meditation, between village monasticism and forest wandering, there arose subtle tensions which passed down through the ages. This is illustrated in a story from the author of the *Visuddhimagga*: A textual scholar went to a forest renunciant for meditation instruction and the scholar was asked how he would find time to meditate given the demands of learning to recite the sutras. Realizing the absurdity of his position, the scholar gave up recitation and became enlightened in 19 years.

The *Visuddhimagga* was written by the most famous Theravada scholar, Buddhaghosa. Buddhaghosa came to Sri Lanka from India with a knowledge of Sanskrit. In Sri Lanka he found a written Canon, which dated from the first century BCE when Sri

Lanka was cut off from India. The Canon may have been written down in Pali for fear of its being lost. There were also a series of commentaries on the Canon in an old form of Sinhalese (the spoken language of Sri Lanka). These were no longer easily understandable because the Sinhalese had changed so much. Buddhaghosa's rendering of the commentaries into Pali was intended to freeze them in time for the use of scholar monks. He used the 400-year-old local Canon as the basis of the *Visuddhimagga* and his commentaries. His commentaries and the Pali Canon he revived are believed by Theravadans to be the authentic sources of Buddhism.

The *Visuddhimagga* was Buddhaghosa's monumental codification and interpretation of Buddhist meditation practice, "The Path of Purification." Buddhaghosa epitomizes the scholar monk. He laid out the rules of monasticism and the techniques used by monastery monks who practiced the asceticism of attitude, mentioned above, that is, using strict adherence to the rules, rather than ascetic forest life, as a way to study the mind's reactiveness. Because Buddhaghosa intended to cover all practices the *Visuddhimagga* also describes the rules of forest renunciation. Some of the practices come from the sutras; others may have their origin in what renunciants were actually doing at his time. Buddhaghosa lists 13 ascetic or *Dhutanga* practices.[82]

1) wearing clothes made only of refuse rags.
2) three robes sewn as cloaks of patches.
3) gather lumps of alms food offered.
4) gapless wandering: collecting from each and every house without preference.
5) one meal a day to be eaten in an uninterrupted session.
6) food mixed together in one bowl.
7) refusing any food offered after the meal.
8) dwelling in the forest.
9) at the root of a tree or

10) in the open air or

11) in a charnel ground.

12) sleeping wherever assigned (when in a monastery or temple).

13) never lying down (sitting up through the night even if asleep).

Dhutanga is derived from the expression "shakes off," that is, to get rid of the defilements. The practices are voluntary. A monk or nun can choose to do whichever seems appropriate. There are three degrees of severity with which each might be done: easy, moderate, or strict. The descriptions of the practices are vivid, often picturing how vile, say, refuse cloth might be. Cloth might come from the charnel ground, a shop, the street, a garbage dump, or birthing cloth. It may be scorched by fire, gnawed by cattle, ants, and rats, produced by supernormal powers, borne by the wind, presented by deities, or salvaged from the sea. The benefit of wearing robes made from such materials ranges from not craving good clothes to no fear that a robber will steal them.

> *While striving for Death's army rout*
> *the ascetic clad in rag-robe clout*
> *got from the rubbish heap, shines bright*
> *As mail clad warrior in the fight.*[83]

The benefit of gapless begging from every house is that the mendicant will "always [be] a stranger among families and is like the moon."

To dwell in the forest is defined as living at least two stones' throws from a walled house, a bucket's throw from an unwalled house, or 500 hundred bow lengths. This distance is hardly one chosen by those who wanted forest solitude. It could easily be adopted by a village monk. The reason for the criterion of walls and a bucket's throw has to do with sewage. Buddhaghosa goes on to say that living in a remote abode an ascetic will be neither distracted nor anxious. The ascetic abandons attachment to life and enjoys the bliss of seclusion.

> *The tree dweller is protected by deities.*
> *And when the tender leaves are seen*
> *Bright red at first, then turning green,*
> *And then to yellow as they fall*
> *He sheds belief once and for all*
> *In permanence.*[84]

The benefits of the open air dweller:

> *The open air provides a life*
> *that aids the homeless [monk's] strife,*
> *Easy to get, and leaves his mind*
> *Alert as a deer, so he shall find*
>
> *Stiffness and torpor brought to a halt.*
> *Under the star bejeweled vault*
> *the moon and the sun furnish his light*
> *And concentration his delight.*
> *The joy seclusion's savior gives*
> *He shall discover soon who lives*
> *In open air; that is why*
> *The wise prefer the open sky.*[85]

"The wise prefer the open sky": Buddhaghosa appreciates the poetry of the eremite's setting. The mind is a wild beast, and concentration is likened to taming that beast. He adds that "a great leopard king lurks in the grass [and] seizes wild beasts," as forest monks wait in the forest to "seize the highest fruit of all." Although Buddhaghosa makes a bow to forest sentiment, his aim is to codify practice for cenobites. What little we know about

Buddhaghosa's life comes from his own report. He mentions how royalty in Sri Lanka supported his massive endeavors by supplying him with helpers and luxurious accommodations. And historians place him in the sect that enforced its Canon over all others.[86] Much of the *Visuddhimagga* describes concentration practices for cultivating wholesome states that are discussed in the *Abhidamma*, the text on Buddhist psychology. Such a state might be loving kindness, and the corresponding practice would be concentration on the mantra: "May I (or possibly all beings) be happy. May I (they) be peaceful. May I (they) be free from suffering." Because of the encyclopedic character of his work a number of experienced meditators have wondered whether Buddhaghosa himself undertook much meditation practice. While he may not have done so it seems likely that he or some of the monks who worked under him had access to others who engaged in serious practice, because for centuries the *Visuddhimagga* has been used as a guide to meditation. Even today monks in Burma apparently learn complex concentration and serenity practices from reading it.

Although the *Vimuttimagga* was able to encapsulate formal cenobitic meditation, it seems likely that that Buddhaghosa never undertook forest practice per se. His rendering of the *Dhutanga* rules and the circumstance of his life are evidence for this. As was mentioned above, there is no information about *Dhutanga* as a living practice in Buddhaghosa's time, and his presentation of the ascetic rules are not rich in the kind of detail that might be expected from someone who actually experienced life in the forests. In addition, he lived a life of luxury inconsistent with forest sentiment. It seems he codified ascetic rules as a gesture to their charismatic role in the sutras, similar to how the Church preserved the symbol of Christ's poverty, despite its wealth. He also borrowed from an earlier, second century CE, Indian commentary that survives only in Chinese translation. It is called the *Vimuttimagga* or *The Path of Freedom* and contains similar

ascetic practices, although with less elaboration.[87]
Buddhaghosa added a twist, to highlight a distaste for nature. This attitude was shared by both Buddhist cenobites and eremites. Although Buddha was a *samana*—a recluse, a forest seeker who regarded nature as an important teacher—much of early Buddhism expressed an aversion to nature. Buddhaghosa expressed this with a vengeance. He seemed to relish the vileness of bloody, vomit-smeared cloth to be used for ascetics' robes. Yet he ate royal food, which it was unlikely he mixed together in his bowl and ate in lumps as another *Dhutanga* rule dictates. He presented images of nature as cruel and disgusting. In common with early Theravada perceptions, the intrinsic corruption of the world, the body, and the objects of desire when exposed by close examination is seen as reason enough to forsake craving. What follows is my metaphoric attempt to put Buddhaghosa's technique of using foulness to arrest the desire Buddha claimed underlay human suffering in perspective. Buddhaghosa's technique can be made more contemporary. I quote from my notes, composed while listening to a National Public Radio documentary:

During a battle in Vietnam, a correspondent describes hauling a man who was hit with napalm out of a foxhole and having his boots and then his flesh come off. Is this any different from the contemplation of the foulness of the body or of decay? The commanding officer: My job was to lead troops, I never thought of my family or anything else. I knew we would prevail. I never had it in mind to make a personal deal with God for myself or my men. I knew we would win. In the morning we walked over the bodies of the enemy.

In using the images he does, Buddhaghosa seems almost to celebrate repulsiveness. It appears as if he wants to shock and to scare. It has the tone of two children trying to see who can be the most shocking by describing the yuckiest, most disgusting thing of which they can think. "Just as a baby's excrement... is the color of turmeric... and just as the bloated carcass of a black dog thrown on the rubbish heap... is the color of ripe palmyra fruit... and its fangs are like jasmine buds... still their odor is directly repulsive." Or: "Just as the pot herbs that grow on village sewage in filthy places are *disgusting to civilized people* [italics added] and unusable, so also head hairs are disgusting since they grow on the sewage of pus, blood, urine, dung, bile, phlegm and the like. And these hairs grow on the heap of the other thirty- one parts as [fungi] do on a dung hill. And owing to the filthy place they grow in they are quite unappetizing as vegetables..."

Now on the radio there are descriptions of the Normandy landing: men with hipbones sticking out:

He looked at me and said, "but you don't seem to understand, I never wanted to get wounded"... you don't think about being maimed or wounded or being a cripple or anything like that. There was a medic there, we dragged this man over and they had plasma and morphine... I saw the first American dead there... floating with blue eyes shining... it was a very sobering sight... The number of dead were enormous... They brought their bodies in bloated... the 'corpses' chest with maggots all over the place... those are not scenes you would report to the people back home. It would do no good.

—-growing on a charnel ground."[88]

Even though Buddhaghosa did not understand life in the wild, he was familiar with city life of fifth-century Sri Lanka. In using the phrase "disgusting to civilized people" we get a sense of a gentleman having to walk through the streets of town. Until the nineteenth century towns were strewn with garbage and had sewage running down the streets.[89] Buddhaghosa introduces us to urban life through which a monk was required to walk on his daily alms round. An ascetic leaves the woods (which need be only a stone's throw outside of the village walls):

[T]hat are not crowded with people, offer the bliss of seclusion, possess shade and water, and are clean cool delightful places, and he must set out for the village in order to get nutriment, as a jackal for the charnel ground. And as he goes thus... he must tread on a carpet covered with the dust of his feet, gecko's droppings... [the doorsteps] often fouled with the droppings of rats, bats, and so on... [or] terrace... smeared with the droppings of owls, pigeons... the grounds... defiled by old grass and leaves blown about... by sick novices' urine, excrement, spittle and snot, and in the rainy season by mud and so on... [on the way] perhaps the sight of an elephant's carcass... a human carcass... a snake's carcass... assailed by the smell of them.

... [H]e has to wander in the village streets from house to house like a beggar with a dish in his hand. And in the rainy season wherever he treads his feet sinking in water and mire up to the flesh of his calves... In the hot season he has to go about with his body covered with dirt, grass and dust blown about by the wind... he has to see and even to tread in gutters and cesspools covered with bluebottles and seething with all species of worms all mixed up with fish washings, meat washings, rice washings, spittle, snot, dogs' and pigs' excrement... from which flies come and settle... on his bowl and on his head.

... Some give yesterday's cooked rice and stale cakes and rancid jelly sauce... Others [shout], 'Go away you bald-head.'[90]

Which may be a quite accurate description of city life in Sri Lanka 1,500 years ago. In such a setting the ascetic sees how repulsive even eating is:

And when he has dipped his hand in and is squeezing [his food] up, the sweat trickling down his fingers wets the crisp food there may be and makes it sodden.

And when its good appearance has been spoilt... and put into the mouth... It gets pounded there with the pestle of the teeth like a dog's dinner... then the thin spittle at the tip of the tongue smears it... and filth from the teeth in the parts where a toothpick cannot reach smears it... [It is] reduced to a condition as utterly nauseating as a dog's vomit in a dog's trough.[91]

What is one to make of this? Extreme is the contrast between the idyllic woods where the monk meditates and the filthy town where he learns to vanquish desire. It turns on its head the forest renunciant's assumption that in nature one can come more easily in touch with the processes of life. What we have in Buddhaghosa is an example of *the scholar monk*. This monk dwells in a village and in this case is also a royal monk who creates techniques analogous to those of the forest renunciant. But the scholar monk, away from the wilds, digs out nature as he finds it, unruly even in the bosom of civilization. The forest monks took to the woods to unmask a natural reality covered up by the luxury afforded by agriculture and hidden by the promises of social life. Buddhaghosa's asceticism of the spirit exposes nature's disease, decay, and death where they lay even in the heart of a kingdom's capital.

Buddhaghosa's techniques are, I think, analogous to the reaction of my college-age meditation students when I assign them the task of formal eating meditation. They are asked to eat very slowly and pay attention to the subtle feelings of each experience in a meal. A number of students report that doing this spoils eating for them, especially when they find themselves paying close attention to the McDonald's-style food available in the campus cafeterias. When they pay attention to what they eat, it becomes unpleasant. They would rather not pay close attention and thus enjoy their meals. I ask them to consider whether their enjoyment comes from eating their food or eating their ideas.

Buddhaghosa's practices are examples of the importance to ancient Buddhism of not glossing over the harsher realities of the organic character of life. In a way, Buddhaghosa embraces the forest monks' desire to face nature but downplays the context in which they would do so. When not describing nature in unreal romantic terms the civilized Buddhaghosa, recipient of royal patronage, sees nature negatively. This is illustrated in the *Visuddhimagga*'s charnel ground meditations:

> *This filthy body stinks outright*
> *Like ordure, like a privy site;*
> *This body men that have insight*
> *Condemn, is object of a fool's delight.*
> *A tumor where nine holes abide*
> *Wrapped in a coat of clammy hide*
> *And trickling filth on every side,*
> *Polluting the air with stenches far and wide.*
> *If it perchance should come about*
> *That what is inside it came out,*
> *Sure a man would need a knout*
> *With which to put the crows and dogs to route.*[92]

While Theravada's aversion to nature is evident in this method of teaching, the monks also used their observations of death and decay in a constructive way to help maintain the health of the community and to doctor, treat, and minister to the larger society which sustained them. In the sutra, *The Four Foundations of Mindfulness*, the Buddha presented meditations on the body. These involved either observation of bodily sensations or visualization of interior anatomy. The natural places to learn about interior anatomy in India were the charnel grounds, where dead bodies were disposed of. The Buddha is quite poetic in his descriptions of charnel ground practice. He describes the body being degraded by the forces of nature. Animals tear off the skin; the muscles and organs are exposed. Rot strips the corpse down to the bones, which are eventually reduced to dust that blows away in the wind.

By watching corpses decay and "butchers at the cross roads," as the Buddha suggested, monks learned how the body is put together and what disease symptoms looked like. From the sixth century BCE on wanderers likely possessed general medical knowledge, but the Buddhists incorporated it into their religion and monastic rules.[93] Direct observation and the adoption of existent folk medicines of the time led to a rational compilation of medical knowledge. Indian Buddhist monks introduced cataract surgery into China in the fifth century CE.[94] In the early texts monks were instructed to tend to each other. The Buddha allowed fats from bear, fish, alligator, swine, and donkey to be used as medicine. Buddhaghosa, living almost a millennium after the Buddha, expands this to all edible animals and elephant, horse, dog, snake, lion, tiger, leopard, bear, and hyena. The medical texts of his time stated that the fat of swamp-dwelling animals appeases flatulence. Jungle animals and those with split hooves were applied to treat hemorrhagic disorders, and bird fat was used to remove phlegm. Roots, extracts, leaves, fruits, resins, and salts were also prescribed. For spiritual possession raw swine flesh and blood were used. Incantation was prescribed for snakebite. Remedies for cracked and bleeding bare feet—particularly relevant to wandering forest monks—included ointments, massage, and the wearing of sandals. (This may have been a luxury or considered to be so. The forest monks of late nineteenth-century Thailand often did not wear sandals as they wandered.)[95] Even though the sutras allowed forest monks only cattle urine as medicine it was likely that they were knowledgeable about medicinal wild herbs.

If the aversion to the nature that existed in towns was counterbalanced by the application of medical knowledge, how did early Buddhists feel about nature in general? It should be held in mind that our attitude toward what we call "nature," as opposed to human built things, is deeply influenced by both the romantic poetry and Darwinism of the nineteenth century. Despite the fact that these sentiments slip into the last hundred years of translations of Buddhist texts, "nature" was not so special or revered in the time period we are considering. There were villages and towns; there were wastelands and forests, but no nature per se.

Even though forest monks engaged in a special form of practice they shared a set of beliefs about the order of existence with monastery monks. In Buddhism all mundane existence is regarded as unsatisfactory. This applies especially to organic life, which is marked by pain, death, and impermanence. Everything in existence, from individuals to whole species, will perish. The web of life is not accorded any ultimate value. Early Buddhism, especially, was otherworldly. "The only reasonable attitude... is to leave things and creatures in peace... and cautiously help... in case of emergency without damaging others."[96] Fitting into the agricultural society from which it derived, Buddhism regarded the wild as dangerous and formulated rites for protection against those dangers. Animals were not excluded from salvation but, because they lacked discriminating intelligence, they needed to be reborn as human to gain a chance for enlightenment.

Buddhists thought animal existence more unhappy and painful than human. On a tour of the Boston aquarium a "forest" (indicating in this case one who belonged to a sect rather than an actual-forest dwelling) monk from Burma was fascinated by the fish. He conversed with the whales and sharks swimming in large glass-enclosed tanks. When he got to a large eel, his comment was, "Strange karma!" (This might be translated as, "What did it do in past lives to deserve such a strange rebirth in this one?") Animals also suffer, because they are enslaved by man and mistreated. In the wilds they kill each other. Predation by the stronger of the weaker is seen as particularly malevolent and, therefore, evidence of lower status. Animals should be treated with compassion, but existence would be better off if they did not exist. Except for artificial birds there are no animals in some Buddhist paradises!

In Theravada,

> [W]e cannot fail to recognize a strong rejection of nature... Every aspect of such a life cycle in the state of nature is miserable: birth, sickness, aging, death, parting from the agreeable, meeting with the disagreeable. Happiness is suffering because it is ephemeral... Every evolutionary form of life is vividly depicted as suffering: the hot hells, the cold hells... the... realms of inconceivable hunger and thirst, the animal realms of one eating another, the human realms of strife, frustration, and death... Contemplation of these world-rejecting teachings generates an intense revulsion, [and] a will singly devoted to transcendence at any cost.[97]

This contrasts radically with how hunter-gatherers view their surroundings. For Buddhists, animals and humans inhabit the world in crucially different ways. They both possess animal nature, but humans have qualities of consciousness not available to animals. Both humans and animals suffer, but the animals are bound to their suffering with little relief. If they live with generosity and little harming, essentially overcoming their animal nature, they have the possibility of being reborn as humans.

I think early Buddhists viewed animals one-dimensionally. They must have been familiar with death in the wild, but they focus only upon elements of predatory violence and deprivation. If one were to ask a Nunamiut Eskimo hunter of the American Arctic about the range of behaviors and expressions of wolves, a complex picture would emerge akin to how the Nunamiut thought of themselves.[98] There would be differences in degree, but for the Nunamiut, wolves, like humans, have individual personalities. They play, nurture, hold grudges, and torture. It seems likely that forest renunciants also would have been familiar with the behaviors of the tigers, monkeys, and elephants with whom they shared the forests. Or it may be that because they were meditating and putting their attention on their practice, they did not observe animal habits. I tend to doubt this because of the years they spent in the woods and the alertness they required to survive. If forest monks' more nuanced understanding of the wild was not preserved textually, it may either be because of scholars' biases or because forest monks did not bother to contradict accepted beliefs.

All early Buddhists, eremites and cenobites alike, lived in an agricultural society that bordered on the wild. They could not help but have some knowledge about nature as it occurred in their surroundings. But in building a religion the monastics disregarded many parts of mundane life, not including them in the sutras. They took plants and animals for granted, even though their environment changed as centuries went by. While eremites may have genuinely believed that animals suffered more than humans, their daily experience dealing with the forest must have tested that belief; and the lore they passed on to neophyte forest renunciants must have contained information incorporating harrowing experiences of human survival in the wild. As we will see in a later chapter, this was indeed the case for the forest monks of nineteenth and twentieth-century Thailand. One Thai forest monk was aware of the different levels of danger from wild and domesticated elephants which both roamed the forests.[99] For early Buddhism I need to argue by analogy, because evidence is lacking. The sutras place humans above animals because humans can overcome their defilements through careful investigation and can tame behaviors that engender bad karma. This is unavailable to animals except via rebirth. Animals are locked into their suffering for the duration of their existence. Animals are thus especially worthy of compassion.

Because animals are sentient beings capable of rebirth and because they recoil from pain and have fear of death like humans, there was a prohibition against killing or injuring them. This led to Buddhist vegetarianism. Later on, especially in Mahayana, kinship with animals was emphasized, because in the endless cycles of rebirth a given animal may have been one's mother or son. But this idea was not widespread in early Buddhism. In the monastic code a monk may accept meat or fish as food if he has not seen, heard, or suspected that the animal was expressly killed for him. Monks and nuns were also prohibited from injuring plants because they are the home of insects. Buddhaghosa says killing a big animal creates worse karma because it requires greater aggression than the destruction of a small animal. While the prohibition against doing work accords with a prohibition against injuring seeds and plants, in no place in the early Theravada texts thought to be foundational are plants, earth, and water said to be sentient, i.e., to have feelings.[100] But by abstaining from taking life, even to the extent of risking starvation, ascetics and renouncers removed themselves from the cycle of killing and, therefore, from the need for ritual appeasement. Farmers who kill and eat animals, they believed, would have to atone for their actions. This can happen by embracing monasticism or being reborn as one who becomes a monk.

In contrast to Buddhist beliefs hunter-gatherers saw themselves as part of nature. Their ritual acts functioned as reminders of that fact and as communications to their animal prey and their own predators. Rituals underscored that the taking of life was to be done in accord with balance in nature. The early Buddhist emphasis upon loving kindness acted as a parallel ritual, informing wild animals that the renunciant was partici-pating as little as possible in the cycle of eat and be eaten. As the sutras put it, "He who gives safety to countless sentient beings receives, in his turn, safety from them, and snakes and other dangerous animals do not bite or injure him who encompasses them with friendship or benevolence."[101] While this had some relevance for cenobites it was crucial for forest renunciants. Placing themselves in the midst of danger, loving kindness was their only protection. More practically, "monks are prohibited from eating the meat of dangerous animals like snakes because they may take revenge... or of beasts of prey like lions, tigers... because these... may attack the monk on account of the smell of the meat they have eaten."[102] We will look more closely at strategies for forest renunciants' survival in nature when we examine the lives of the forest monks of Thailand.

The picture that emerges of the Elders' relationship to nature is that of an early Buddhism arising from forest renunciation, which had respect for nature but looked on nature as repulsive. Forest asceticism, which likely preceded the Buddha, was regarded originally by Buddhists as a pure form of practice. As Buddhism developed, however, it became a religion of village monks bound by a monastic code and relying on scholars to maintain its beliefs and act as agents of its dissemination. This cenobitic tradition enshrines the forest tradition but, never-theless, relegates it to a subsidiary role. In fact, village monks looked on the forests much as did their non-monastic neighbors. The woods were dangerous places and only people of lesser sensibility and worse karma would abide there. (This antedates the similar views of European imperialists by several thousand years.) In the sutras a disciple admonishes a trapper that he shouldn't hunt red deer and a deva (a minor deity) calls him, "A silly trapper, dull of intellect."[103] Moreover, cenobites had little familiarity with or respect for nature to temper the fundamental aversion central to early Buddhism. Theravada Buddhism, as it emerged under the dominance of scholar monks, truly thought nature, the wilds, and those who dwelled therein were disgusting and not worthy of concern.

Among the scholars meditation was carried on, but it played a minor role. The *Visuddhimagga* is a monumental text on practice and yet, for monks and nuns trained to memorize text or engaged in debate, for monks who cared for village shrines and conducted ceremonies, for monks who worked in the great monasteries and Buddhist holdings bestowed by royalty—for the overwhelming majority of monastics in the 2,500 years of Theravadan Buddhism, there was little time or predilection for meditation. Our knowledge of Buddhist history comes largely from non-meditating, non-forest monks and scholars who have nonetheless preserved what we know about forest renunciants and their practices. Meditation within Buddhism has been a thin thread strung mostly from teacher to student for more than two millennia. That meditation survived Buddhist religion is due to the commitment and depth of those who, like the Buddha himself, felt compelled to look into the nature of suffering.

The forest tradition is an even finer thread. Shortly after the time of the Buddha it vanishes from view. Perhaps it survived, passed on as oral tradition. We do not know. Because forest renunciants were dedicated to practice and kept no records we have only the word of scholars who did not record its existence. Theravadan forest practice is simply not seen again until a renais-sance of forest monasticism in late nineteenth-century Thailand. The details of forest renunciation, like those of solitary *Pratyekabuddhas*, were not made known, not established, not unveiled, not explained.

Immediately after the Buddha there were forest practitioners who provide a link to the Mahayana Buddhism that developed in China and then Japan. Mahakasyapa stands preeminent among the Buddha's disciples. In the Pali Canon the monk is pictured as ordinary. Three other non-canonical texts suggest that he, rather than the Theravada designate, was the Buddha's rightful successor. Similarly, one expert sees another disciple, Sariputra, the supposed author of the *Abhidamma* and a master of subtle argument, as having forest roots which are covered up in the Pali Canon in order to present him as the ideal monastery monk. The style of the Pali Canon may conceal a world of individual charismatic forest saints deriving purity from their setting and charisma from their meditative accomplishments.[104] *Mahalla* monks were those who were ordained later in life. They were often associated with rebelliousness or lechery. They were wild old meditators who sometimes let their hair grow long and wore ragged hemp clothes.

The unkempt Upagupta appears in Sanskrit Buddhist sources and in Mahayana texts but not in the Pali Canon. He may have lived somewhere between the third century BCE and the first century CE. He emerges later as an apocryphal saint in Theravada cultures. Upagupta's childhood is said to have been spent in the forest climbing trees. He had no fear of wild things. He never participated in settled monastic life, although he had contact with monasteries.[105] Even the Pali Canon has monastic rules from which one can infer that there were monks out in the wild living off the land. It is not an offense for a monk to eat the remains of an animal kill, but Buddhaghosa warns that one must wait until the predator is gone, not only because of the danger but because it is not compassionate to eat another animal's meal in its presence.[106] Because Buddhism took root where devotion, prayer, and magic were already part of people's lives, it was these aspects of the religion, not meditation or the Buddha's rational investigation, that attracted converts. These aspects kept alive the myth of the forest renunciant who braved the dangers of the wild and possessed special powers to subdue nature. It may well be that most forest practice done after the Buddha was magical. We are not interested in following the merely magical side of Buddhism. Our interest continues with those who, like the Buddha himself, chose the path of meditation, using nature as a master teacher.

Chapter 3

Chinese Recluses

The next time and place that forest meditation appears in Buddhist history is in China some three to four centuries after the Buddha's death. Buddhism came to China by four different routes. The first passed through northwestern India, present day Pakistan, over the mountains into Central Asia and then along the Silk Road into western China. The second route, existing only for a brief period, was a shortcut through Tibet. Third, Buddhism filtered through Assam and Burma into Yunan in southwestern China. Fourthly and finally, Buddhism came by sea across the Bay of Bengal, stopping in Sri Lanka, the Malay Peninsula, or Java on its way to Canton or Tonkin in south China.

The first and the fourth routes were its major pathways. During Asoka's reign, Buddhist missionaries were sent to the northwest, Sri Lanka, and perhaps Burma. In the first century CE, 150 years later, Buddhism-embracing kingdoms thrived on the plateaus of Central Asia. These kingdoms stretched along the Silk Road and cultivated what were then fertile valleys or grazed animals on endless prairies. Ringed by high mountains to the south, bordered by the Steppes and impenetrable Siberian forests, the taiga, to the north, spread out around formidable deserts. These kingdoms prospered on a risky trade that exchanged Chinese silk for Roman glass. Political and economic life throughout Central Asia differed greatly. Kingdoms vied with kingdoms. Horse-riding nomads from the periphery invaded and settled. The Chinese to the east, Indians from the south, and peoples from the west conquered and were conquered. Whole societies migrated when neighbors drove them out of homelands. Some kingdoms lasted centuries longer than many European empires. These civilizations came to an end when the weather became drier, undermining agriculture, leaving the desolate landscape we now associate with Central Asia. From the eighth century on the Muslims conquered the area and destroyed what remained of the cultures that had prospered there. The exotic kingdoms of Scythia, Parthia, Bactria, Khotan, and Kusan are today known only as myths in the West, yet they thrived for centuries and played a crucial role in the transmission of Buddhism.

After arriving in Central Asia in the first century BCE Buddhism spread eastward, becoming an important, if not the predominant, local religion. It was adopted as the state religion by some kingdoms. Monasteries were built and many texts composed. Alongside of Buddhism were religions from Persia, Greece, and India. Some Central Asian pictures show the Buddha with black hair and curved Mongol mustaches. In others his disciples have features like Christ in Byzantine paintings.[1] The Buddhism of Central Asia came from northern India and was made up of disparate elements that slowly emerged as Mahayana. Coexisting with this was a non-Pali Theravada, whose canon survives in Chinese. Doctrines were preserved in Sanskrit and local languages.

Buddhism first made its way into China from Central Asia, and it was Mahayana Buddhism that the Chinese embraced. On the eastern end of the Taklamakan Desert stood the town of Tun-huang, the gateway to China. There in the hills caves were dug to house traveling missionaries bringing their religions to China. A hundred years after the Pali Canon was written down Buddhism began to make its way into China. Sometime between 2 BCE and 166 CE monks from Central Asia began to settle in China and recruit Chinese followers. By the end of the third century CE Buddhism was thoroughly established throughout the domains of the Han Dynasty. Centers in the north descended from the Silk Road and several in the south came via sea from India. The Chinese adopted Buddhism with vigor. Between 307 and 312 CE imperial census takers counted 3,700 clergy. During 317–320 CE there were 24,000. By 500 CE the number had grown to around 100,000. And a census in 572 CE recorded 2 million Buddhist clergy![2]

The China into which Buddhism entered and the kinds of Buddhism which prospered there were very different from their Indian counterparts. A thousand years before the Buddha, when Aryans were just entering the northwest of India, the first Chinese dynasty covered tens of thousands of square miles. Based on stone tools, agriculture, a warrior caste, and horses, a monarchy with a rudimentary bureaucracy held sway over numerous small communities. There was human sacrifice and a written language. By the time of the Buddha the Chinese population had grown to 20 or 25 million, and there were written chronicles of dynasties. About the time Asoka was consolidating power in India, the Ch'in Dynasty created a large, tyrannical, central state. The Ch'in dynasty's conquests extended from the Mongolian steppes south into Indochina. Along the Yellow River plain aboriginal vegetation was uprooted and wildlife consisted of animals who could survive on degraded steppelands. The great fertile, Loess Plateau near the northern capital of Chang-ang may have originally hosted forests, grassland, or a mixture of jungle, savanna, and riparian forests where rhinos and tigers roamed. Because of intensive agriculture, these disappeared early in Chinese history.[3] In the Dabie Mountains to the south the fertile, warm, Chinese "Land of Plenty" had frequent fogs. Hot summers allowed triple cropping and dense populations. Here the wild was progressively eliminated. The Ch'in Dynasty mobilized hundreds of thousands of peasants as soldiers and laborers to build the Great Wall and other grandiose projects, including land clearing for agriculture. In the first century BCE the Han Dynasty, which governed during the introduction of Buddhism, had a bureaucracy of 130,000 officials who helped rule a widespread state. A few hundred years later the population grew to 50 million and the capital, Chang-an, had a population of 2 million.

When Buddhism entered China virgin forests remained in the far north and some in the heart of China as islands in a sea of civilization. Any hunter-gatherers who may still have survived in them were too insignificant to warrant mention. The acceptability of the woods as a place of human habitation had dimmed in the proto-towns of early Buddhist India. Five hundred years earlier hunter-gathering was fading from Chinese reality, and by the time Buddhism arrived in China, civilization was so thoroughly entrenched that, except where the Chinese conquered barbarians in the south, the old life of foraging in the wilds was no longer even a remote dream.

China has greatly altered its landscape, from the changes before and during the Hsia Dynasty (2205–1766 BCE) to the gigantic Three Gorges project now under way. This is similar to Asoka's clearing the forests.[4] In a spirit akin to the Mahabharata the Chinese warred upon the wilds. Fire was used in prehistoric China for hunting and then clearing land. Chinese farmers set forest fires to deprive dangerous animals of their hiding places. An early tale illustrates this. "Shun committed to Yuh the direction of the fire to be employed, and Yuh set fire to, and consumed, the forests and vegetation in the mountains and in the marshes, so that the birds and beasts fled away to hide themselves."[5]

As God of the Old Testament gave Adam's heirs the world to cultivate, there was no doubt about the role of wild places for a Duke in 522 BCE: "The trees of the mountain are maintained for your use... the reeds and the rushes... the fuel, for fire of the thickets."[6] With growing rice production, increasing population, and an expanding well-organized state, an infrastructure of civilization was built regardless of the environmental impact. To make road building more efficient cart axle widths were standardized under the first Chinese emperor in 221 BCE. Roads were literally chiseled by hand out of mountain passes. In the eighth century one pass was transformed from a formidable mountainous trail to a broad stone paved road with tunnels. It was used daily for commerce.[7]

A few Chinese looked aghast at what was happening to the land. One regarded the middle of the second century BCE as, "an age of decline when tunnels were drilled in rocks to seek treasure; gold or jade were cut about and carved, to form implements for man... Man melted copper and iron... From the wombs of animals man cut out beings yet unborn, they put to death young animals... Man drilled with metal and stone to make fire, he laid a structure of timber to build his edifices, he burnt down the forests to trap animals; he drained lakes to catch fish."[8] A millennium after this was written Chinese mastery over nature was epitomized in the story of Han Yu's address to the crocodiles. "In ancient times it was the practice of our former Emperors to set the mountains and swamps ablaze, and with nets, ropes, spears, and knives drive beyond the four seas all reptiles, snakes, and malevolent creatures noxious to man." But because of weak rulers the crocodiles came back. "[Y]ou, bubbled-eyed crocodiles, you were not satisfied with the river depths. You take every opportunity to seize and devour people and their livestock, bears and boars, stags and deer, to extend your bellies and multiply your line." Bragging of his great power, Han Yu gives the crocodiles seven days to leave or be annihilated. They depart.[9]

Like nature, the Chinese peasantry was subjected to control. As early as 1600 BCE, because of famine, the government undertook forced resettlements and colonists were sent to occupy new areas.[10] From 455 BCE onward these colonists were used to secure and expand frontiers and absorb conquered peoples. Between 100 BCE and 100 CE the Han dynasties moved 1.5 million people north. Migrations were sometimes planned in details that included how to distribute land and the building of canals, irrigation projects, and houses. During the Han Dynasty many Chinese were on the move. Among them were herdsmen, slash-and-burn farmers, merchants, itinerant craftsmen, vagabonds, and migrant laborers. Whole communities traveled for work in winter, returning to their farms in the summer. In times of war, famine, and natural catastrophe urban populations fled to the countryside. From the middle of the first millennium BCE to 500 CE the government created a more homogenous population by forcefully assimilating conquered peoples and supporting the marriage of soldiers and immigrants to locals. China was quicker than India in subduing and eliminating remnant tribals, except on the fringes of dynastic rule. In Indian cities, even today, one can see exotically dressed tribals who may still sustain themselves by foraging, if only by selling wild products.

In the south, where Imperial China was expanding, we get a glimpse of how the Chinese related to what they saw as uncivilized nature. The Han Chinese were hemmed in by nomadic warriors to the north and west and blocked by the mountains to the southwest. This left the hunter-gatherers and rice-growing tribals in the south to feel the brunt of Chinese expansion. During the age of Confucius, the Miao of what is now Vietnam were characterized as savage, hardly different from wild animals. By the fourth century BCE their rice-growing Thai neighbors adopted some Chinese ways but were forced progressively southward by Chinese expansion. The Chinese invaded the rich valleys and killed or subdued the natives.[11] The diaries and reports of Chinese colonial administrators read like their British counterparts 1,200 years later. Some were impressed by the beauty of the tropical forest which they encountered, but they disliked the discomfort, worried about disease, and felt the majesty of the landscape was wasted on barbarians who did not appreciate it. They made sense of the environment by applying the same principles used for the rest of China.

This understanding was Taoist. Taoism may date from just before the time of the Buddha. Of its originator, Lao Tzu, there is only myth. Confucius, a contemporary of Buddha, created a second set of beliefs, and the Tao may be thought of as a response. While Confucius' ideas of order, honor, responsibility, and merit were fundamental to running dynastic bureaucracies, the Tao made "doing what is natural"—going with the flow, as we might say today—the primary value in life. Later, I will discuss the importance of this dialogue in the lives of Chinese recluses. To understand the Chinese outlook on nature there is another aspect of Taoism we need to look at first: Esoteric Taoism, which was also connected to the idea of being natural. This developed from the third century BCE on and came to represent much of what Taoism was in Chinese history. Concerned with attaining immortality and understanding the energies of life, esoteric Taoism analyzed the workings of nature, including foods, geology, and weather. Diet, yogic practices, and landscape were factors thought to determine the length and quality of life. Underlying material existence were vital principles or energies, like yin and yang, which could be augmented or reduced. By manipulating these vital energies through medicines, diet, and living arrangements, immortality could be achieved. Unfortunately, some people, including emperors, died from taking Taoist tonics supposed to insure immortality. Yet, despite the danger of Taoist promises of immortality, Taoists really experimented with health. They cataloged the healing powers of herbs and developed practices such as acupuncture.

And when the Chinese administrators of the southern colony tried to understand the countryside called then Nam-Viet, they used Taoist concepts. The tropical jungles and animals were seen as a result of emanations from the soils. Minerals and nature had various energies: "[T]he tangerine south gives way to the thorny lime of the north."[12] Different locales were energetically connected, and a person could travel through channels in the earth. Although esoteric Taoist geography was questionable, to say the least, Taoist knowledge of healing plants could be efficacious. And what they observed was found in great abundance. In China 1800 species of plants are used for oil, fiber, and fruits, tanning, and starch. There are 300 usable wild yams, palms, and beeches. Wild fruit trees include bayberry, lychee, longan, kiwi, date, and buckthorn, some of which the Chinese domesticated. The Chinese used 7,000 species of wild medicinal plants. Three thousand of these latter occur in the southern, more tropical areas. Of these, 500 species are still used medicinally.[13] Herbals and pharmacopoeias go back to the fifth century BCE. With the lowland forests of Nam-Viet that the Chinese occupied now gone, it is hard to tell from the descriptions what the forests were once like. Old Chinese pharmacopoeias prescribe antidotes for the poisonous plants of Nam-Viet but give only vague descriptions of the plants themselves. The trees described by colonists emphasize useful ones like palms. From this we get the sense that the Chinese understanding of nature was esoteric, medicinal, and utilitarian.

In the West, Taoism is seen as nature-friendly. This may be a misconception, although Taoism certainly appeals to the ways of nature. From the successful book *Tao of Pooh* to books on the Tao of business, resting back into or giving oneself up to the natural is taken as a formula for success without stress. The *Tao de ching* is written in an archaic Chinese, so it is difficult to know exactly what it means, but central to its themes is the idea of naturalness. Naturalness draws some of its meaning from images of nature.

Nature does not have to insist,
Can blow for only half a morning,
Rain for only half a day,
And what are these winds and these rains but natural?
If nature does not have to insist,

Why should man?
It is natural too
That whoever follows the way of life feels alive,
that whoever uses it properly feels well used,
Whereas he who loses the way of life feels lost,
That whoever keeps to the way of life
Feels at home,
Feels welcome
Whoever uses it improperly,
Feels improperly used:
"Fail to honor people,
they fail to honor you."[14]

From reading this and other translations one gets a sense of the Tao as a nature idyll. But is that what it is? Non-doing is cast as the cultured Chinese art of relaxing, that is, not doing anything of civil significance in an idyllic rural setting. This translation only mentions nature in poetic generalities, such as "like waves in the sea." The metaphors are invoked without any sense of how threatening such phenomena may be. At the time it was composed, travel by sea was an extremely dangerous undertaking. The earliest descriptions evoke images more akin to the seas in a Turner painting, overwhelming and treacherous rather than "nature does not resist." It strikes me how Confucian, civilized, and orderly the Tao is. It is, I think, more likely written, not out of a primordial communion with nature, but to ease the stress of Confucian bureaucrats, poets, and gentry, immersed as they were in the state, commerce, and family. What is proposed as a remedy is not nature in all its roughness but a country estate where one relaxes and does not strive to achieve civil ends. Nowhere in such a prescription is notice taken of the harshness of seasons, the violence of nature, or the effort and boredom of foraging.

The Tao is concerned with being receptive to nature, but from within society. "If you receive the world, the Tao will never leave you and you will be like a little child." "Do you want to improve the world? I don't think it can be done." A moderate man is, "tolerant like the sky, all pervading like sunlight, firm like a mountain, supple like a tree in the wind."[15] In contrast, real nature might be a hail storm on Lama Mountain when on a warm sunny day the temperature drops forty degrees in a couple of minutes and the hail stones come plummeting injuriously down; nature may mean spending half the summer drying salmon to feed the dogs you need to pull you around, so you can hunt the next winter. Strip away the fortress of civilization and nature is revealed as a struggle of life and death, not a picture postcard or a comfortable view from a window.

Lao Tzu's greatest disciple, Chuang Tzu, was a real historical figure who lived 200 years after the time Lao Tzu was reported to have lived. Chuang Tzu's images of nature, familiar to citizens of a developed agricultural state, include the names of birds, insects, and animals, along with mythical beasts. Although distant from the wilds, for third-century BCE China nature was important as metaphor. Master Tung-kuo asks Chuang Tzu where to find the Way. To his increasing amazement he is answered that it resides in ants, grass, and even "piss and shit."[16]

Chuang Tzu moves further into esoteric Taoism. One of his translators noted that Chuang Tzu takes one on

A romp through ancient Chinese nature lore... the seeds of things have mysterious workings. In the water they become Break vine, on the edge of the water they become Frog's Robe. If they sprout on slopes they become Hill Slippers. If Hill Slippers get rich soil, they turn into Crow's Feet. The roots of Crow's Feet turn into maggots and their leaves turn into butterflies. Before long butterflies turn into insects that live under the stove; they look like snakes... Green Peace plants produce leopards and leopards produce horses and horses produce men. Men in time return again to the mysterious workings. So all Creatures come out of the mysterious and go back into them again.[17]

Lao Tzu and Chuang Tzu do not describe real nature but poeticize it into a strange force that humans can then emulate. Doing so, humans reunite with nature. According to Chuang Tzu: "The myriad of creatures, all that live, let their territories merge together… men lived in sameness with birds and animals, side by side as fellow clansmen… In sameness, knowing nothing."[18] Taoists see rivers, rock, and clouds as sentient. They are co-transmutable with humans. Mountains and rivers are thought to have mystical energy: The larger the mountain the greater its power, especially if the mountain is named.[19] Taoists were not concerned so much with the landscape as with what it represents for, and in contrast to, the civilized world.

The archetypal Taoist master is a cave-dwelling recluse who collects wild herbs and engages in esoteric practices, such as fasting and controlling breath, which were thought to amplify the life force. Such recluses were known for their magic, the fruit of which was immortality. They were called "ancients," the "men of old," or the "immortals." One scholar argues that the roots of Taoism derive from Neolithic Chinese shamans, who may have used cannabis (marihuana) in ecstatic rituals. They were marginalized by the bureaucracies of the third millennium but survived as hermits in the mountains. Recluses have long been esteemed in China for their mystical powers. Throughout Chinese history royalty, gentry, and bureaucrats who fell out of favor withdrew from politics, sometimes even retreating from civilization to try the life of a recluse. As the story is told, in either 1100 or 300 BCE, two officials who were critical of the rulers left in protest, becoming recluses. Their attempt to subsist entirely on doe's milk and ferns failed (some ferns are toxic; others are common Chinese food). They starved to death.[20]

As this story exemplifies, most Chinese were so dependent

upon their civilization that citizens aspiring to be recluses did not know how to survive in the wilds without rice. In fact, the landscape had become so domesticated that even the environment of the recluses' was developed. In the mountains the government or patrons built Buddhist temples, and there were Taoist hermitages, group retreats, and huts of mountain dwellers. These were reachable by paved rock paths, stairways cut into mountainsides, and bridges made out of rock or carved trees. They were close enough to towns for the residents to procure supplies. Some recluses' habitations were no more than crude lean-tos with pine needle or straw beds. Although the way to them was arduous, discouraging visitors, they were located along well-worn footpaths, 20 minutes to several hours walk from each other. In general, the Chinese state saw to it that pathways through the mountains were dotted with hostels and temples that provided the traveler or pilgrim with shelter and food. Recluses gathered abundant Chinese edible wild plants, grew vegetables and some grains, and obtained supplies by begging, barter, or from patrons and nearby villages. Unlike mountain men of the early American West, most lived on the edge of society rather than outside of it. Visitors and gatherings of recluses were common. Recluses had, after all, been around for more than 2,000 years. Nonetheless, Taoist recluses were portrayed romantically:

Even if you found them they probably wouldn't talk to you... They prefer to meditate. They are not interested in conversation. They might say a few words to you then close the door and not come out again... Sometimes they eat once every three days, sometimes once a week. As long as they are able to nourish their inner energy, they are fine, they don't need food. They might meditate for one day, two days, a week, even several weeks. You might have to wait for a long time before they come out again.[21]

Meanwhile, on the Buddhist side, Mahayanist monks from Central Asia walked across the deserts or monks from India sailed across the Bay of Bengal and the South China Sea, both arriving in the civilized Chinese world. It has been said that when Buddhism met Taoism and Chinese culture, three syntheses took place. One, Buddhism absorbed some of Taoism, becoming more mystical. Two, Taoism began to define itself as a formal religion in contradistinction to Buddhism. And three, Buddhism became thoroughly Chinese.

We will concentrate on the first and third of these changes. As mentioned earlier, many different schools of thought arose within Buddhism. At the Second Council of monks, held in India a hundred years after the Buddha's death, divisions arose which eventually led to the elaboration of Mahayana doctrines. These divisions involved doctrinal differences that later became the rallying cries of sectarian struggles. Mahayana and Theravada have stereotyped each other for over a thousand years, variously claiming priority or more authentic revelation.[22] Mahayana sects also battled with each other for religious hegemony, sometimes resorting to intrigue and violence. Behind these contests were intricate theological disputes unimportant to the task at hand.[23] Here we need only sketch some of the central ideas of Mahayana which support a different attitude toward nature than was represented in Theravada. This is done in order to look more closely at the uses of nature in the meditation practices of the Chinese recluses.

Three Mahayana ideas are relevant: the doctrine of emptiness, the concept of Buddha-nature, and the Bodhisattva ideal. The doctrine of emptiness has many different interpretations in Mahayana. Its simplest presentation is in the *Heart Sutra*, a fundamental Mahayana text that distinguishes Mahayana from Theravada. The *Heart Sutra*, composed many years after the original sutras, begins:

Sariputra, all [basic meditation categories] are marked with emptiness...

Therefore, in emptiness, no eyes, no ears, no nose, no tongue, no body, no mind, no color...

and so forth until no realm of mind consciousness.

No ignorance and also no extinction of it and so forth until no old age and death and also no extinction of them.

No suffering, no origination, no stopping, no path, no cognition,

also no attainment with nothing to attain.

The *Heart Sutra* denies the basic units of meditation presented in the *Abhidamma* (the psychology of Theravada). It claims they are empty of any intrinsic existence. This emptiness also applies to all other Buddhist concepts, including the Four Noble Truths, Dependent Origination, the doctrine of emptiness, and emptiness itself.

The second idea, Buddha-nature, comes out of arguments concerning the uniqueness of the Buddha into whom Siddhartha was transformed by meditation. In Mahayana Siddhartha's Buddhahood is seen as only one, although special, of many expressions of the fundamental essence, Buddha-nature. This Buddha-nature is expressed not only in the lives of the Mahayana saints who came after the Buddha but also in every sentient being. Humans and animals have Buddha-nature and their progress toward awakening depends upon their ability to recognize and manifest their Buddha-nature. People already possess the essence of Buddhahood, though they don't necessarily see it. While Theravada restricted sentience to animals, some Mahayana masters in China extended Buddha-nature to plants and even inanimate objects. Thus, not only do all things have the potential for enlightenment but existence itself is an expression of Buddha-nature. If a person were able to embrace existence, in the form of rocks or insects or a dying child, in a completely open way, that person would see the message of the Buddha.

The third important component of Mahayana is the Bodhisattva ideal. A Bodhisattva is a Buddha who is short of the final stage of enlightenment. In Theravada there was some ambiguity about what daily life on earth would be like for an enlightened being. Complete Theravadan enlightenment would seem to take a being away from the world of decay and karma. In contrast, Mahayanists enjoy many Bodhisattvas who stopped just shy of complete enlightenment in order to dedicate themselves to the enlightenment of all other sentient beings. As one Zen mantra puts it, "Beings are numberless, I vow to save them all." In Mahayana compassion is brought to the fore. Without it meditation is considered dry and selfish. Mahayanists have often felt that Theravadans suffer from a limitation of empathy, whereas Mahayana masters—coming up just short of complete enlightenment for the love for all sentient beings—are regarded as paragons of Buddhist compassion.

A recent ecstatic description of the three components of Mahayana indicates how they intertwine:

All beings suffer, teaches the Buddha. Sentient beings are, therefore, the inspirers and recipients of heartfelt compassion and are, in this sense, benefactors or even mothers of the Bodhisattvas who vow to liberate them from suffering. [This is] the root principle of Mahayana. The relative truth of existence is that it is an expanse of suffering beings, a condition which is the motivation for the precious Mahayana commitment to universal conscious awakening. This relative truth of suffering must not be swallowed up, even subtly, by the absolute truth that Reality is an inherently selfless expanse, an infinite empty space, intrinsically peaceful and blissful. Relative truth and absolute truth must remain in a subtle balance or even in perfect unison.[24]

In Mahayana the world is a bigger place and the role of untamed nature more important.

Although the Mahayana we know today is thoroughly steeped in the cultures of East Asia, some scholars see its roots going back to the forest traditions of post-Buddha India, between the first century BCE and the third century CE. The early Mahayana texts claim to date directly back to the Buddha's highest teachings.[25] There was abundant *Heart Sutra* literature by the first century BCE, preserved by recitation, in the same way as the Pali Canon. They were both written down around the same time. We cannot determine which was more authentic. The metaphors characterizing the forest practice of the Elders referred to an isolated individual. They include a lion roaring in the jungle or a solitary rhinoceros. Forest Bodhisattvas created a new language of emptiness and compassion. "Although... physically secluded from others, his mind never abandons them. In his solitary retreat... he practices meditation... and gains true wisdom to save others... He returns among them, father, mother, husband, or son, master or servant, school master, god, man, or even animal."[26] The early forest Bodhisattvas lived outside the centers of the various religious movements. It is hard to know whether they were *Samanas*, Brahmans, or Buddhist. They need not even have been monks. "[U]ntamed, uncontrolled, not devoted, not diligent... [meditating]... like the wind in the sky," they dwelled in the wilds.[27] But because of the Bodhisattva ideal, the Mahayana texts speak of the importance of bringing the forest mind back to the city.

Given the centuries between forest renunciation in India and the beginnings of Chinese Buddhism, and given the pathways of transmission, it is impossible to know if original forest practice was carried directly to China. The monks we know of, who walked east across Central Asia, were scholars or travelers in the company of merchants. There is no mention of forest renunciants. We do not even know if the tradition existed in Northwestern

India or in Central Asia. Although many caves used by Buddhist monks have been discovered, these caves may have been similar to the hotel-like quarters at the western gates of China or may have been used by genuine eremites. Forest practice may have traveled to China through Southeast Asia. By the fourth century CE Buddhism was flourishing in western Nam-Viet, whose jungles were conducive to forest practice as the forest monks of Thailand showed in the nineteenth century. Although there is little direct evidence, one scholar envisions "monasteries and missionaries deep in the primeval forest surrounded by demons and headhunters." But by the fourth century Canton was becoming a notable shipping hub: "more Indian monks could be seen in the sea-ports than in the mountains."[28] The first indication of a recluse tradition in China comes over the sea from south India, rather than from Central Asia. Although there may have been no direct transmission, forest practices were mentioned in the sutras and outlined in the *Vimuttimagga* that was translated into Chinese.

Since forest practice embodied the original spirit of Buddhism it is possible that over hundreds of years some meditators tried it. To see how this might have occurred, we can look at the natural setting through which scholar monks walked across Central Asia on their trek to the civilized world of China. The only records we have were left by Chinese traveling the opposite direction, westward, to visit the cradle of Buddhism and gather manuscripts. Fa-hsien's (340?–420?) diary is the earliest known description. He went in search of a purer monastic code because he felt Chinese Buddhism was lax. He made a round trip through Central Asia returning to south China by sea. Sixty years old when he started, he traveled through a region which rested peacefully under Buddhist influence. Leaving Tun-huang, the gateway to China, he walked 25 days through the Taklamakan Desert. He described it as having "burning winds... No birds fly overhead, no animals run across the ground... nothing to guide

[one]; only the dried bones of the dead serve as trail markers."[29]

Crossing the Sefid-Kuh range through icy winds, a fellow traveler dies frothing at the mouth. Of a ruined pilgrimage site he writes, "white elephants and lions stalk the road in terrifying manner. It is no place in which to travel about idly." He climbed the steep slopes of the Pamir Mountains, "covered with snow both winter and summer. [With dragons who] call forth poisonous winds, cause snow to fall, or send showers of sand, gravel, and stones flying." Not many travelers survive. The locals referred to the dragons as Snow Mountain people. He traversed the terrifying scaffolding and hanging bridges of the gorges of the upper Indus leading to the plains of India. "The trail is precarious and the cliffs and escarpments are sheer, the mountains forming stone walls that plunge thousands of meters to the valley below." This part of the trip took six years. He then spent six more in India collecting manuscripts and visiting monasteries and shrines. He returned to China by sea, spending time in Sri Lanka and getting blown off course to Sumatra or Java. Seventeen years after departing he returned home. He was then 77 years old.

Although Chinese visitors in the next 300 years reported Buddhism's decline, during Fa-hsien's travels it was thriving in Central Asia and India. By the end of the twelfth century Buddhism had all but vanished in India. Scholars debate the causes. From the fifth century CE on Buddhism began to borrow tantric practices of Siva cults and became more and more esoteric. Some scholars feel Buddhist monastics became aloof from the masses, while Brahmans were adopting devotional beliefs and coming closer to common people. This combination was the foundation of an emergent Hinduism. When the Muslims completed their conquest of India in the twelfth century CE, they destroyed monasteries and universities, burned libraries, and put monks and nuns to the sword. There is a story of the Muslim destruction of one of the last monasteries. They killed all the shaved-headed residents of what they thought was a fortress and then discovered a collection of manuscripts which they could not read because all the monastics were dead. Although Buddhists and Brahmans were treated very much the same way, Buddhism, in its decline, did not survive the destruction of its institutions, whereas Hinduism was allowed to continue among the common people.[30] Whatever forest practice may have existed was wiped out. After that, Sanskrit Buddhism survived only in its East Asian, Tibetan, and some minor Southeast Asian versions. Theravada, based on the Pali Canon, continued in Sri Lanka and Southeast Asia.

Although Fa-hsien, the scholar, came face to face with nature in his travels, it did not affect his Buddhism. His interest was in sacred places, relics, and Indian texts. In China, the rigors of travel were progressively diminished by an expanding population and economy. Still, for monks who traveled there walking was their means of transport, though they might rest for the night in conveniently located hostels or monasteries. When one left the developed part of the Chinese state, nature became more imminent and more dangerous. But whether in or out of Chinese civilization, weather and shear physical effort put the traveler in much more intimate contact with nature than Westerners tend to experience, except perhaps while backpacking.

As Buddhism grew, the Chinese recognized four different categories of monks. First there were the official monks that the government supported. Second were private monks under the patronage of wealthy families. Third were monks who lived in towns or in the forest. Finally, by the sixth century there were monks living not only in the great monasteries but also in a large numbers of hermitages, recluse huts, and local shrines.[31] Buddhist immigrants had transmitted their beliefs to the peasantry. It was a religion that grew from below. Peasants — often illiterate, undisciplined, or sought by the authorities —

sometimes adopted the guise of wandering monks. From time to time the Chinese government tried to register monks to control the beggars. The haphazard spread of Buddhism did not always include its core ideas.[32] Also, local cults and wanderers practicing magic or astrology mixed Buddhism with esoteric Taoism.

In its early days the Chinese considered Buddhism to be a Taoist sect that forsook esoteric practices. By the end of the second century the differences between Taoists and Buddhists became clearer. Taoism focused on immortality using exercises, incantations, rituals, and herbs to achieve immortality, whereas Buddhists meditated as a means to end suffering.[33] Ideally, Buddhists lived by precepts and strove not to harm, while the Taoists merely aimed toward virtue in an undefined way. Monasteries of the Chan sect (which became Zen in Japan) forbade begging and became self-sufficient to counter Confucian criticisms that they drained society's resources. This policy was summarized in the aphorism: "a day without work is a day without food."[34] Wandering monks gathered wild foods and grew their own.

As early as the fourth century CE a number of monasteries were established north in the Shan mountains. There are references to asceticism and meditation and, by the second half of the century, scholar monks are reported wandering. "I go over the mountain peaks to gather medicinal [herbs]... to escape from disease."

Chains of mountain peaks over thousands of li;
[one li equals four tenths of a mile]
The slender forest girds the tranquil fjord.
When the clouds move on, the distant mountains fade away;
When the wind comes, the wild-growing brushwood becomes [even more] inaccessible.
The thatched roof [of a hermitage] hidden away, is not visible,
But from the sounds of chickens I know there is someone

[living there].
When I slowly walk along the path
I see firewood left behind everywhere [by the recluse]
And then I know that, after a hundred ages,
there are still people from primal times.[35]

The language of this poem illustrates a mixture of Taoist and Buddhist themes. Although esoteric Taoism, is evident in the reference to herbs and "people from primal times [i.e., immortals]," the Taoism of this Buddhist meditator is mostly philosophical, with its concern for naturalness and non-doing—aspects of the Tao which dovetailed with Buddhist meditation and gives a particularly Chinese slant to meditation's relation to nature.

Meditation practices from the sutras were introduced in the fourth century by scholar monks worried that in the flurry of translation and new ideas Chinese Buddhism would be left without a solid foundation. One of the foremost translators in the capital, Chang-an, was Buddhabhadra, who also trained people in meditation. Several centuries later a master of one of the large Chinese Buddhist sects described four styles of practice: perpetual sitting, walking and venerating a Buddha image, half walking-half sitting, or neither.[36] The first derives from meditation as expounded in the sutras. The second finds its expression in more devotional forms of Buddhism and among those seeking good fortune or solace for the tragedies of their lives. This constituted most of Buddhism in China. One example is Pure Land Buddhism, where the image of the Pure Land is used as an object of contemplation and prayer. Another is the cult of Buddha Amitabha. Followers chant the name of this Buddha for salvation and prosperity. Although the recluses we consider may have been adherents of one of these devotional sects it is their use of "perpetual sitting" that reveals their connection to nature.

It has been conjectured that the otherworldliness of Buddhism appealed to the Chinese especially during times of chaos and disaster that so often punctuated Chinese history. Because Buddhism was concerned with suffering and offered salvation by turning inward, it may have been appealing to the more educated and introspective Chinese who saw their world being torn apart by uncontrollable forces. To the populace as whole it was probably Buddhist magic and the promised rewards of devotion that were most attractive. Buddhist texts are filled with stories of monks besting shamans, spirits, and wild ones.[37] Because Buddhism in China was Mahayana and permeated by Chinese culture, the meditation practices involving nature developed in China had a particularly Chinese character as well. The tradition which reflects this most prominently is Chan.

The First Patriarch of Chan was Bodhidharma, and the myths which surrounded him gave flavor to the tradition he founded. Although Bodhidharma seems to have been a real person, most stories about him are of questionable authenticity. Unlike the Theravadans, Mahayanists give great credence to the lineages of their post-Buddha enlightened masters, each of whom is credited with original revelation. Bodhidharma is supposed to have come from India as the 28th Indian patriarch in a lineage dating back to the Buddha. All the texts agree he arrived by sea in south China before 479 CE and went north between 480 and 495, staying there until 516–526. Nothing else is known with any accuracy.[38]

Bodhidharma arrived in Canton, a cosmopolitan port frequented by Buddhist monks arriving from India and traders from as far away as Persia. Bodhidharma was renowned for being elusive. To evade a king who sought his advice, he left the city by crossing the Yangtze River and went into the mountains. He dedicated himself to a ferocious practice of meditation. There he stood facing a wall for nine years and did not give in to the appeals for instruction from the man who eventually became his successor until the latter hacked off his own arm as a dramatic gesture of the depths of his desire to learn.

Bodhidharma represents a number of elements of meditation practice. One is that enlightenment comes about without study or ritual. The first Indian patriarch in Bodhidharma's lineage is Mahakasyapa, who we encountered earlier as the foremost of the Buddha's forest disciples. Once, while addressing an assembly of monks, the Buddha held up a flower and smiled. Only Mahakasyapa is said to have understood Buddha's gesture, becoming enlightened by it. This direct non-discursive transmission became a model for Chan and, later, Zen. Such learning was characterized in a Chan text as:

A special tradition outside the scripture;
No dependence upon words and letters;
Direct pointing at the soul of man;
Seeing into one's own nature and the attainment of Buddhahood.[39]

After Bodhidharma Chan Buddhism developed in complex ways. Two schools emerged. One embedded the non-discursive core of Chan into an ideal of sudden enlightenment that sprung from outrageous acts which stop the mind. The Chan of Lin Chi (Rinzai in Japanese) involved non-verbal actions more violent than the Buddha's flower, such as a master slapping a student or throwing him in a river. Practices of the sudden enlightenment school included assigning students the task of unraveling a verbal conundrum or kung-an (in Japanese, a koan), such as the famous, "What was your face before you were born?" or "Does a dog have Buddha-nature?" In the intense effort to understand the ineffable, students' minds let go, and they attained clarity. Books filled with koans were used for training monks in Chan monasteries.

The second school was that of gradual enlightenment. Here silence was cultivated through the practice of "just sitting." In

Japan this was associated with Soto Zen. Both schools had elements that cut loose from the confines of daily life. For them both irreverent behavior and raw nature demonstrated Buddha-nature more clearly than proper society could. Buddha-nature is beyond words and ideas.

One of the most famous koans concerns the First Patriarch. It goes: "What is the meaning of Bodhidharma coming from the West?" The responses of some Chan masters are:

Chao-chou: The cypress tree in the courtyard.

Ling-shu Jumin remained silent.

Matsu kicked and knocked down the questioner. To another he said: If I do not strike you, people all over the country will laugh at me.

Hsueh-feng shook the fence he was fixing with the questioner.

Lin-chi (Rinzai) asked his teacher, Huang-po, three times, "What is the real meaning of Bodhidharma coming from the West?" and received three blows. Being hurt by the rough treatment he went off to see a hermit who told him that Huang-po had been treating him with motherly kindness. On hearing this

Lin-chi awakened.

Liang-chieh: It is a big rhinoceros, whose horn often frightens chickens.[40]

When I came across the Bodhidharma koan, while doing research for this book, my spontaneous response was: "Out of the West came the thundering hoof beats of the great horse, Silver. The Lone Ranger Rides Again." The radio program about the Lone Ranger began with these words in the 1940s. The Wests, out of which respectively Bodhidharma and the Lone Ranger came, had related meanings. The Lone Ranger stood for civilization in a wild and lawless West. Later, we will examine how our images of that West are imposed upon Chinese landscape poetry and paintings, reading into the lives of their creators very different experiences of nature than they actually had. In contrast to the Lone Ranger, Bodhidharma cut through the civilization he landed in to find a more grounded reality in the wildness of practice, where behavior was not bound by Confucian civility, the recitation of texts, or the theology of scholars. Practice was meant to penetrate to the essence of existence. Bodhidharma was crude, like the nineteenth-century natural historians' image of nature driven by survival of the fittest. As Tennyson put it, "Nature, red in tooth and claw." Pictures of Bodhidharma show him sometimes with a ferocious grimace and other times with a mournful expression. He represents a confrontation with life and death laid bare of the protections of civilization.[41]

The only response to the Bodhidharma koan above that touches on wild nature is Liang-chieh's: "It is a big rhinoceros, whose horn often frightens chickens." Harking back to the *Rhinoceros Sutra*, where the horn symbolizes being alone in the wild, we might suspect that Liang-chieh's domesticated chickens or civilized humans are frightened of the unadorned reality of life as seen in nature. Although most Chan teaching took place within monasteries, there were Chan eccentrics who, like Bodhidharma, connected practice to nature. Foremost of these was Han-Shan, or "Cold Mountain." He and several contemporaries mocked the Buddhist monastic establishment from their wild mountain retreats.

Cold Mountain, a seventh-century recluse, bore the name of his dwelling place. One of his associates, Pickup, Shih-te, was the janitor or cook in a monastery who would supply Cold Mountain with scraps of food when he came to visit. The two are often pictured making fun of the monks. Cold Mountain is dancing and Pickup is sweeping the monks out of their conventional, stuck places. Cold Mountain and Pickup embody Chan irreverence. A third member of the Cold Mountain poets was Big Shield who, along with Pickup, liked to inscribe his poems on monastery walls. As is the case with so many recluses in Buddhist history, the stories about Cold Mountain and Big Shield are of questionable accuracy. Yet the myths that surround them evoke powerful images. If they indeed lived the life of hermits, abjuring scholarship and tradition, then like others in forest lineages they did not leave, nor would we expect them to have left, detailed records of their lives. What they did leave was their poetry.[42]

As we saw, for centuries mendicants wandered the woods and hills of China. Some lived in solitude. Despite the fact that there must have been intimate contact with nature one scholar feels both that civilized Chinese hated wildness and that before Buddhism educated Chinese had no way to talk about nature. When they adopted the idea of the Buddha-nature of rocks and trees, they acquired a language and sentiment by which they could describe nature.[43] By dwelling in the wild, recluses both confronted the society and used Buddhist metaphors about nature to convey their experiences. Buddhist recluses turned away from "the world of dust," which signified conventional life. This was analogous to Taoists' living effortlessly with nature. They practiced the Way (of the Tao, the invisible formless matrix thought to give rise to endlessly changing forms). For Buddhists the Tao was often reinterpreted as "Buddha mind," i.e., an attitude toward life rather than a condition of material existence. Other recluses were curmudgeons, simply rejecting conventional ties.

The Cold Mountain poets' emphasis on solitude was likely greater than they actually experienced. Han-Shan presents us with a problem encountered with other recluses, and that is how much were they merely posing as dwellers in nature and how much did they actually do it? Literary analysis indicates that Han-Shan's poems may have been written by two persons. He also may have been a failed civil servant and married. His command of classical Chinese allusions and standard Buddhist imagery can be taken to mean that he is repeating canned themes, rather than living experiences.[44] Despite these caveats, the Cold Mountain poems strikingly convey how living in nature can be a teacher of the essence of Chan.[45] Unlike other recluses, who composed poetry or painted and were dependent on towns for the perishable materials with which they preserved their creations, the Cold Mountain poets inscribed their poems upon trees and walls in the countryside.

Whatever their dependency on civilization, recluses faced all manner of hazards, and their lives stood as a challenge to civilized Chinese. They embraced inclement weather, illness, and hunger. Han-Shan has been pictured in different ways. In one painting he is emaciated, with tattered clothes, birch bark cap, and wooden clogs. He may have had a limp. In other paintings he is fat and jolly. The challenges of life out of doors dominate his life.

I settled in Cold Mountain long ago
Already it seems like years and years.
Freely drifting, I prowl the woods and streams
And linger watching things themselves.
Men don't get this far into the mountains,
White clouds gather and billow.[46]

If I hide out at Cold Mountain
Living off mountain plants and berries....
All my lifetime, why worry?
One follows his karma through.
Days and months slip by like water,
Time is like sparks knocked off flint.
Go ahead and let the world change...
I'm happy to sit among these cliffs.[47]

If you are looking for a place to rest,
Cold Mountain is good for a long stay.

The breeze blowing through the dark pines
Sounds better the closer you come.
And under the trees a white-haired man
Mumbles over his Taoist texts.
Ten years now he hasn't gone home;
He's even forgotten the road he came by.[48]

staying below Cold Cliff
the surprises really amaze me
taking a basket to gather wild greens
lugging back a basket of fruit
sitting down on a straw to a simple meal
munching on magic mushrooms
rinsing a gourd bowl in a clear pool
making stew from scraps
sitting in the sunshine wrapped in a robe
scanning poems of the ancients.[49]

What gives these poems the feel of real experiences of nature is the detail with which they portray daily life in the woods. Although the poets often make light of the difficulties, the harshness of changing conditions is a constant theme, no doubt reflective of real experience.

Men ask the way to Cold Mountain
Cold Mountain: there's no through trail.
In summer, ice doesn't melt
The rising sun blurs in swirling fog.
How did I make it?
My heart's not the same as yours.
If your heart was like mine
You'd get it and be right here.[50]

wanted to go to the eastern cliff

for so many years till today
finally grabbed a vine and climbed
met mist and wind halfway
the path was narrow clothes hardly passed
the moss was slick shoes wouldn't advance
stopped beneath this cinnamon tree
and slept with clouds for a pillow.[51]

... A recluse needs to be willing to live with:
Thin grass does for a mattress,
The blue sky makes a good quilt.
Happy with stone under head.[52]

None of which is easy, except in the imagination of those who have never done it: wild greens, scrap stew, grass mattress, slick moss, stone pillow, and dark pines. Han-Shan's heart does not yearn to forget mortality with a full meal at a warm hearth in the bosom of family: "Ten years now he hasn't gone home; He's even forgotten the road he came by."

Hints of the Cold Mountain poets' meditation practice are found in their poems.

laughable, these wooded springs
miles from the nearest home.
mists drift up the towering peaks
where Ribbon Falls cascade down the scarp.
monkeys cry out a long song of the Tao
and the roar of tigers keeps men at bay.
the pine wind sighs sharp and mournful
while birds chatter and gossip.
all along, I skirt the rocky torrents
or take a solitary stroll along the ridge
sit and meditate against a standing stone
sprawl back to look at creepers up the cliff.

in the distance I see moat and walls
can almost hear the city's bustling rattle.[53]

Meditation includes sitting in silence, repeating a mantra, or reading texts: "sitting in the sunshine wrapped in a robe scanning poems of the ancients." Along with these is a special kind of practice which connects recluses to their setting. This is the attempt to simply stay present with the nature that surrounds them and defines their existence. There are two aspects to this practice.

One is that when a recluse's or, for that matter, anyone's mind quiets down he or she becomes aware of the surroundings. With a silent mind nature becomes apparent. We can see the fruits of the Cold Mountain poets' uncluttered attention in the compelling images of nature they evoke. Remember how often you walk through a natural setting thinking about this or that problem in your life, hardly aware of your surroundings or the scurrying insects at your feet. Henry David Thoreau reminds us, "Of course it is no use to direct our steps to the woods, if they do not carry us thither... it sometimes happens that I cannot easily shake off the village. The thought of some work will run in my head and I am not where my body is... I am out of my senses."[54]

One day I climbed a 1,500 foot hill near my California home. I spent an hour or so at the top meditating in the warm sunshine. I encountered no one on my ascent or descent. On the way down my mind was very quiet and I was walking slowly, attentively. As I rounded a curve on the fire road that was my path, I encountered a female mountain lion and a kitten. We three stood quite still. Then the kit went over the side of the trail. I was a bit concerned, not wanting to be caught between mother and offspring. When I was sure the kitten was not behind me, I did what you are warned not to do, I sat down. I had no fear, just the stillness of my meditation. While I was seated, the mother approached me slowly. Then we engaged in a little dance. I stood and she backed away a bit. I then approached her slowly. After I had taken a couple of steps in her direction, she gave a low growl. I backed away a few steps and then my mind got in the act. I thought that I might need a bit of protection, so I bent down and picked up two rocks, intending to throw one behind the lion to distract her if she approached too close and the other to throw at her if I had to. The moment I picked up the rocks the communication between us changed. The she-lion became super alert and quickly vanished over the edge of the hillside. I knew immediately that my thinking had ended our encounter. I had little fear, except perhaps when she growled. She weighed about 65 pounds and did not feel intimidating. Later I saw a biologist's video footage of a male mountain lion in the same area. It weighed about 150 pounds, a real lion. I am not sure the quiet of my meditation would have been sufficient to overcome the fear he might have inspired.

The second aspect is that nature constantly reminds the recluse of its indifference to human concerns. The troublesome mind of the recluse and the occupations of the society from which a recluse has fled are of little import in this larger context.

Clouds and mountains all tangled together up to the blue sky
a rough road and deep woods without travelers
far away the lone moon a bright glistening white
nearby a flock of birds sobbing like children
one old man sitting alone perched in these green mountains
a small shack the retired life letting my hair grow white
pleased with the years gone by happy with today
mindless this life is like water flowing east
Ahead the green creek sparkles as it flows
toward the cliff a huge rock with a good edge for sitting
my heart is like a lone cloud with nothing to depend on
so far away from the world's affairs
what need is there to search for anything[55]

"Go ahead," sentimentalizes the poet, "and let the world change... I'm happy to sit among these cliffs." Or perhaps the Cold Mountain poets are not sentimentalizing:

Among the thousand clouds and ten thousand streams,
Here lives an idle man,
In the daytime wandering over green mountains,
At night coming home to sleep by the cliff.
Swiftly the springs and autumns pass,
But my mind is at peace, free from dust or delusion.
How pleasant, to know I need nothing to lean on,
To be still as the waters of the autumn river.[56]

these woods and springs make me smile
no kitchen smoke for miles
clouds rise up from rocky ridges
cascades tumble down
a gibbon's howl threads the Way
a tiger's roar transcends mankind
the pine wind rushes clear
birds discuss singsong
I walk the winding gorges
and climb the peaks alone
sometimes sit on a boulder
or lie and gaze at trailing vines
but when I see a distant town
all I hear is noise.[57]

There is no avoiding the Buddha's teachings in nature. Impermanence and the insignificance of the human sense of self are seen at every turn. It is only when the recluse's mind is separated from the setting that discontent arises. Nature reveals the universality of Buddha-nature. In civilization, as Pickup notes above, "all I can hear is noise." Nature allows the noise to settle out. But this is by no means an easy practice. Recluses are constantly challenged by nature and by the chattering of their own minds.

Over the years I have spent time in remote and isolated parts of the world. In such places I met men who could not live around other people. Their outward appearance might lump them with the Chinese recluses, but inwardly they had no practice. Their minds, as the Buddha put it, were "whirled away." In isolation their inner monologue overwhelms them. In spite of the fact that they often possessed impressive bush skills, they appeared to dwell in delusion. They talked to me as if talking to themselves. Some had little but anger and bitterness to share with their visitor. They are examples of how isolation without strong practice can lead to madness.

The Cold Mountain poets touch on this. A chattering mind is balanced by meditation's insistence on remaining present, if only to a breeze.

when I can't stand the stirring of birds
I lie in my grass hut then
while the cherry's still dark
and the willows still fuzzy
the rising sun mouths a blue ridge
clearing clouds wash a green lake
who'd think of leaving the dusty rut
and heading south up Cold Mountain[58]

a hermit's heart is heavy
he rues the shift of years
looks hard for roots and mushrooms
but running won't make him immortal
the court is wide the clouds just curling
the forest bright the moon just full
why doesn't he go back

cinnamon trees detain him[59]

Rough and dark Cold Mountain trail,
Sharp cobbles the icy creek bank.
Yammering, chirping always birds
Bleak, alone, not even a lone hiker.
Whip whip the wind slaps my face
Whirled and tumbled snow piles on my back.
Morning after morning I don't see the sun
Year after year, not a sign of spring.[60]

Loneliness may be the greatest challenge: "In the wilderness, mountains and seas are all right, But I wish I had a companion in my search for the Way." If you don't discipline your mind, loneliness gives rise to madness as in the case of the "bushed" hermits I met. Even for practitioners who aspire to the compassion of the Bodhisattva bitterness is hard to avoid.

pigs eat dead human flesh
humans eat dead pigs' guts
pigs don't mind that humans stink
humans say pigs smell fine
throw dead pigs into the river
bury dead humans deep
when neither eats the other
lilies will bloom in boiling soup
all I see are fools
storing wealth and grain
drinking wine and eating creatures[61]

Nature separate from civilization's comforting womb is a harsh master.

The Cold Mountain poets set a standard against which to compare Chinese attitudes toward nature. Two different stances can be gleaned. One was taken by practice-recluses for whom, like Cold Mountain himself, direct experience of wild nature was a crucial ingredient of practice. The other attitude is that of the aesthete-recluses for whom nature had a symbolic and artistic value.

Several centuries after Cold Mountain, Master Liang-chieh, who answered the Bodhidharma koan with the Rhinoceros metaphor, added, "Every step [a monk] takes should be free from attachment to his dwelling place." He asked a monk where he came from.

"I came after wandering from mountain to mountain."
"Have you reached the top?" asked the Master.
"Yes, I have reached it," answered the monk.
"Is there anyone there?" said the Master.
"No, no one is there," replied the monk.
"If so, it means that you have not reached the top," said the Master.[62]

Both examples hint at wandering, at least, as part of practice.

Despite Cold Mountain's solo practice most Chinese Buddhism, including Chan, was associated with temples and monasteries. While monks did travel by foot from place to place and nature was much less mediated for people who did not have central heating, air-conditioning, or modern insect screens, the symbolism of nature nonetheless rarely came from an immediate experience of living away from the tens and then hundreds of millions of Chinese farmers or its great cities. What distinguishes practice-recluses is their familiarity with the detail and immediacy of nature in its less pleasant attributes. Examples of both the practice and the aesthete-recluses' attitudes toward nature are found among the Nine Monks collection of poems from the seventh century.

Within the pass the living grasses freeze;
South Mountain wears ten-thousand withered trees.
Long space where human hopes are cut;
In lonely snowdrifts search the distance out.[63]

And

Bug tracks bore into obscure holes;
Moss roots join broken ridgepoles.
My reflections turn to a hidden place, deep.
Then down from the top of the peak,
Step by step.[64]

In contrast to,

Zen heart peaceful and still
Inside white clouds.
Autumn floods and spring mountains
Aren't the same yet.
It's just the pine wind
Whistles another tune.
Deep night white moon,
Drizzling already.[65]

The latter poem expresses a general sentiment without much indication that the monk experienced the fullness of life in raw nature. In contrast, the author of the first poem knows winter well and seems to speak from experience about trying to find human hope in the bleakness of winter's destruction. We will return to this problem of teasing out authenticity in our discussion of aesthete-recluses.

In Chan monasteries images of nature were used in meditation training. The Rinzai or koan tradition instructs students to respond to a koan or saying referring to nature with a mind that does not rely on thought. This is the "before thinking mind" or "beginner's mind" to which modern Zen teachers refer when they try to get students to answer koans without thinking about them.[66] On first reading it would seem that a collection of several thousand Chan koans, sayings, and sutra verses from the T'ang and Sung Dynasties (626–1279) represents a tradition of recluses rather than cenobites.[67] Images of nature are prominent, as the translator explains, "To the enlightened eye, everything explains vividly the unexplainable and transmits the untransmittable. All nature, as it is, is seen as the manifestation of *satori* [Japanese for an instant of great clarity]." Examples might be: "Rain bamboo, wind pines; all preach Zen;"[68] or "The sounds of the valley stream wash your ears clean; the canopy-like pine trees touch your eyes green."[69]

While most of the collection's references to nature are rather clichéd, some have an authentic ring: "Sitting quietly in a hut… White clouds rising over the mountain;" or "Old age deepens the love of mountain life. Dying by the cliffside: my bones will be clean." On the whole, the collection is not that of a recluse tradition. One saying makes clear that involvement in the Chan community is what was important, not being a recluse: "The accomplished hermit hides in the town; The immature hermit hides in the mountain."[70] This reflects the early Mahayana idea that a meditator, having attained Bodhisattva-hood in the forests, returns to society to work for the salvation of all beings. Although most Chan monks skipped the forest stage, we have two examples of monastic careers which proceed from early training in a monastery to forest dwelling to life as teacher.

Stonehouse lived from 1272 to 1352 during the Mongol Kublai Khan's imperial reign when Buddhism was in favor. Stonehouse chose to go to a monastery instead of preparing for the civil service. At age 17 he went to a temple in southern China then off to study with several masters in the mountains. After 12 years of koan practice he felt stuck and decided to leave. On his way down the mountain he saw a storm shelter and things became clear to him. When tested with a koan by his teacher he responded that the koan was merely dead words. His teacher then asked what he understood. Stonehouse's reply was, "When the rain first clears in late spring, the oriole on a branch speaks distinctly." This won his teacher's approval. At age 41 he turned down the abbacy of a famous monastery and moved to a hut just below the peak of 1,350-foot-high Redcurtain Mountain, 15 miles from the city of Huchou, now Wuhsing. He refused to beg and went without when there was no food. He did not respect monks who begged. After 20 years of being a recluse he was goaded by the argument that Bodhisattvas are supposed to return to society into taking charge of a temple. This lasted seven years, and then, at age 66, he returned to Redcurtain Mountain, where he lived as a recluse until his death at 81. He wrote most of his poems during this last period.[71]

He sustained himself by foraging, gardening, and bartering wood for grain.

> *head of white hair body of bones*
> *versed in all aspects of daily living*
> *I pound mountain thistles in fall in a stump*
> *sun-dry vine buds in spring in a tray*
> *buy solomon-seal from someone below*
> *eat seaweed when a foreign monk arrives*
> *but I never guessed at seventy-seven*
> *I'd dig a pond to grow lotuses and cress.*[72]

His isolation was only relative: "few visitors brave the cliffs. I haul wood to market... drip with sweat lugging rice back up;" and, "old ladies steal my bamboo shoots[;] boys lead oxen into my wheat."[73] Late in life disciples came to learn from him. He occasionally refers to raw nature as the source of his inspiration.

I was a zen monk who didn't know zen
so I chose the woods for the years I had left
a patched robe over my body
strips of bamboo around my waist
mountains and streams explain the Old Man's meaning
flower smiles and bird songs reveal the hidden key
sometimes I climb the rocks on the ledge
cloudless afternoons once a month.[74]

But the effort to subsist takes most of his attention and becomes an important ingredient of his practice:

a hoe provides a living
for a [monk] in the mountains
usually tending bamboo
he doesn't have time for flowers[75]

What is so telling about Stonehouse is that his intimacy with nature grows out of a meditative discipline, which he maintains in the face of the difficulties that come with practice.

forty-some years I've lived in the mountains
...
satisfied at noon by a bowl of wild plants
...
till someone asks why Bodhidharma came east
and I hang out my wash[76]

He seems to understand meditation, although which techniques he uses is not clear: "guarding against evil breaking the horse of will/exiling thoughts taming the monkey mind." He goes beyond his earlier formal practice by living the koans: "over the years I've used a hundred crocks of pickles/I plant pines for beams."[77] For him daily activities may be more important than formal practice.

> Movement isn't right and stillness is wrong
> and the realm of no-thought is confusion instead
> [Bodhidharma] didn't have no-mind in mind
> any thought at all means trouble
> a hut facing south isn't so cold[78]

He does mention his meditation cushion and describes himself sitting:

> all day... facing mountains/nothing else comes to mind.

In a series of poems one gets a sense of the deepening of his understanding of life.

> reasoning comes to an end
> a thought breaks in the middle
> all day nothing but time
> the whole year undisturbed
> in empty mountains cloud let go[79]

Stonehouse uses metaphor to hint about unusual experiences that sometimes occur during intense meditation practice: "beyond the door I made but doesn't close I glimpse strange birds fly past." We will see more such references in the cases of the Zen hermits and Thai forest monks.

As in any authentic practice, there is Mara, the doubt which the Buddha faced:

> the stove is quiet the smoke has stopped
> the spring's frozen speechless the sky says snow
> facing a wall my concentration gone
> again I think about begging in town.[80]

and the boredom of so much time without distractions:

my hut in the cliffs is like a tomb
barren of even earthly thoughts
despite wearing cloths and eating rice
I seem to be dead just waiting for cremation[81]

four or five naps every day
still don't exhaust my time[82]

and disease:

shivering I sit up to burn some pine.[84]

old age:

old and spent I've gotten lazy
no more folded hands at dawn [i.e., formal meditation]
guests arrive and I face them speechless[85]

and his death poem:

corpses don't stink in the mountains
there's no need to bury them deep
I might not have the fire of Samadhi [concentration]
but enough wood to crown this family line[86]

For all a human being's struggles what the life of a recluse boils
down to is:

I sing a Cold Mountain song after zazen [meditation]
sip some valley mist tea after dinner
and when something lingers I can't express
I cross the ridge for a basket of vine buds.[87]

Stonehouse is an apostle of the everyday life of a Chan recluse. Many of his poems are about the changing wind, time, and season. The only animals present seem to be gibbons, who steal his pears, and cranes and other birds. He sees tiger tracks, but wild animals do not seem to be a threat. He lived not too far from the civilized world, yet he attended closely to the nature he had. It was his teacher.

There is little evidence in English of any significant practice-recluses for the next 500 years, although Chan practitioners must have wandered. The last well-known Chinese recluse was Empty Cloud, who is claimed to have lived from 1840 to 1959, 119 years. He studied Taoism as teenager. He took to the road at 19 and was ordained as a Buddhist monk. Between ages 28 and 31, he reported, "I stayed in a grotto... my food consisting of pine needles and green blades of straw... My eyes were bright and those that saw me took me for a ghost and ran away... In the first and second years of my seclusion, I had many interesting experiences; I did not regard them as strange but turned by singleness of mind to look and to repeat the Buddha's name. Deep in the mountains and in the marshland, I was not molested by tigers and wolves, or bitten by snakes and insects."[88]

"Lying on the ground with the sky above me, I felt all things were complete in myself; I experienced great joy... In the third year... As there were mountains to stay on and herbs to eat, I started wandering from place to place." While searching for a teacher, he was told that his ascetic practice had been a waste of 10 years. He had only tamed the body and not the mind. "If by staying in a grotto and drinking water from mountain streams, you succeed in living ten thousand years... You will still be far away from the Tao." So from age 31 until 43 he took to eating rice gruel and practicing meditation at many different temples. At 43 he undertook a pilgrimage of penance, out of guilt for having abandoned his parents. With incense sticks in hand he "walked by day... no matter whether it blew, or rained and either in fine or bad weather. Thus prostrating myself at every third step, with one thought in my mind, I repeated the name of the Bodhisattva." He walked thousands of miles in the next three years. "Each time I had the chance of checking my mind in adverse conditions, and the more trouble I had, the more my mind was at ease." He settled for two years, practicing Chan in a monastery, then took to the road again.

He walked to Tibet, traveling among Tibetans, Mongolians, and wild tribes. It took him a year to walk to Lhasa. "Often I did not meet a single man for days when I climbed the mountains or crossed the streams." He didn't like Tibet and so walked to Bengal and took a boat to Ceylon and then Burma, finally returning to China. He visited shrines and magic places. He traveled 4,000 miles. "I forded streams, climbed mountains, braving gales, frost and snow. The scenery changed every day but my pure mind was like a bright moon hanging solitary in the sky. My health grew more robust and my steps were rapid... An ancient rightly said that after reading ten thousand books one should walk ten thousand miles." At 56 he was enlightened. At 61, during the Boxer Rebellion, he retired to a cave, changed his name to Empty Cloud and, "had to drink snow and eat wild herbs which I cultivated." "But even though I lived alone in a poor hut, my mind was completely unaffected. One day, after putting a pot of potatoes on the fire to cook, I sat cross-legged waiting until they were done. Suddenly I entered [deep concentration]." Some days later, neighboring monks came to check on him and finding tiger tracks before his hut, opened it to discover him still sitting there. They struck a chime and he awoke. Being hungry, he went to get his potatoes, "As I lifted the cover of the cauldron, I found the potatoes covered with an inch of mold."[89]

Mirroring the ideal life cycle of a Bodhisattva, the rest of Empty Cloud's time was involved with temples and religious politics. He lived until just before the Cultural Revolution and was tortured by the communists, which contributed to his death.

Empty Cloud is an archetype. Taoist, Buddhist monk, devotee chanting the name of the Buddha as his meditation practice, a man of extraordinary energies, it is hard to assess the depth of his wisdom. As with Stonehouse, we can ask what he saw in nature and how it contributed to his understanding of life. Stonehouse's poetry is a testament of his connection to nature. For Empty Cloud all we have are his claims that his life as a recluse contributed to his enlightenment and made possible his long life, his energy, and his role in maintaining Buddhism in China. We know little of how his experiences of nature contributed to these outcomes, although I suspect that they must have played an important role.

Even though the communist regime destroyed much of Buddhism, a contemporary writer tracked down some surviving recluses in China. Some live alone in the mountains, while others belong to loosely knit communities. "There have been hermits in the Chungnan Mountains for three thousand years... Taoist hermits, Buddhist hermits, and intellectual hermits... Pure Land hermits... [all who] usually spend their lives in the mountains, while Zen hermits stay only in the mountains until they find the Way, then they come down. Before they become hermits, monks and nuns usually spend several years in a monastery... when they finally begin to get somewhere in their practice, they go live in a mountain hut for another three or four years. Sooner or later they become enlightened."[90] These recluses gave many reasons for going into the mountains. "The mountain was majestic and beyond the sounds of dogs or roosters or the sight of the dusty world. Living there alone in a hut, a person could easily forget the humdrum world." The writer asked one isolated monk if he got lonely, "No, not as long as I have the wind and the moon, the water and the mountain for my companions."

Living on bare subsistence another monk said, "usually I have enough by planting a few potatoes and gathering wild plants. There is enough firewood but there isn't much water. Sometimes in the summer I have to carry water up from far below... the path is hard and dangerous. Only someone in good health whose mind is set in the Way can survive here." And for practice, "Do you chant the name of the Buddha or meditate?" Chi-ch'eng: "I just pass the time... Ever since I was young, I preferred quiet, and I've always loved the mountains. I don't like the flatlands." And from a nun who grows vegetables and walnuts, which she sells: "Trying to stay alive keeps me pretty busy. But I get up every morning before dawn and chant the *Lotus Sutra* and the *Titsang Sutra*. At night I meditate and chant the name of the Buddha."[91] The author found a Buddhist monk subsisting on grass and wax candles. When he was imprisoned by the communists he said he didn't mind it so much because he had just enough to eat and plenty of time to meditate. Again, it is difficult to assess the character of the practice of these recluses and how it involved nature. There are many reasons people withdraw to the woods. During hard times, such as the Depression in the United States, just after World War II in Germany, or the great famine and Cultural Revolution in Maoist China, people who were not socially integrated or could not generate income sought refuge in the woods where they could eke out subsistence.[92] In China the long tradition of recluses provides a convenient rubric under which this was done. Besides the few famous examples we have considered, little is known of the lives of practice-recluses throughout the vast expanse of Chinese history.

Those who are often thought of as the true heirs of Cold Mountain were the other recluses mentioned, the aesthete-recluses. The most famous among them were the Chinese nature poets. We know significantly more about this group. Icons of Chinese culture, they are the subject of much scholarly writing. Along with the Chinese landscape painters, they give much of the sense we have in the West of Chinese attitudes toward nature. In the early 1960s I attended the first large art exhibition in the West of the paintings that the Chinese Nationalists, driven from the mainland by the communists, brought with them to Taiwan. I was awed by misty, mountainous landscapes dotted with small figures and an occasional hut. I had never seen nature in that way before. The eyes with which the Chinese saw their landscape seemed so different from how I had looked at America. I concluded that the Chinese saw the natural world in a way I did not understand.

Then one morning in the early 1970s I hitchhiked in the back of a small pickup truck from the Mexican border into the mountains of northern Guatemala, and I understood what the Chinese painters had been seeing. From the bed of the pickup, careening down torturous roads, the steep, mist-covered hills around me seemed to have come out a Chinese painting. Such landscapes, informing the aesthete-recluses' relationship to nature, is well captured by the Irish poet, William Butler Yeats, in his poem "Lapis Lazuli."

Two Chinamen, behind them a third,
Are carved in Lapis Lazuli,
Over them flies a long-legged bird,
The symbol of longevity;
The third, doubtless a serving man,
Carries a musical instrument.
Every discoloration of the stone,
Every accidental crack or dent,
Seems a water-course or an avalanche,
Or lofty slope where it still snows,
Though doubtless plum or cherry branch
Sweetens the little half-way house
Those Chinamen climb towards, and I
Delight to imagine them seated there;
There, on the mountain and the sky,
On all the tragic scene they stare.
One asks for mournful melodies;

Accomplished fingers begin to play.
Their eyes mid many wrinkles, their eyes,
Their ancient, glittering eyes, are gay.

Serving man, half-way house, distant snow-covered mountains, cherry trees, musician, and the melancholy of those born to privilege and responsibility who have seen much too much of the world—such are important symbols of Chinese high culture. The poem touches on the Taoist-Confucian dialogue to which Buddhism added the question of the meaning of life. As mentioned before, the *Tao de ching* written by Lao Tzu seemed to challenge Confucian ideas of duty to state and family and encourage people to live naturally, without efforting. Before we turn to this, let us look at the image of nature in the poem which was so important to Taoism and which inspired the aesthete-recluses.

Before the Common Era, Chinese imperial rule spread southward into Kwangsi Province and the hills south of the Yangtze River where lay Lu Mountain, as well as the Huang, Heng, and Wuyo mountains. Here they came upon the landscape we know so well from Chinese paintings. "Because of extensive faulting and folding these mountains have formed remarkable shapes, with sheer precipices, overhanging rocks, rapids and waterfalls... the mountains rise precipitously from a flat landscape."[93] The mist-forming, humid, subtropical region had evergreen forests, crocodiles, and bamboo. The landscape made a lasting impression on Chinese artists. Rather than the loess plains to the north, where most of the Chinese originally lived, or the steppes leading to Central Asia, on whose edge sat the early capitals, this mountainous landscape became the icon from which artists drew their images of nature. Although Chinese nature art and writing is too rich to be treated comprehensively in this book let us touch upon some of the ways it connects to meditation and nature.

Landscapes in Chinese paintings fit into a Taoist under-standing of nature as imbued with mystical qualities. The misty, jagged, vertically ascending hills of Kwangsi make excellent subject matter for artists who believe geology expresses unseen forces. These artists presented the landscape as much wilder and more remote than it actually was, as did the practice-recluses. Some of the barren jaggedness of the hills may have been the result of erosion that had been caused by extensive deforestation. More than one scholar has noted how, "The landscape of the gentry is that of landscape artist and gardener. Of Taoist and Buddhist inspiration, it is less a view than an enveloping atmos-phere to which the scholar-official can escape for short periods of time."[94] What appears in poems and paintings as isolated wilderness is close to centers of population. It is more the local sojourn of the urban citizen than the escape of the hermit cutting himself off from society. We noted before that Buddhism gave the Chinese a way of speaking about nature which had not been available within the Taoist-Confucian dialogue. Nature was seen to embody Buddhist understandings of existence.

The best example of the relationship between landscape painting and nature in Chinese Buddhism I know of occurs in the works of a Japanese Zen painter who made the customary pilgrimage to China as part of his meditation training. Of his travels, the aesthete-recluse, Sesshu Toyo, (1420–1506) said: "I went to China with the thought of receiving instructions from masters, yet I found no masters but the mountains and waters of China."[95] Sesshu's painting, *The Long Scroll,* is considered one of the major works of Zen or Chan nature painting. In it there are stark rock formations with mist and trees jutting up from the barren landscape. Sesshu painted *The Long Scroll* from the sketches and memories he had of his trip to China 18 years earlier, when he was so impressed by the Chinese landscape. The scroll, scholars have noted, represents the Zen themes that rocks, trees, mountains all have Buddha-nature and that humans are insignificant in this larger world.[96] When I look at the scroll I do so with American eyes influenced by the Lone Ranger galloping through the seeming emptiness of the American West. On first glance I see dramatic pieces of landscape, apparently inhospitable to agricultural or domestic pursuits, situated in remote areas, which require hazardous journeys to get to them. The hilly background of the scroll strike one as far away in the wilds.

Closer examination reveals something quite different. Although the scroll progresses through seasons rather than through space, each of the seeming wilder parts is either situated between villages or structures of humans or has within them the infrastructure of society. In one direction the pictorial sequence of the scroll shows a steep hillside with steps carved out of rock on an excavated ledge (representing years of labor), a walled town under mountains, and a steep, scraggly treed hillside, again with steps carved out of rocks on the occupied side. Two people are ascending the steps at the base of which appears to be a cave with lots of people and an inn where there is a celebration going on. Then there are more hills with a path ascending to a temple, sheer cliffs, and a curved Chinese-style stone bridge over a stream. Although most of the scenes in the scroll are pictured below misty mountains, which suggest wildness, the foreground is almost always punctuated with a village, temple, or well-worn human-constructed pathways. It does not feel nearly as remote as an American National Park, with concessions at its base and groomed trails leading away into what might be weeks of hiking in woods and mountains without coming upon another facility. The network of inns and hostels that the government or Buddhist orders erected every 10 miles or less across the Chinese countryside is frequently portrayed in Sesshu's landscape. He depicts a nature void of nonhuman animals.

In the mid-1970s while walking down the escarpment in Chiapas, Mexico from the cloud-forested mountains to Palenque on the tropical jungle floor I encountered a cluster of palm-thatched houses every few miles. Along the way I met Indian children walking through the mountains to school and Indian porters carrying heavy loads. The nearest roads were 20 or more miles away. One would have to be quite familiar with that countryside to know the extent to which wildlife still existed and whether or not there were areas one could consider natural alongside of those of continuous human use. The same applies to Sesshu's nature painting.

After looking at the paintings of Sesshu and Chinese landscape artists I began to see the world around me through their eyes. In my wanderings while doing research for this book it dawned on me that high-tension-power-line towers are the pagodas of our era. At the time I was homeless, or I should say a vehicle person. Having temporarily lost the place where I was staying in Berkeley, I tried to find places to sleep in my van. This would have been no problem in the land of Sesshu's paintings, for there was open space around the villages, but then there would have been nowhere a three-thousand-pound vehicle could go, not even down the rutted main streets of a village. While the infrastructure of the San Francisco Bay area provides plenty of places for the van to travel, there is almost no open space in which to leave it to function as my bedroom. Two nights before on a large turnout off of a quiet road in exurbia, I was awakened by a policeman at 2:00 a.m. who informed me that a county ordinance prohibited sleeping in a vehicle and that since, he forcefully informed me, I had better be passing through, he would let me sleep the night and tell the other patrolling officers not to bother me. I thanked him. The next night I sought refuge at China Camp State Park, a bit of open land on the Bay on the edge of urban San Rafael. The overnight fee was $14, enough to keep the street people out, but then again, no police and only one person trying to crash for free. China Camp was refreshed by the salt water of San Francisco Bay and there was little city noise.

China Camp: a funny coincidence, Sesshu's paintings were

inspired by the scenes of China. About an hour after sunrise I walked out to the Bay but saw no shore birds. It was almost November. There were ducks way out on the water, no real bird-watching, so I climbed the hills that separate the park from San Rafael. I had been told the view from the top was great: One could see the whole Bay area. It was a misty morning. Had I been Basho, the Japanese poet (we will meet him in the next chapter), I would have been disappointed—all that effort and risk (it was a heart-pounding climb and living in my van has its dangers) and not much view because of the fog. But other things greeted me. The trail and then the old construction road on which I walked were carved out of the side of the hill, just like Sesshu's paths. One could see how much material had to be excavated by looking at the drop from the upper edge of the cut. Since a caterpillar tractor had to be able to make it up my path, a lot of material had been moved. Some was pushed over the lower edge and could still be seen some thirty or so years after the work had been done. Similarly, Sesshu's paths through the hills are extraordinarily wide for just recluses wandering off into the mountain's traffic. I wondered whether or not they were also roads for carts pulled by oxen or water buffalo or maybe even horses. At times the Chinese government set standard dimensions for roads and carts. And there is another similarity. In order to give the feeling that the road drops away as it climbs into the distance, Sesshu added parallel lines that almost look as if they were carved-out steps. On my road, the marks of machinery and the wear of bicycle tires and human shoe treads gave a similar sense of perspective.

If I had the skill I could paint a scroll of China Camp which, though it is in the midst of a densely crowded urban area of 5 million people, would have the appearance of Sesshu's nature paintings. From atop the ridge looking out through the small openings in the madrone trees, the few houses I can see along the Bayshore and the San Francisco hills off in the misty distance could easily be the natural view of Sesshu's painting. A smeared-together cluster of houses in the distance with one building sticking out looks just like Sesshu's village surrounded by water and distant mountains. Then the tower of a power line sitting atop a hill in the mist maybe a mile away, with its ceramic insulators spread with the curved slope of a roof, looks just like the pagoda in *The Long Scroll*, a serene resting place in the midst of wilderness. Of course one has to factor out an element that cannot be represented in Sesshu's art, except by implication when he portrays a marketplace. That is the sounds which float up to the China Camp hilltop: a pile driver in the distance, a truck shifting gear as it goes uphill, and the ever-present background noises of cars and airplanes.

Of course thirteenth-century China was incomparably less industrial than contemporary America, but it is hard to say to what extent it was less crowded. There were undoubtedly margins in abundance around the villages, but, nonetheless, the noises of villages reached the monks' retreats. And the sounds of passing porters or the commerce of peasants could easily undermine the sense we have when looking at the paintings that it was a wild landscape. If the capital, Chang-an, boasted a population of 2 million 800 years before Sesshu and China's population during Sesshu's travels was more than 100 million, our sense of the nature he portrays as wild may be quite different from what it was actually like as the Bay Area, with its traffic jams, is quite different from my misty morning's imagined painting.

The reality behind the illusion of wildness in Sesshu's scroll is further illustrated in an early twelfth-century painting by a southern Song Dynasty court painter, Zhu Rui. Entitled *Bullock Carts Traveling over Rivers and Mountains*, the painting appears to be a close-up of the commercial roadway that was Sesshu's mountainous path. It portrays "the upward struggle of heavily laden carts and the life of the inn at the top."[97] Although painted in the south with an archetypal southern landscape, the painter indicated it was a northern scene by portraying camels resting in the courtyard of the inn. Camels were only used in the rolling landscape of the north, not the precipitous hills of the Yangtze. As in Sesshu's scroll, the path ascends into distant misty mountains. Although seen as wilderness by Western eyes, the mountains experienced by the Chinese were tamed by hostels and commercial traffic and given the different levels of technology no more wild than is China Camp. *Bullock Carts Traveling over Rivers and Mountains* illustrates how much the Chinese representation of nature was a romantic artistic convention. Artists maintained the fiction for centuries after the landscape of the Yangtze no longer bore its earlier wildness. While the Yangtze had been forested in the first century, by 353 CE the flatlands had been cleared for cultivation, although the hills were still wooded. Between the eighth and thirteenth centuries even the remotest regions fell to the axe.[98]

The Buddhist sermon Sesshu presents was inherited from the great aesthete-recluse Chinese nature poets and painters, some of whom lived hundreds of years before him. Their names include Wang Wei, T'ao Ch'ien, Li Po, and Tu Fu. Most led lives which swung between "rustic seclusion" and the royal court. One scholar characterizes their creations as "versions of pastoral" rather than true nature poetry. Their activities included managing their estates, gathering potent Taoist herbs, drinking parties, fishing, and hunting. "We drank and sang [and expressed] our subtlest feelings." The fourth-century Buddhist monk Chih Tun wrote, "Once I loved the quiet of a hut in the wilds and had ideas about digging up herbs. So I dwelt alone there. I climbed the mountains and gathered herbs and knew all the joys that crags and rivers afford." [99] Many of the early poems are Taoist, seeing mountains as places of power, magic, and immortality. "I would like to ride upon the whirlwind." "Without knowing it I rise and stride upon the air." The wealthy poet Hsieh Ling-yun may have even lived in the mountains.

At dawn I took my staff and sought the rugged crags,
At dusk I halted and spent the night in the mountains.
On this distant peak I have built a lofty house
Facing the mountain and overlooking winding streams.[100]

These represent, "Taoism seen through the haze of half-appre-hended Buddhism."[101] Their practice is clichéd, if it exists at all. They paste Buddhist ideas onto a landscape only partly experi-enced.

In this deep forest the slightest sound can be heard.
When sadness has gone thought returns again.
When Understanding comes Passion no longer exists.[102]

When the Tao dissolves it become rivers;
When it coagulates it becomes mountains.[103]

"My knife meets only with emptiness. I see the ox but not as a whole. I concentrate my thoughts on these mysterious crags and sing a clear song about the long rivers."[104]

Wander where you will you rarely meet with spirits,
Their subtle goodness being naturally akin to darkness.
Yet when you reach this place of the wisdom of emptiness,
A mysterious hill has formed here from the dust.
All the mountains lie in silence,
A single peak cuts through the air.
Misty sunlight falls along the crags.
...
There are men who cross these heights.[105]

Among the aesthete-recluses we find poets who clothed the

Confucian-Taoist dialogue in Buddhist rhetoric. Their lack of practice is illustrated in self-defeating sentimentality rather than disciplined examination of the nature of discontent. They romanticize their withdrawal, describing neither the luxury of their lives nor their engagement in an ongoing social and political world. This does not mean that some did not encounter difficult circumstances or that their human concerns were not real, but rather that they did not avail themselves of the ways meditation might address their suffering nor engage nature as a resource on such a path of practice. Hsieh Ling-yun (385–433) retired from court to his estate and lived the life of a recluse but then got drawn up into politics and was eventually executed for rebellion. While in retirement he spent time in monasteries, studied sutras, and wrote commentaries. He spent two years with a friend, "feasting on mushrooms and herbs"

> Together climbing the heights and looking down,
> Pushing aside boulders to clear the streams,
> Trimming branches to thin out the woods.
> In the distance we gazed out over layered crags[106]

He spent much of his time on his estate directing its landscaping. In his life Confucius won out. "I only regret my gentlemanly resolve/Has not found surcease upon the mountains."

There was a mixed message about the ancients, who were so venerated for their "naturalness." Although it was regarded as exemplary to withdraw from imperial service and seek the meaning of life in nature, nonetheless, early in Chinese history sages were acclaimed for rescuing foragers or early agriculturists from their primitive conditions. "They suffered from cold and damp in winter and heat and insects in summer, the sages proceeded to build houses of clay and wood for them."[107] Sages were also honored for clearing land for agriculture. The *Book of Changes* says that, "in primitive times men dwelt in caves and lived in the wilds," later in roofed shelters with ridge poles, then in hills and gardens, and finally surrounded by city walls. While progress is both bemoaned and admired, Taoist withdrawal, according to aesthete-recluse Hsieh Ling-yun, was not to live close to nature as a forager might. This he regarded as savagery. Withdrawal was a refined search for Taoist naturalness.[108] As we have seen, what is meant by naturalness is different from nature, although Hsieh Ling-yun and other Taoists rely on a blurring of the two to give power to their imagery. He doesn't mention that he walked into the hills accompanied by a serving man or that time in nature meant relaxing at a country estate.

One of the most famous aesthete-recluses, Wang Wei (699–759), exemplifies this. While a bureaucrat he was banished for allowing a performance of a forbidden dance. He felt unfairly singled out. His wife died in 730 and he took a vow of Buddhist celibacy. He was a Chan student for 10 years, during part of which he wandered as a monk. He wrote city poems full of pathos and longing. His nature poems expressed Taoist senti-ments. Politics changed and he returned to public service. Quite a civilized man, he seemed more afraid of raw nature than observant of it. From his post as imperial censor in a town on the edge of the Gobi Desert he wrote: "frontier sadness blows from a painted horn. It takes years to get through the Dry Sea of the Gobi Desert... when you set out as an envoy to the Tatars be careful: You may be drinking from a bowl made from the skull of the Yuezhi king."[109] Melancholy and shock at the crudities of barbarians are more prominent than Buddhist investigation of life. After all, the Gobi Desert could represent Mahayana emptiness and Tibetan Buddhists drank out of the skulls of their dead teachers to remind them of the meaning of death.

Participating in court politics caused Wang Wei much mental anguish. Yet he found his country estate, hardly a recluse's remote hut, a place of loneliness. "The thin haze of evening is saddened with the whine of cicadas. No one calls. My cane [bamboo] gate desolate. Alone in the empty forest, I have an appointment with white clouds." He seeks solace in nature and never really finds it. "[N]eeding to lodge among people, I shout across a brook to a woodcutter." On occasion he did settle into the silence: "there are silent words deep in hill water, a long whistle over the summits." But he can't let go of the moment when it has passed: "I fear I will lose this refuge forever so at daybreak I fix it in my mind." Not a very good strategy if one is striving to accept Buddhist impermanence. It is more reflective of the artist's goal to preserve what is beautiful. He walks a lot and occasionally sleeps in a cave. Unlike the Elder Monks and Nuns, who use nature as a teacher and sit quietly in wind and rain, Wang Wei romanticizes nature and seeks relief from its challenges. When the heat of the day bothers him he seeks relief in a shady place. "I know my heart is not enlightened."[110]

On hearing a tiger roar a monk whom he was visiting sends him packing. "In still night [the monk] sits in an empty forest."[111] Wang Wei leaves out of fear of the tiger.

T'ao Ch'ien (365–427) called himself a hermit, in spite of the fact that he lived in the country raising grain and caring for his many children and relatives.

Why should I, a hermit,
Gaze vacantly at the change of seasons?
The ministers are ashamed of their empty grain jars...[112]

For a long time I was in a cage,
But now I am back with nature.[113]
He is more a poet of agriculture than of the wilds.
I'll search out sheltered streams and quiet pools,
follow mountain paths up through the hills.
...

in these ten thousand things, each following its season
away perfectly, I touch that repose in which

life ends, done and gone.

...

My dream is to walk out all alone into a lovely
Mornings—maybe stop to pull weeds in the garden

...

settling into my breath, or sit writing poems beside a clear stream.[114]

For him the garden represents nature, and he has what we now call a drinking problem.

In the morning, without wine, I can not get up.
Every day I want to stop drinking.
but if I do, my body will not run in good order.[115]

His Taoism worships the natural and the goal is to be natural in one's life's actions, but in the shadow of a posture of naturalness lurks discontent. "It's loving family voices that make me happy/*koto* [an instrument] and books that keep worried grief away."[116]

I remember when I was young and strong;

...

In no time I went down into old age.

...

How much is left of my journey?

...

The men of old held every minute of time to be precious;
When thinking of this, I am frightened.[117]

Indulging in drink and fear may be compatible with a casual Taoism. T'ao Ch'ien lived in a time when Buddhism was rapidly penetrating Chinese society. Though he may have stood for naturalness over against monastery Buddhism, he was not able consistently to face his discontent with the commitment to attention and insight which are the heart of a practice-recluse's Buddhist meditation.

There are further examples of the aesthete-recluses. Some wrote beautiful nature poetry. Some were drunks. Some experienced calamities. Others were sentimentalists or struck artistic poses. According to one translator, "[Li Po] tried almost all avenues available to become prominent... [and] ended in failure... Li Po's life as a recluse partly resulted from the current idea that the loftiness of the recluse was prized both by society and by the government and, therefore, would lead to eminence... When frustrated in his political pursuits, he would turn to Taoist activities for consolation."[118]

The birds have vanished down the sky.
Now the last cloud drains away.
We sit together, the mountain and me,
until only the mountain remains.[119]

Nice verses but, drowning one's disappointment, ambition, and fame are hardly the stuff of a genuine Buddhist recluse.

Tu Fu (712–759) suffered from the hard times of the Tang invasions, defeats, and catastrophes. He lost his son to starvation and died broken in poverty. Perhaps better seen as a Confucian commentator on the tragedy of the times than a meditator, he wrote:

I lie out flat on the river pavilion
reciting poems or dreaming.
Water roars by, but my heart remains still.
Clouds drift over and my mind responds lazily.
...
How can I retire to my forest home again?
To dispel my melancholy, I write another poem.[120]

It is sometimes difficult to tell from their poems whether a recluse engaged nature through practice or was an aesthete. Han Shan te-ch'ing's (1546–1623) poems contain more of the feel of both practice and nature than the previous aesthetes.

IV.
it only took a single flake
to freeze my mind in the snowy night
a few clangs to smash my dreams
among the frosted bells
and the stove's night fire fragrance
too is melted away
yet at my window the moon
climbs a solitary peak
V.
through a face full of clear frostiness
raw cold bites
through a head overstuffed with white hair
a gale whistles
and over the world from the flowers of emptiness
shadows fall
but from my eyes the spells of darkness
have completely melted
VI.
in the sh sh murmur of the spring
I hear
moon clear the primal Buddha pulse
come from the West
with motionless tongue
eternally speak
how can I be sad again?
how strange.[121]

In the first lines of the poem serene concentration leads to seeing hope as another delusion. This is an insight with which the Buddha would agree. Throughout the poem nature's discomforts are acknowledged as expressions of Buddha-nature. In the end Han Shan te-ch'ing wonders how it could be that the mind becomes sad again after moments of clarity when attuned to nature. The fact that the writer reports this puzzle of meditation practice, that one's mind and body create uncomfortable emotions notwithstanding profound insight, lends credence to the authenticity of the writer's experience. Many aesthete-recluses' reports read more like Buddhist slogans. Han Shan te-ch'ing seems to be harvesting the fruits of the Buddha's prescribed forest practice.

From the perspective of modern natural history the nature seen by practice-recluses is partial. This is even more true of the aesthete-recluses. They create dynamic images of weather, season, and landscape. They mention the passing of time of a day or a life and the sounds of nature, but they have little to say about the interactions of animals, the lives of predator and prey. The only changes in the environment over time that I have encountered are the mention that mining and agriculture have ruined the landscape of the ancients and that the silting in of the Yellow River delta caused the land to march into the sea (almost one hundred miles). The recluses' images are beautiful, but they capture only some aspects of a vibrant, subtly interacting world. From the point of view of the civilized Chinese, interactions which go into making up the survival of the fittest do not seem to be worthy of comment. The Chinese leave out the world of insects and decay. Nowhere have I found pictures of a tattered butterfly on its last legs or rotting wood with its myriad of beetles and other decomposers.

Some practice-recluses really lived out in nature and knew well the woods, which may not have been all that wild. They give us a slice of that world, but there is much more there that may have been relevant to their practice. Part of this are the animals who had been so thoroughly included in the Mahayana universe but do not draw much attention in the Chinese landscape. Unlike early Buddhist India, bubble-eyed alligators and other dangerous wildlife were eliminated from the centers of Chinese culture. Practice-recluses mention the sounds of tigers and gibbons in some poems. The tiger is a prominent symbol in China. Dragons were the bringers of rain, but tigers represent drought. To arouse the dragon farmers dragged a tiger skull through pools of water.[122] All four Asian subspecies of tiger live in China. On China's northern border live Siberian tigers and on the southern borders Indochinese and Bengal tigers. The center of China was the home of the ancestor of them all, the South China tiger. This most common of tigers was present south of the Yangtze until the 1950s. It persisted in remnant grasslands and forests, preying on livestock and humans when deer and other natural prey were reduced by hunting and habitat destruction.[123] Official gazettes going back several thousand years report numerous attacks. Peasants had ambivalent feelings about tigers, sometimes regarding them as valuable spirit beings or protectors of the forest and other times collectively pursuing them when they wreaked havoc. Tigers were felt to be harmless in times of good government but aroused when the country was not well governed. Tigers, like Chinese Buddhism, thrived on suffering. The aesthete-recluse above who fled the woods when hearing a tiger roar may have been acting with appropriate caution. Nevertheless, practice-recluses expressed little fear of tigers. In the twentieth century Empty Cloud was neither bothered by tigers who passed his cave nor had any fear of them. This may be because he, like other practice-recluses, faced his fear as the Buddha suggested or that, unlike the forests of the renunciants, dangerous animals were so scarce that there was little need to practice loving kindness as a protection. Although there were places in China were peasants had plenty of opportunity to observe tigers, Chinese paintings of them are caricatures. Most wildlife was regarded similarly in Chinese high culture.

This view of nature is further evident in Buddhist stories where rebirth as an animal was punishment for misbehavior. In a koan (Zen conundrum) used to train monks the patriarch Pia-chang was reincarnated as a fox (an animal held in low esteem) for asking whether enlightened monks could become animals. "Not falling into causation. Why was he turned into a fox? Not ignoring causation. Why was he released from the fox body? If you have an eye to see through this, then you will see the former head of the monastery did enjoy his five hundred happy blessed lives as a fox."[124] And in 1571 on Mt. Yu-ch'i in Hangchow Chu-hung, who began as a Chan monk and then turned to Pure Land Buddhism, settled near a ruined monastery that the locals rebuilt for him. Tigers killed 20 people and many animals. Chu-hung pacified them with tantric rituals but had to do so again when the trouble reoccurred. "[Someone] came from our village and asked me to pray for relief. I believe that human beings and tigers originally possess the same nature, and the cause for the destruction lies in hatred inherited from the past. If we capture the tigers, then we harm one other. If we drive them away, then what is the difference between us and other people? [T]herefore fasting and creating merit... transform them silently and the harm will disappear... I beseeched those who had harmed the lives of tigers in their previous lives to renounce their anger and resentment, so that the tigers would not seek retribution. I hope those who are attacked by tigers today can all be reborn into one of the good realms... Neither do tigers want to injure men on purpose, and we hope they will speedily live out their present incarnations and depart the wheel of suffering."[125] Chu-hung calls upon the loving kindness which the Elder forest renun-ciants practiced, but he also uses tantric magic. In neither case is much revealed about the actual life of tigers. It would be inter-esting to know what would have happened had the peasants adopted Chu-hung's advice.

In their relationship to nature most Chinese recluses adopted a tone different from that of the Elders. The natural world of the Elders was more limited, yet their attention to that limited domain was more precise. Forest renunciants focused minutely on the interplay between nature and mind and guarded against the defilements of the mind. In the jungles the renunciants attended to the existential meaning of eating and being eaten and the inevitability of decay. Mahayana criticized the way they expressed this. In the *Vimilakirti Sutra*, a fundamental Mahayana text, Vimilakirti corrects a Theravada disciple of the Buddha. The disciple says, "I see the great earth, with its highs and lows, its thorns, its precipices, its peaks, and its abysses, as if it were entirely filled with ordure."[126] Vimilakirti accuses him of seeing things in a limited way. "Those whose minds are impartial toward all living beings and whose positive thoughts towards the buddha-gnosis are pure see this buddha-field as perfectly pure."

For Mahayana the ability to see through and beyond the world's appearance of being spoiled is a test of one's understanding of Buddha-nature. With its inclusion of lower animals, and even rocks, as sentient beings, with its idea of emptiness, and with its Bodhisattva ideal Mahayana claims a truer grasp on reality. In painting nature with broad strokes the Chinese recluses tended toward a romanticism which glossed over the unpleasant parts in which it felt the Elders were mired. It strikes me that the forest renunciants' careful observation of decay is a crucial part of the original Buddhist emphasis on facing death-steeped nature on its own, often harrowing, terms. Yet Mahayana may be less dour in its fuller embrace and a relief from always having to see impermanence behind what feels like a safe and joyous day. From this survey of Chinese recluses, we now turn to Japanese Zen hermits who cultivated an even more expanded view of nature and yet maintained astute attention with their practice.

Chapter 4

Zen and Nature

Japan is more like China than China was like early Buddhist India. China gave birth to a Buddhism which was thoroughly Chinese. The Chinese did not look to India as a continuing source of Buddhist inspiration. In the fifth century Fa-hsien's mission was clear. He went on a pilgrimage to holy sites, but more important was to bring back manuscripts to be translated into Chinese. The West from which Bodhidharma came and the Western Lands of Pure Land Buddhism were not real countries like India but symbols for enlightenment. By the tenth century there was little Buddhism in India to be held up as a model. Japan, on the other hand, derived much of its culture, its Buddhism, and its meditation practices from China. For long periods of time China cast a shadow over Japanese history. It was often looked to as a font of knowledge and culture or viewed as a foreign influence from which the Japanese felt compelled to differentiate themselves.

The Japan to which Chinese meditation came was geographically different and less civilized. China is a huge, diverse country with broad plains divided by mountain ranges. Japan is not very big and 80% of its landscape is mountainous. Twenty-eight percent of Japan is lowland with only 30% habitable. Forests cover 66% of the land mass compared to the world average of 29%. In this, it is like Finland with 69% or Sweden with 53%. Only 16% of Japan is cultivated, in contrast to Europe where 30–50% is cultivated. Japan gets lots of rain and has mild temperatures. The soils are poor, but because of its wet, temperate climate, vegetation is lush. Japan has many steep mountainous slopes incised by dense river-valley networks. The rivers are torrential. Japan has no long continuous mountain chains.

Smaller mountainous areas need to be traversed to travel from one part of the main island, Honshu, to another. The mountains are dotted with volcanoes, 60 of which have been active in historical times. Mt. Fuji is its highest peak at 12,388 feet. It dominates Japan's largest upland plain, about 70 miles square, around one of its historical capitals, Edo—modern day Tokyo.

In parts of Japan weather and landscape give the country a special character. On the mountainsides facing west toward the Sea of Japan there is a gloomy winter monsoon with heavy snows. Some places in the mountains of central Honshu get up to 160 inches of rain. The Pacific side of the mountains experience dry windy winters. The weather patterns switch in the summer. Each year Japan suffers half a dozen typhoons, which twice saved Japan by destroying invading Mongol fleets. The vegetation of Japan is dominated in the north by a laurel evergreen forest. It contains live oak, camellia, and holly. Above 2,300 feet there used to be 2,000-year-old stands of cedar. A deciduous forest grows above 3,300 feet, descending lower in the north. Its major trees are beech, katsura, maple, oak, and birch. These are strikingly colored in the fall. At even higher elevations there are conifers, and above 8,000 feet one finds alpine meadows. Cherry trees, which play a prominent role in Japanese portrayals of nature, are found in wild stands but have also been planted all over the countryside. Among Japanese wildlife are bears, wild boar, raccoon, wolves, foxes, deer, antelope, hare, and weasels. There is one wild monkey, the Japanese macaque, which is widespread. Japan has two poisonous snakes. The rest, including a five foot rat snake, are harmless. Besides an abundance of shore birds, there are 150 songbirds. The image of nature portrayed by Japanese Buddhism was very much influenced by this landscape with its wildlife, cherry trees, mountains, and brooding weather.

From 30,000 to 10,000 years ago waves of humans of mixed Asian and Polynesian ancestry migrated into this setting. Neolithic culture in Japan lasted until about 300 BCE. The

Neolithic Jomon peoples, whose elaborate pottery was patterned with plaited cord, hunted, gathered, and fished in deep waters. They probably engaged in a rudimentary form of agriculture. Between 250 BCE and 250 CE wetland rice was introduced from China, and simple flood control and irrigation projects were constructed along the lower floodplains of the western rivers. About 100 BCE, iron tools were imported. Some scholars have speculated that the shift to rice production came because the growing population of Jomon people was exhausting the wild resources around the settlements. In China rice had been grown since 3000 BCE and iron used since 600 BCE. Japan did not make its own iron implements until 300 CE when the iron sickle was fabricated. Iron was not in general use for farming until 700 CE. Japan imported much of its material culture from China, shortening development times. In the fourth and fifth centuries CE Korean immigrants brought large-scale irrigation and sophisticated iron working technology that contributed to the expansion of rice cultivation. Farm animals including oxen, horses, and chickens were introduced. Living standards went up. These developments came to Japan a thousand years later than China. Buddhism first made its way to Japan a little after the Korean migrations.

The attitude toward nature which Buddhism encountered in Japan was different than in China. Civilized China made war on nature and, although tempered by Taoist romanticism, cultured Chinese feared and hated the wild. The Japan into which Buddhism entered was much closer to its hunter-gatherer past, had had much less impact on its environment, and thus sat more comfortably in its relationship with nature. Prehistoric Japanese hunter-gatherers likely shared animism with other Paleolithic peoples. As agriculture spread the animism was embedded in a series of beliefs which later became identified as Shinto. While the Taoists saw universal energies expressed in mountains and herbs, pre- or proto-Shintoism contained beliefs in a large number of kami, gods or spirits thought to reside in every natural thing. The kami embodied a fundamental goodness that nature was thought to possess. Humans maintained this by living in harmony with the kami. Kami presence in great mountains, waterfalls, or trees was especially important. The Japanese kept their lives in order by ritually propitiating the kami. This was done near the object in which the kami resided. While originating in animistic beliefs, kami worship indicated a different relationship to nature than hunter-gatherers possessed.[1] The latter feel a kind of equality with their totemic animals, whereas the kami of agricultural Japanese possessed divinity.

While harmony with the natural world so conceived was important, there were also harmful kami which had to be appeased. There are so many kami, and they are so ill-defined, that even modern Shinto priests say quite different things about the same named kami. This suggests that Shinto arose from many local beliefs in which different locales had their own sets of kami that changed over time. Objects of nature were often thought to be the children of kami.[2] While the kami of the sun, the moon, and mountains like Fuji are particularly revered, kami are everywhere. There are mid-mountain kami and swift mountain-dwelling kami. There are goddesses of water channel demarcation piles and inconspicuous river kami. Swift-flowing places have kami that need to be propitiated. Before cutting trees woodcutters pray collectively to all of the relevant kami, because there are too many to name individually. The number of kami is overwhelming.

Japanese agriculture grew relatively rapidly from hunter-gatherer society and, as it did so, earlier animistic beliefs easily carried over into farming activities. Kami that resided in nature were domesticated. Agricultural activities from planting to harvesting required rituals so that the governing kami would grant a successful harvest.[3] Families had their own kami, and shamans were called upon to invoke powerful foreign kami. With the introduction of rice cultivation, the society that succeeded Jomon went from independent villages to federations and, finally, to a central authority owning all the land it periodically redistributed. The central government adopted a state religion which included rural practices.[4] Proto-Shinto formed gradually in the fourth to sixth centuries. With immigration from Korea elements of Taoism and Korean shamanism were also mixed in.

The official date for the introduction of Buddhism to Japan is 552 CE. In 593 CE it was adopted by royalty and made a state religion. Unlike China, where Buddhism was spread among the masses by thousands of anonymous immigrants, Japanese Buddhism remained a royal activity for hundreds of years. As a court religion, Buddhism could not avoid politics. The building of monasteries and monuments by patrons had little to do with its theology or practice but more with royal consolidation against princely power. As elsewhere, the major appeal of Buddhism was its magical promises and its aesthetics. From the upper classes it gradually drifted downward, conflicting with Shintoism, which, like Taoism, found it necessary to consolidate into a religion in order to meet the new competition.

From the sixth to the ninth centuries Japanese royalty had increasing contact with China. They adopted Chinese script, Confucian ideas, and Buddhist beliefs. With each diplomatic mission to China went Buddhist monks to study and bring back Chinese ways. In 805–806 CE two of the most famous Japanese monks, Saicho and Kukai, returned from China to establish what, for several hundred years, were the most important Buddhist sects, Tendai and Shingon. While most adherents to these were gentry, the practices sometimes went beyond the ritual and philosophic narrowness of early Japanese Buddhism to incorporate devotional chanting. Buddhism did not really penetrate into mainstream Japanese life until the twelfth century with the spread of Pure Land Buddhism and the introduction of Zen. Pure Land Buddhism involved the cult of the Amitabha

Buddha (Amida), a Bodhisattva of compassion. Peasants chanted the Bodhisattva's name, "Namu-Amida-Butsu" or "Nembutsu" to gain help with their everyday problems. Zen, on the other hand, appealed to the rising Samurai of that time. It was a discipline for warriors who, if they did not fraternize with commoners, nonetheless influenced their lives as a result of the political struggles in which Samurai played important roles. Chan, from which Zen derived, was already couched in the language of nature. So the Japanese, who were closer to the wild, had a ready-made tool with which to explore the relationship between Buddhist practice and nature more deeply than had their Chinese predecessors.

From the sixth to the twelfth centuries life in the narrow cultivable areas of Japan became more developed. All potential farmlands were occupied, and yields improved. Animal-drawn plows were introduced, replacing the iron hoe and allowing for uniform triple tilling. Animals had been grazed in wooded wastelands, but now such areas were more valuable as potential farmland or for raw material extraction. This led to feeding animals rice stalks in stalls and collecting the manure for fertilizer. Owners of plow teams became wealthier. From the eighth century on, the aristocracy and Buddhist temples—harvesting firewood, lumber, salt, fish, vegetable oils, clay, and chestnuts—began to encroach upon the unoccupied lands. They denied free access to the peasantry.[5] A labor tax for public works and rice-land development was instituted, which was used to build great manors for the gentry and grandiose religious institutions. The oldest standing wooden building in the world is Hōryū-ji, built in 607 CE. Huge beams were cut nearby for this and other government buildings.

By 638, 46 Buddhist monasteries had been constructed. Such massive construction continued into the eighth century. One temple used enough timber to build 3,000 1950s-style Japanese houses. By 850 all harvestable timber in the areas accessible from urban centers was used up. Thereafter metropolitan temples were more modest and great monasteries began to be built in remoter forests closer to the supply of wood.[6]

The years 1050 to 1550 saw another era of major exploitation, followed by a period during which the forests were finally depleted of most harvestable lumber (1570–1770). In the nineteenth century the Japanese government began systematic reforestation. As part of their industrial policy after World War II the Japanese replanted with cedar in order to make the country self-sufficient. Today Japanese cedar forests are the largest in the world. More than 10 million acres of cedar produce large clouds of pollen which come floating off the sides of Mt. Fuji into Tokyo, creating allergic reaction in 10% of the population. Dense cedar stands prevent the growth of other plants, and wildlife in them is less diverse than in mixed forests.[7] In much of the rest of contemporary Japan oceans are diced, mountains are paved, and almost every river channeled in concrete.[8] Our image of the Japanese's rapport with nature comes from the hermits we are considering and dated Japanese painting and poetry. It has little to do with the realities of modern industrial Japan.

In contrast to China, until relatively recently Japanese towns and agricultural land lay near what appeared to be wild forests. Thus, Japanese reverence for nature and nature spirits had ready reinforcement. Nature was accessible and imposing, not degraded islands of wilds surrounded by seas of agriculture.

The rugged, wooded mountains stood within a few days' walk, and although they may have contained varying degrees of wildness, they were easily experienced and less subject to the vagaries of romantic fantasy. Like the Chinese, the Japanese associated numerous personalities with mountains. Hijiri or holy persons included wandering shamanesses, Shinto priests, mountain ascetics, magicians, artisans, bards, and singing nuns. Parenthetically, it has been postulated that the figure of the shaman in various cultures enjoys his prestige due to being a human representative to nonhuman nature—a more crucial job in societies closer to their hunter-gathering roots, as the Japanese were.

In the eighth century a tradition of Mountain Asceticism, Shugen-do, was founded by En-no-Gyoja, who may or may not have been a Buddhist. The rigorous ascetic praxes he prescribed sometimes involved meditation and incantations and were intended to develop magical powers. As in many places that Buddhism spread, monks had to come to terms with local beliefs.[9] Temples were built near Shinto shrines and were dedicated to nearby kami. Kami were referred to as Bodhisattvas or devas. Buddhism incorporated both Shinto and folk practices, and Shinto priests adopted Shingon Buddhist rituals. The Japanese appealed to kami for daily assistance but turned to Buddhism for salvation.[10] Emperor Temmu (622–686) underwent austere Buddhist training on a mountain. He may have practiced using nature as the object of his concentration.

The snow is falling constantly,
The rain is falling ceaselessly;
Constantly as falls the snow,
Ceaselessly as beats the rain,
Ever thinking I have come,
Missing not one turning
Of that mountain-path![11]

By not missing one turn of the mountain path one is able to conquer the constant and ceaseless activity of the mind.

Other noted Buddhist monks such as Taicho (682–767) underwent mountain austerities, achieved great power, and gathered followings. Both the Shingon and Tendai sects valued remote mountainous places as sites for temples. The Shingon priest Shobo built a mountain place of worship near the capital and improved access for pilgrims.

Kukai (774–835), a young aristocrat drawn to Buddhism, became dissatisfied with the religious politics of the capital. He may have joined what was called the Natural Wisdom School, a group of monks who built temples in secluded mountains to practice meditation. At age 20 he abandoned his studies, and for the next 10 years he wandered. Of this period his biographer waxes:

The blue sky was the ceiling of his hut and the clouds hanging over the mountains were his curtains; he did not need to worry about where he lived or where he slept. In summer he opened his neck band in a relaxed mood and delighted in the gentle breezes as though he were a great king, but in the winter he watched the fire with his neck drawn into his shoulders. If he had enough horse chestnuts and bitter vegetables to last ten days, he was lucky. His bare shoulders showed through his paper robe and clothes padded with grass cloth... Though his appearance was laughable, his deep rooted will could not be taken away from him... Not being obliged to his father or elder brothers and having no contact with relatives, he wandered throughout the country like duckweed floating on water or dry grass blown by the wind.[12]

Although he read a lot and wrote a treatise on Buddhism, what exactly his practice was during this time is not clear.

Like many monks of his time, he traveled to China. There he was certified as an enlightened teacher. On return he solicited royal funds to build a monastery. "Only a few priests practice meditation in high mountains, in deep forests, in wide canyons, in secluded caves... When young, I, Kukai, often walked through mountainous areas and crossed many rivers. There is a place called Koya... High peaks surround Koya in all four directions; no human tracks still less trails are to be seen there. I should like to clear the wilderness in order to build a monastery there for the practice of meditation, for the benefit of the nation and those who desire to discipline themselves."[13] The place chosen was not very accessible: "I came to the peak last month on the sixteenth day in order to practice silent meditation. The mountain is high, the snow deep, and walking is painful." Construction of the monastery created financial difficulties. All the building materials, except wood and water, had to be brought in by porters.

Although I do not doubt that Kukai may have meditated deeply upon the natural settings in which he resided, his later life illustrates how those settings became domesticated, and how the picture of nature painted in romantic Buddhist poems is not an accurate portrayal of the actual Buddhist activities there. During the period of construction Kukai wrote that he didn't belong to any family or country; that mountains and birds spoke to him and monkeys performed gymnastics.[14]

Yet his whole operation was dependent upon the royal household, the government, and contributions from the aristocracy, and he often had official responsibilities in the capital. He was called upon to lead Shingon initiation ceremonies. He pined to be released from his duties in the capital. Only in the woods could one attain "the great void."[15]

Yet he remained bound into realms of power and utilized them to tame the wild. His view of nature was influenced by Shinto: The peaks challenged his strength but therein dwell gods and tree spirits.[16] And Kukai was struck by the intense experiences he had during concentration practice: Sitting in the forests he thought he heard a bird but realized it was only his mind.[17] Such experiences can happen when a meditator's mind quiets.

In Kukai's era Buddhism centered more on ritual, philosophy, and esoterica than the current popular idea of meditation concerned with concentration and insight. It was a time of Yamabushi: "those who repose in mountains." The Yamabushi had special dress and magical instruments. Although they were

Buddhist priests, some married long-haired shamanesses who went into trances. To obtain spiritual power they went on pilgrimages to the peaks of sacred mountains.[18] These mountain ascetics were called upon to subdue demons. Late tenth-century hermits were so sought after in the capital that some hid in smaller towns to avoid the notoriety.

As pilgrimages grew in popularity hijiri became entrepreneurs and tour leaders. During medieval periods mass pilgrimages became popular. Specialists at fairs and other gatherings gave theatrical performances of the pilgrimages of famous priests. In the tenth century a community of several hundred hermits lived at Kumano, dwelling in exotic looking huts.[19] As Buddhism developed in Japan from the Middle Ages on, monasteries, hermitages, and ascetics spread throughout the mountains. Among these were practitioners who wove the natural setting into their meditation practice.

One hermit became the Japanese equivalent of Cold Mountain, the archetypal Chinese practice-recluse. He was Saigyo (1118–1190), born into a powerful clan family. As a young man he was a good horseman and became captain of the guards. In that role he was exposed to the seamy side of royal life. At 23 he abandoned the court to become a Buddhist priest, taking the name Saigyo, which means "west-go." He spent the rest of his life as a hermit living in nature.

During his early travels he was supported by temples and a widespread network of kin. He returned to the capital on occasion and sent his poems to other poets for their comments. We know little more of his biography than what he related in his poems. During his life an era of peace came to an end in a series of natural catastrophes and violent struggles. The spread of Pure Land Buddhism and of Zen shortly after his death may have been a response to the hard times. D. T. Suzuki argued that Saigyo anticipated Zen. Later Zen hermits took Saigyo as their inspiration. Saigyo himself looked up to Kukai as a model and made pilgrimages to places the latter had visited.

With Saigyo we begin to see how much further than their Chinese counterparts Japanese hermits took the use of nature in their meditation practice. In Saigyo's poetry we find both distinct elements of a meditation practice that utilized nature and detailed descriptions of how his daily life was embedded in the natural world. Although scholars have not figured out exactly what Saigyo's meditation practice was, he left us some hints and tells us directly of its role in his life. "I visited someone who had renounced the world... We conversed about the importance... of uninterrupted daily practice."

> *Linked worlds,*
> *Linked lives: on an*
> *Upright shaft*
> *Of bamboo every joint*
> *Is strong and straight.*[20]

This harks back to the Buddha's suggestion that a forest monk find a spiritual friend. For Saigyo only an eremite would do, because monks in the city, the cenobites, were lost in the world.

> *Back in the capitol*
> *We gazed at the moon, calling*
> *Our feelings, 'deep'*
> *Mere shallow diversions*
> *That here don't count at all.*[21]

Saigyo's meditation practice seemed to involve gazing at the moon. It has been called moon disk meditation, and Saigyo is thought to have spent long periods of time contemplating the moon until it penetrated his being.

> *So taken with*

The faultless face and radiance
Of an alluring moon,
My mind goes farther... farther...
To reach remote regions of the sky.[22]

Without direction
Before the moonlight, my mind
Grows bright and clear,
And what will be the end of this
Is something that I cannot tell.[23]

Like all successful meditation practices that strive to come to terms with human discontent, Saigyo's practice brings out unresolved parts of his life which remain sources of suffering.

No pock nor shadow
On the moon's face, so just then
I recalled yours—clear
Till tears from my own mind
Defaced the moon once more.[24]

And then there is the tendency of the mind, which the Buddha recognized, to form likes and dislikes in response to experience. Even moon meditation becomes for Saigyo an example of how quickly clinging and aversion arise.

In spring I spend the day
With flowers, wanting no night;
It's turned around
In fall when I watch the moon
All night, resenting the day.[25]

In the world to come
I shall reveal what it is

in my heart
The radiance of the moon
That is never enough for me.[26]

The detail and sensitivity with which Saigyo describes nature makes his poetry convincing to others who have shared that life experience. This is missing from the Chinese aesthete-recluses and their Japanese counterparts who present more disembodied, if romantic, pictures of nature. The poet Gary Snyder worked in the woods as a young man and climbed many of the peaks in the Sierras and Cascades. He also spent years training in a Japanese Zen monastery. He now lives in the foothills of the Sierra Nevada Mountains of California, where he practices Zen and is engaged in defending his home bioregion from the onslaught of industry. Of Saigyo he says: "To anyone who has moved on similar paths, it is clear that Saigyo had in fact entered deeply into nature in an experiential way... No temple-bound monk could write of climbing a cliff by clutching wild azaleas, or of wading a deep river and 'feeling washed clean to the base of the heart.' The richness of his knowledge of watersheds, seasonal cycles, and organisms brings one back to the question, why all these moons and flowers?"[27]

The moons of Snyder's rhetorical question are Saigyo's object of meditation, and the poem to which Snyder refers is:

Scaling the crags
Where azaleas bloom... not for plucking
But for hanging on!
The saving feature of this rugged
Mountain face I'm climbing.[28]

Hanging on is a part of bushwhacking through a trail-less countryside, very different from walking Chinese mountain roadways accompanied by a serving man. Listen to Saigyo describing an out-of-the-way retreat of Kukai: "the dangers faced in making the climb up to that spot are really unusual. I made my way up to the top by crawling on all fours."

Lucky to make it:
Here at this point where
Holy ones met once
To make pledges on abrupt
Precipices above it all.[29]

As Snyder points out in an essay on crawling, there are few better ways to connect to nature than to navigate the woods the way wild animals do.[30]

And,

So steep and dangerous
Is Mount Arachi that there's
No way down the valley…
Till one is made for snowshoes
By white snow fallen over all.[31]

This resonates with my attempts at snowshoeing as a form of Buddhist walking meditation. The winter woods come alive. Unobstructed by leaves, the woods open like a meadow and animal tracks become highways through snow-covered, impenetrable brush. It is hard to get lost because you can always backtrack along your snowshoe prints. In the snow-made silence I have meditated for hours.

We see more of Saigyo's intimacy with nature in his observations of the subtle changes of season. The quality of the haze on the hills heralds spring:

Ice wedged fast
in the crevice of the rock

this morning begins to melt
under the moss the water
will be feeling out a channel[32]

This poem suggests Saigyo spent many days out of doors in the early spring, where winter cold, which lingers on the ground, is met by the newly warm rays of a spring sun. In the shadows it is cool, but the surfaces of rocks with southern exposures are warm. Where the two seasons meet, the warmth begins to thaw the winter ice, which freezes again as the temperature drops at night.

Of the gloomy winter monsoon on the mountains which face the Sea of Japan, Saigyo also knew a great deal. The fifth-month rains covered walking stones and turned meadows into a muddy wash.[33]

The Buddha prohibited monks from wandering during the monsoons because of farmers' complaints that the monks were destroying the rain-soaked fields. In nascent Indian civilization economics dictated the rains retreats. Whereas in the wilds the rainy season not only made travel difficult but affected a hermit's mood. As was noted earlier, the Buddha warned that for a renunciant of the wrong disposition, "the wilderness would whirl away his mind," leading to "the hopelessness of forest-life for one who fails to gain tranquility of mind." Stonehouse touched upon these difficulties. Saigyo explores them further: He could "barely get [...] through the days," of fifth-month rains. From his understanding of Buddhism he knew that he should be able to use his circumstance to gain clarity, but nonetheless his mountain top, "is a cheerless place."[34]

He expresses a sentiment with which I have had occasion to empathize:

In a freezing cabin reading Saigyo:
Walking to the open oven door for heat.
The wood's wet and there's no kindling.

An orderly life's not real.
Cursing hot Buddha, cursing cold Buddha.

Saigyo may have been better than I at the practice of learning from discomfort, rather than being overwhelmed by it. Harder than physical duress is loneliness, which for the Buddha was to be examined rather than escaped from in the pleasure palaces of the gentry or the family TV room. Giving up on visitors and feeling that there was no fit place to live he would live "no place" in his "hut of sticks flimsy as the world itself."[35]

To live "no place" is a practice no less relevant in town than in the woods. "No place" in the woods is more apparent because of more obvious human impermanence. The apparent permanence of town lends credence to the delusion it is a fit place to live.[36]

Saigyo worries that he has become too much in love with nature, rather than viewing it with equanimity.

It was bound to be:
My vow to be unattached
To seasons and such...
I, who by a frozen bamboo pipe
Now watch and wait for spring.
Now seen... now gone
the butterfly flits in and out
Through fence hung flowers
But a life so close to them
I envy... though it's here and gone.[37]

The moon at night in the winter sky
cleared up after the storm! Indeed
you are a friend of the lonely man
who lives alone in the shadow
of a remote mountainside.[38]

Some critics feel nature was more his teacher than Buddhism, but as a committed practitioner he uses moon meditation to loosen this attachment too.

Winter has withered
Everything in this mountain place:
Dignity is in
Its desolation now, and beauty
In the cold clarity of its moon.[39]

This has a ring of truth to it. I recall significant full moons of my life: a sub-zero walk across a frozen cornfield, a lighthouse promontory in Newfoundland, a New Year's Eve on the streets of Havana, kneeling in prayer in the woods above the Kettle River, and under the stars on Lama Mountain after a day of traumatic community meetings. The complete indifference of the moon to both our romantic projections on to nature and the cherished meanings of human life were as starkly demonstrated in these as it is in Saigyo's poem.[40]

Saigyo's is the way of the recluse immersed in, and learning from, nature.

By imagining
These mountain depths, some men think
They come and go there;
But, not living here themselves,
Can they know real pathos?[41]

Saigyo's takes on life as directly as possible. He looks askance at people in their hovels unaware of nature, keeping away the mosquitoes with smoky fires.[42] For him nature is a good teacher. The wind blows away his dark daydreams.[43]

Today's satori:

Such a change of mind would
Not exist without
My lifelong habit of having
My mind immersed in blossoms.[44]

But the struggle does not end just because the mind sometimes becomes clear. Nature stands as metaphor for the mind's capriciousness.

Thought I was free
Of passions, so this melancholy
Comes as surprise:
A woodcock shoots up from marsh
Where autumn's twilight falls.[45]

He persists in using the symbols of nature to characterize his practice. Not even marking his trail he forges he way on a mountain to find a place "where bad news can never reach me."[46]

The place without bad news is a metaphor for awakening, as the trail is a metaphor for practice. The next poem perhaps is to be taken with a sense of humor. It is not clear whether he refers to a scene really viewed or his own mind.

Deep in the mountains
Sitting upright on moss used
As a mat for himself
(With not a care in the world)
Is a gibbering, chattering ape.[47]

Then, traveling a few years before death, he attained some sense of peace:

Bending to the wind

The smoke above Mount Fuji
Vanishes in the sky—
The matter of destination
Is nothing my thoughts know.[48]

Saigyo's moon meditation continues to intrigue me, especially on retreat. March, 2004:

The moon is not quite full, as it was seven hundred years ago for Saigyo, but it brightly lights the snowy remains of winter which dot the woods in Barre. I walk the loop, the great circle that meditators take on their perambulations after lunch. The roads were once farmers' cart trails connecting them to each other, their fields and faraway markets. Down Pleasant Street toward Peters-hamlet I walk. I turn down Mill Rd. without thinking, the habit of years, then by the pond where a lumber or grist mill must have stood, though even the old folk did not tell tales of it. I stop to gaze at the pond made daylight by the ice still covering it. I grasp for Saigyo's moon meditation to calm my soul flooded with memories stirred up by the beauty of the night and lifetimes I trod this way. The concentration of the retreat has slipped away. Alas Saigyo left us no hint of how he contemplated the moon, only that he did and it soothed his being. I listen for coyotes, but none break the silence. There is only the crashing of a branch on the ice. I proceed by the once dark pine woods, now dotted with the lights of meditation center housing. Why did they choose the cold north side and not the warm south, where I built a house in my fantasy when the old Russian lady who used to own the pond was telling me about the herbs and mushrooms she gathered in the woods?

Passing the pond, I come to Harold and Hazel's farmhouse, standing at the corner of Mill and Old Stage Roads. I heard that Harold had died in the three years since I last walked this way. Was wrinkled Hazel alone in the darkened house, lying in the bed in which she bore her children, in which her husband was born and one of his parents too? It must be more than 70 years since she came to teach in the schoolhouse on Pleasant Street and he, the farmer's son, wooed her. Now most of the fields have gone to woods or houses or were sold to the local dairyman. Into his 80s Harold still grew verdant vegetable gardens. I often stood among his rows talking of kohlrabi and raspberries and admiring his crops. Now the weeds of the abandoned garden poke through the snow. Then down Old Stage Road, which names its long-dead function. For how many years now has the traffic sped down Pleasant Street, leaving the old stage road quiet? A hundred yards or so further stands Paul's house. We built it with high hopes more than 20 years ago: 'the maximum house for the minimum money.' Twenty-four foot on a side, three stories high, it stood there as a dark silhouette for the many years Paul did not live in it. The woods that hid the old Winnebago trailer with 'Steamed Hotdogs' on the side and broken windows are gone, as is the trailer. Many a night in the dead of winter I slept there, my dog curled in the snow under the front stairs. In the morning we would make our way up to the meditation center after hearing the bell ring through the cold predawn air. Paul too is gone, but no one seems to know where. There are lights in the house now and a jungle gym outside. It no longer haunts the loop on which the meditators walk often asking, 'Who lives there?' At Paul's house I turn back. My mind is quieter now. I can feel the moon and silence of the night. I still wish I knew Saigyo's secret. It might bring me to a deeper peace.

Not all those who became hermits were as successful as Saigyo. Kamo no chomei (1153–1216) was a court poet who fell upon hard times. He lost his large estate, then a smaller house. The

chaos of his era was thought to be a predicted Buddhist apoca-
lypse. At 50 he became a monk and retired to a 10-foot square
hut. He wrote bitterly of the catastrophes taking place. Much of
the area around his hut was brush and trees, "But I have a clear
view to the west which is some aid to my meditation." He
chanted the name of Amida's Western Paradise. "When I tire of
intoning *nembutsu...* I simply give myself a rest... There's no one
to stop me and no one to feel ashamed on my account. Though
I've taken no vow of silence, since I live alone, I escape creating
bad karma with my tongue. I make no special effort to keep the
precepts but given my surroundings what occasion would I have
to break them?... At the foot of the mountain is a rough shack
where the keeper of the mountain lives. He has a little son who
now and then comes to visit me... my friend and I go off
rambling. He's ten and I'm sixty... Sometimes I dig cogon grass
sprouts, pick rock bear cherries... gather baskets of cress or
tubers of wild taro... When I hear the voice of the pheasant, I
wonder if it is not the voice of my father or mother."[49]

Paraphrasing a Saigyo poem, he writes, "When I see how
friendly the deer... have become, I realize how far removed I am
from the outside world... Matters of food and clothing I handle
in the same way. A robe of wisteria fiber, a quilt of hemp... I use
whatever comes to hand... Starwort from the meadows, nuts
from the hilltop trees... just so it's enough to keep me alive. I
never feel ashamed of my appearance."[50] Except, "I feel ashamed
whenever circumstance obliges me to go to the capital and beg."
Kamo no chomei's practice does not seem to work for him: "My
fondness for quiet and solitude must be a block to my salvation...
You say you've abandoned the world and come to live in the
forest hut so you can discipline your mind and practice the Way.
But however much you imitate a saint's appearance, your mind is
still steeped in impurity... This is because you let the poverty that
is your lot in life distract you... At that time my mind could give
no answer. All I could do was call upon my tongue to utter two

or three recitations of Amida Buddha's name, ineffectual as they might be, before falling silent."[51]

One can speculate why his practice was ineffective. Kamo no chomei feels that he personally failed at it. It may be that his devotional practice is less suitable for the realities of a hermit's life in nature than was that of the early Buddhist forest renunciants. They were committed to concentration and inquiry into the character of mind and body as both unfold while sitting quietly in the midst of the wilds. Kamo no chomei did not have the foundation of a rigorous monastic meditation training that supported many hermits through the difficulties of hermit life. It seems that Saigyo's moon meditation kept him alert to the interactions of mind and body. He was able to study the impermanence of life experiences as the Buddha recommended. He also seemed attuned to the insubstantiality of self.

Kamo no chomei, on the other hand, seemed to want chanting *nembutsu* to transform him. He was disappointed when it didn't. He never really studied his "disappointment." So the mind which found life in a violent world so disappointing was also disappointed with his lack of spiritual progress. While nature did not "whirl his mind away," he did succumb to "the hopelessness of forest-life for one who fails to gain tranquility of mind."

After some tentative beginnings, Zen came to Japan in the exchanges with China during the twelfth through thirteenth centuries. The invasion of China by the Mongols sent a number of Chan masters fleeing to Japan, even as many Japanese monks still ventured into China. The most famous was Dogen Kigen (1200–1253), who is revered in both Soto (just sitting or gradual awakening) Zen and Rinzai (koan or sudden awakening) Zen.

Dogen is the most challenging figure to try to understand in exploring the relationship between nature and meditation. Dogen was never really a Zen hermit, yet many of his teachings were cast in a haunting language of nature. We need to explore his unusual insights.

As was the case with many monks before Buddhism seeped down into the populace, Dogen came from an aristocratic family. At age 13 he was ordained a Tendai monk and studied scriptures, Tantric rites, and Rinzai Zen. At 23 he traveled to China with his teacher. There are many stories of his adventures, including his meeting with a cook from a monastery who changed his understanding of practice. Dogen became "awakened" — enlightened — when his Chinese Zen master challenged another monk who had fallen asleep while sitting in the meditation hall.

Returning to Japan Dogen avoided the religious politics of the capital by going to a poor country temple. He began writing treatises on practice for which he later became famous. As more people, including commoners, came a larger temple was built for him. After 10 years religious politics drove him to "the inhospitable northern coast," where he was offered land and resources to build his ideal temple and monastery. With the move he produced a series of attacks on established Rinzai Zen, developed the practices of Soto Zen, and laid down rules for running monasteries. The monastery, whose construction he oversaw, was in an undeveloped area. Its construction took most of the rest of his life, so that he only spent a few years there after it was completed. He returned to the capital once for a couple of years and again left the monastery for medical treatment, which did not cure him.

While Dogen did not do extensive practice in the wilds, a language of nature fills his teachings and he seems to have appreciated how nature impinged upon practice.

Evening zazen hours advance. Sleep hasn't come yet.
More and more I realize mountain forests are good for efforts in the
way.
Sounds of the valley brook enter the ears, moonlight pierces the eyes.
Outside this, not one further instant of thought.[52]

The ancients, "after they passed eons living alone in the mountains and forests, bodies and minds like dead trees, only then did they unite with the way. Then they could use the mountains and rivers for words, raise the wind and the rain for a tongue, and explain the great void."[53] His poetry evokes an existential sweep of life. Of his trip to China he says, "realizing that the eyes are horizontal and the nose is vertical, without being deceived by anyone, I came home empty-handed. Therefore, I returned without a trace of the Buddha dharma and depending on my own destiny, I let the time take its own course. Morning after morning, the sun rises in the east; night after night the moon sinks in the west. The clouds disappear, and the mountains are manifest; the rains pass and the Four Mountains are low."[54] The "four mountains" are birth, old age, sickness, and death.

His teaching is wrapped in the language of nature. What might it be like to take Dogen literally? Maybe not very different from the observation that life in the nature is uneventful, even achingly boring. A restless mind has little to grab hold of.[55] An experience of this came while sitting on the side of a hill in San Anselmo one afternoon in the warm sun, the air cold on the lungs as I climbed. A sense of silence overcame me. Nothing but the sun, the mist, the buildings in the distance with the harsh noise of some machine below hidden by the trees. "Morning after morning the sun rises in the east; night after night the moon sinks in the west."

Dogen chooses the place for his final monastery because of its proximity to nature, its harsh climate, and the trees and hills, which he feels are important for practice. But Dogen goes about domesticating the wild and uses nature more as symbol than reality. He transformed the landscape to build his monastery, and his writings explode the idea of nature to make his points. Images from nature represent the teachings, but it is no longer actual nature.

Mysticism creeps in. As Paul Williams writes, "For Dogen the world of phenomena really and quite literally is the Buddha-Nature." Quoting Dogen:

The real aspect is all things. All things are this aspect, this character, this body, this mind, this world, this wind and this rain, this sequence of daily going, living, sitting, lying down, this series of melancholy, joy, action, and inaction, this stick and wand, this Buddha's smile, this transmission and reception of doctrine, this study and practice, this evergreen pine and unbreakable bamboo... This very world of impermanence is the Buddha-nature... The impermanence of grass, trees and forest is verily the Buddhahood. The impermanence of the person's body and mind is verily the Buddhahood. The impermanence of the country and scenery is verily the Buddhahood.[56]

To which we might add that the Buddhahood also includes the impermanence of survival of the fittest and the subatomic world of particles. Dogen brings Rinzai-like contradictory koans about nature into the silence of Soto contemplation,

The moon
abiding in the midst of
serene mind
billows break
into light.[57]

as contrasted with:

All my life false and real, right and wrong tangled.
Playing with the moon, ridiculing wind, listening to birds...
Many years wasted seeing the mountains covered with snow.
This winter I suddenly realize snow makes a mountain.[58]

and:

> Mountains have been the abode of great sages for the limitless past to the limitless present. Wise people and sages all have mountains as their inner chamber, as their body and mind. Because of wise people and sages, mountains appear... You may think that in mountains many wise people and great sages are assembled. But after entering the mountains, not a single person meets another. There is just the activity of the mountains. There is no trace of anyone having entered the mountains. When you see mountains from the ordinary world, and when you meet mountains while in mountains, the mountain's head and eye are viewed quite differently. Your idea of the mountains not flowing is not the same as the view of dragons or fish... One time mountains are flowing, another time they are not flowing. If you do not fully understand this, you do not understand the true wheel of the [Buddha].[59]

Or, "[Water] is not that which flows down. To regard water as *flowing* only is tantamount to slandering water... [Saying flowing] will force you to say *not-flowing*. Water is water only in its thusness... As you penetrate *flowing* and *not-flowing*, the ultimate character of all things is instantly realized."[60] Dogen says that until you have seen mountains flowing, you have never really seen mountains. From a common sense point of view, this is confusing. For Dogen you can only understand Buddha-nature in all things when you see that the ordinary is not at all ordinary and yet is completely ordinary. This "doubleness" of the ordinary and the mystical was central to Zen, distinguishing it from mystical traditions whose practitioners set their sights more keenly on the otherworldly.

To Dogen Buddhism was inseparable from "mountains and waters" but this was not a worship of nature, which he would have regarded as an a limited view binding the mind as other delusions do.[61] Dogen has been called a Zen metaphysician or ontologist and has been the subject of much philosophic speculation. He uses koan-like statements to cut away at the mind and its tendency to posit causal relationships:

> Some beings see water as wondrous blossoms, but they do not use blossoms as water. Hungry ghosts see water as raging fire or pus and blood. Dragons see water as a palace or pavilion. Some beings see water as the seven treasures of a wish-granting jewel. Some beings see water as a forest or a wall. Some see it as the dharma nature of pure liberation, the true human body, or as the form of the body and essence of mind. Water is seen as dead or alive depending on causes and conditions... water is not just earth, water, fire, space or consciousness...
>
> ... But water as earth, water, fire, wind and space realizes itself.
>
> For this reason it is difficult to say who is creating this land and palace right now or how such things are being created. To say that the world is resting on the wheel of space or on the wheel of the wind is not the truth of the self or the truth of others. Such statement is based only on a small view. People speak this way because they think that it must be impossible to exist without having a place on which to rest.[62]

One learns by penetrating contradictions. For Dogen omnipresent Buddha-nature can be seen in nature, but as the mind tries to grasp what is seen its essence slips away.

> The years of a lifetime are a flash of lightning; who clings to objects? They are empty through and through. Even if you care for the nose hung in front of your face, still be careful and value every moment to work on enlightenment.[63]

This advice is directed to meditators. There is a different admonition for mountain adepts.

The autumn colors of the thousand peaks
are dyed with seasonal rain;
How could the hard rock on the mountain
follow along with the wind?[64]

Although he couches his instructions in the language of nature his monastery was the real container for the practice he established. There monks faced a wall in highly disciplined silent cenobitic meditation and could only experience mountains flowing in the life of a monastery. Despite the fact that some of Dogen's writings appear to be directions for a mountain ascetic, the majority are commentaries on texts used in the training of monks or rules for running a monastery. Still Dogen rarely strays from the Buddha's central concerns. "This birth and death is the life of Buddha. If you try to exclude it you will lose the life of Buddha. If you cling to it, trying to remain in it, you will also lose the life of Buddha, and what remains will be the mere form of Buddha. Only when you don't dislike birth and death, or long for them, do you enter Buddha's mind."[65]

If one is at all sentimental about nature, it is hard to resist Dogen. He hooks that sentimentality and drags you to the limits of your thinking mind, to the limits of your understanding of your own sense of nature. For Dogen this is where real learning begins.

Saigyo lived the life of a Buddhist hermit, utilizing nature in the core of his practice. He also debated within himself whether his attachment to nature overshadowed a deeper practice. Kamo no chomei felt he failed, both as a meditator and a hermit. Dogen seems to be saying that nature is both inseparable from practice and an impediment to it. He provides a remedy for Saigyo's attachment but also never practiced as a hermit. Japanese

Buddhism and Zen in particular are dotted with unusual personalities who for the next 800 years explored these themes. We will
look at some of those for whom information is available in
English.

Muso Soseki (1275–1351) became a national teacher. He lived
in the era of the Five-Mountain, Rinzai monasteries located in the
two major cities of the Kamakura period of Japanese history
(1185–1333). Receiving much royal patronage Zen Buddhism
prospered. Muso was born into the aristocracy. Ordained young
he studied Shingon and Zen then traveled to China. Returning to
Japan he continued his studies, passing required exams and
learning from immigrant Chinese Zen masters. Unsatisfied, he
took to the road and for the next 20 years stayed in one or another
hermitage away from the metropolis. Muso's life represents a
continuation of the Chinese, Confucian-Taoist dialogue. As we
saw in China, gentry born to the Confucian obligation to serve
government and family sought escape, often posturing as hermits
seeking Taoist "naturalness." Their search was often plagued by
internal conflicts. There was anger at not being recognized at
court, despair because of social turmoil, a sense of failure at their
inability to achieve naturalness, and they were boastful and self-
pitying when seeking solace in rice wine. Muso did not have
these failings. He seems to have been genuinely attracted to quiet
practice in places away from the centers of political life. Yet he
allowed himself to be drawn into the limelight.

The solitude Muso seeks is often interrupted. He appreciates
nature but does not explore it intimately. He does not get so deep
into meditation that he does not want guests, nor does he wander.
From his hut he is aware of nature marking the passing of time
and that even though he watches the sea he, "has never seen its
depths."[66]

His characterizations of nature are not very detailed. He often
uses standard Buddhist metaphors. Ice flowers fill the forest
where Bodhidharma's guidepost shines and the Buddha body

"stands in vain in the snow."[67] Muso never really gets to settle into nature and his protest of that feels a bit limp. His abode is not very inviting. It is a cramped fisherman's hut, not suitable "for entertaining the rich and famous."[68] But that did not keep them away. "Though so deep in the mountains there wasn't even a real road of any sort to the spot, much to my annoyance people kept calling [me from] the loneliness of these mountains. [His escape] [f]rom the sorrows of the world."[69]

This prompted my own poetic response. Sitting in my van in a San Anselmo, California park typing about Zen nature poems my mind rebelled against the intrusion of the residents:

Beautiful cold sunny morning,
Gray-haired jogger with dogs
to a young woman, "Good workout!"
In my self-made prison or my dharma hut?

If I really wanted to be far from the world of dust there was little to stop me. While Muso went way beyond the Chinese aesthete-recluses by actually withdrawing and attempting practice, he did not stick to the path of the Taoist ancients. He gave into the Confucian pull of responsibility, citing age rather than the Bodhisattva vow to save all sentient beings. "But as I grow older my body is growing weaker, and now it is little hard for me to sit zazen for very long at a time. The winds of karma have led me to preside over a few temples and to teach students."[70]

At the age of 50 Muso was called to be the abbot of the national Zen temple. Although he protested he accepted the position. As abbot he taught many students and became the most important designer of temple gardens. His gardens were archetypes of how the Japanese sense of nature became domesticated. Japanese gardens are not merely symbolic of nature but are taken for the experience of nature itself.

[A]s long as [people] have made a distinction between landscape and the practice of the Way, they cannot be called genuine Wayfarers... People who believe that mountains, rivers, earth, plants trees, and stones are all fundamental Self may appear to appreciate the landscape, through worldly feelings, but there are those who even make these worldly feelings into the Way for enlightenment and make the changing appearance of the springs, rocks, plants, and trees through the four seasons into meditation work. That is how Wayfarers appreciate the landscape. So it is not necessarily bad to like landscape and not necessarily good. There is no plus or minus in the landscape itself. Gain and loss are in people's attitudes.[71]

For Muso, correct attitude is incorporated in the design of a landscape garden. The guidance needed to pursue practice in nature is built in. It is a bit like Dogen's understanding of mountains while seated in the meditation hall. Although nature clearly exists, even in a garden, wildness is no longer a crucial ingredient. What is important is a certain aesthetic sense. In contrast to Muso, my orientation toward nature would focus in on that wildness.

sitting eating in the rock garden sun,
under an alder.
in the house transcribing Muso,
a shadow follows the swing of my head.
On my glasses hangs a spider.
I remove the web gently
and look in light:
tiny being
too small to see clearly
arms-legs trying to ascend.
I put her outside on leaves.

will she starve there?

Muso was considered a poet of the Five Mountain monasteries. Like the Chinese aesthete-recluses, many of these poets wrote about nature, but in contrast they did not present themselves as recluses. They used a series of code words and expressions to represent Buddhist ideas. The rays of the setting sun were the light of truth.[72] Sleep meant meditation, maple leaves were the illusory world of perception. Poems used images long associated with Zen—certain landscapes, reeds, geese, orchids, rocks, sunset over a village, or fishermen on a bay. The Five Mountain poets tried to describe the world as seen by someone who is enlightened. Their poems had little to do with real nature.[73]

During the first centuries of Zen it was assumed that the depth of one's meditation would express itself in a practitioner's poetry. By the fifteenth century, as Zen became more imbedded in Japanese culture, things reversed. Aesthetes were claiming "Poetry is Zen," despite the fact that Chinese and Japanese Zen masters warned students to stick to practice and not get swept away by the romance of writing poetry whose sentiments far exceeded students' real understanding.

Like Muso, some of the Five Mountain monks fled the city for hermitages or satellite temples in the country. A few used this as a strategy for advancement. It gave them a kind of charisma untainted by the religious politics of town. Many did not like rural life. Their retreats were called Rinka monasteries; the word implied that they were under forests or thickets. The poetry and practice produced by these monks is uneven. There were genuine hermit practitioners such as Jakushitsu (1290–1367), who wandered for 25 years and taught for a brief period. He left little written heritage.[74] And there was Bassui (1327–1387), whom a mountain ascetic warned that desire for seclusion partook of a dangerous pride. Bassui lived in one hermitage for seven years, then moved from hermitage to hermitage for the next seventeen years. He never stayed anywhere for more than three years, because followers would gather around him. In the last part of his life he allowed his following to grow. Although he preferred to live in small mountain hermitages, there is little reference to nature in his work.[75] Most of the other Five Mountain poets skimmed the surface, merely emulating a form. They often had difficulty with what I have considered in this book to be real eremitic practice—that is, meditation demonstrably based on experiences of life in nature.

> The white clouds
> On the mountain-tops
> Poke halfway into this thatched hut
> I had thought too cramped
> Even for myself.[76]

Inseparable from life in the wilds is the discomfort of weather and insects. These overwhelm some of the poets while becoming sources of insight for others:

> My room so miserable with heat and mosquitoes I can't do zazen,
> I kill time pacing the gravel paths, hands behind my back;
> Nothing in the inner garden—something draws my attention—
> Looking closer: a single strand of spider web stretches across the path.
> To escape the heat I sleep upstairs
> Where a slight cool grows in the night:
> ...
> I accept every sound and sight that's offered,
> The more detached, the more I hear and see;
> A time of night I am so truly still
> I no longer notice the mosquitoes buzzing round my ears.
> from a spider's web hangs an empty cicada shell,
> Twisting and turning this way and that in the breeze;

While it was alive one heard only its pleasant song—
Who would have thought that, dead, it could dance like this?
Lotus pods in late winter...
Seeds already gone—children plucked them all.
From an empty hole a wasp emerges, heading for his old nest.[77]

Traveling was a real test. They took to the road seeking poetic inspiration rather than the Buddha's inquiry. An inn might be a refuge from their trials: "Tiring to the feet;" "Eyes filled with yellow dust;" "Freezing in the wind driven snow for the sake of a poem;" A "Broken bridge... a windblown flag [indicating a tavern]."[78] Most of the monks sought social contact. Some kept cats and warned the mice to stay away lest they get caught.

After the Five Mountain period we encounter a number of eccentric Zen adepts. One was Ikkyu or Crazy Cloud (1394–1481), who moved between country and town. Ikkyu defied monastic convention and survived to be a great Zen master. He spent most of his adult life wandering during a period of war and devastation. It was a time when the strict, old order was breaking down and innovative arts were beginning to flourish. Unlike other Zen masters, he delved into sexuality and doubted his own realization. For him, nature was no haven of Buddhist reality.

Ten years spent in brothels, elation difficult to exhaust.
Now, forced to live amid empty mountains and gloomy valleys,
Thirty thousand miles of cloud spread between here and those
delightful places;
The wind in the tall pines around the house grates upon my ears.
Crazy Cloud, who knows to what wild wind he belongs?
Morning, in the mountains, evening, in the city,
If I, at the right occasion, were to wield the stick or shout "Katsu,"
Te-shan and Rinzai would blush.[79]

Although Ikkyu wandered for many years and at one point kept his disciples in the country to insulate them from the temptations of the city, there is little evidence that he attended to the nature in which he resided or used it as a vehicle for practice. He was more interested in sex. While irritated with the wind in the trees, he saw himself connected to female genitalia and procreation by what he called the red thread, and he seemed to understand the nature of emotions as illustrated in his enlightenment statement.

> For ten years my mind was cluttered with passion and anger;
> Even this moment I still possess rage and violent emotions;
> Yet the instant that crow laughed, a [Buddha disciple] rose up out of
> ordinary dust; In this morning's sunshine, an illumined face
> sings.[80]

In the sixteenth and seventeenth centuries there are records of several more eccentric hermits. One like Ikkyu preferred town. Unkei Tosui (d. 1683) vanished from the temple where he had many adherents and was not seen for three years when a disciple seeking him out discovered him living among beggars under a bridge in Kyoto. Tosui made the student help him bury a dead beggar, and when the student balked at eating the beggar's leftover food Tosui drove him away. Tosui went in disguise to avoid his followers. He cared for lepers and earned subsistence doing menial tasks. Lines from a poem he wrote on a night in a "lonely forest shrine" go: "This what is my life is like… A worn-out robe, a broken bowl."[81]

Another, Fugai Ekun (1568–1654), whose name means "outside wind," was a Soto monk traveling for more than 20 years. His paintings of Bodhidharma had sad, ferocious eyes. For several years he lived in caves facing Mt. Fuji. He played with the local village children. He gathered food or got it from villagers. One trick was to hang an ink and brush painting outside his cave and villagers would leave rice for it. He ate out of a dried skull.

Of his experience he said, "This old monk meditates and rests in the empty mountains/With loneliness and stillness through the days and nights," but we know little more about his use of nature in his practice.[82]

We now come to the most famous Zen poet, Basho (1644–1694).

With the scent of plums
... suddenly,
sunrise comes

According to T. Hoover, "This is nature poetry at its finest, full of all the detached reverence of Zen. It is also impressive and accepting: nature is there to be enjoyed and to teach the lessons of Zen."[83] This is how Basho is usually seen in the West. Readers of Blyth's famous, early translations were taken by the beauty, simplicity, and power of Basho's haiku.[84] Basho has come to symbolize Zen. It may be that Basho is indeed "Japan's greatest poet." But to me, at least, it is not so clear that he "is filled with the spirit of Zen."[85] Let us examine this issue.

By the time of Basho both Buddhism and Zen had penetrated most levels of Japanese society. Basho is the first well-known figure we have encountered who was not an aristocrat. Born into a poor samurai family, at an early age he became a retainer of a local lord, whose death left him to wander about Kyoto. There he met a poetry teacher and lived the life of a struggling poet, eventually receiving some patronage. He took the name Basho from the banana tree that stood next to his house. For a year he studied meditation with a Rinzai teacher. Although little is known of what he learned it has been claimed that, "There can be little doubt... that his mind was able to deeply grasp essential elements of the Zen way."[86] Basho lived for years as a struggling poet in Kyoto, and it was only in the last decades of his life that he attracted students and began the series of pilgrimages that generated the poetry for which he later became so famous.

With Basho, we again confront the problem of authenticity that seemed so problematic for the Chinese aesthete-recluses. Basho writes as if he were a hermit experiencing a compelling connection between nature and Zen. In reaction to a "Zennist," or naive enthusiasm, for Basho there has arisen a more critical scholarly opinion.[87] It claims to unmask Basho. Even before I encountered this viewpoint in my research, I became suspicious of the veracity of Basho's poetic experiences. I felt that neither Basho's practice nor many of his descriptions of nature rang true. I began to think that Basho did not actually do what he claimed. We will first look at my explorations, then at some of the scholars' criticisms, and finally at how a Zen Master, both whose practice and understanding of nature I regard as genuine, reconstructs Basho as authentic Zen.

Upon reading Basho's classic travel diary, *Back Roads to Far Towns*, I recorded the following in my notes:[88]

Basho's diary provides a context for the haiku poems, which, when standing alone, appear to represent the epitome of Zen characterizations of nature, that is, clear, immediately powerful Zen insight into the meaning of existence as reflected in the natural world. Basho's most famous poem

frog by the pond — plop

expresses reality so simply and so true to the natural process that it is like a momentary enlightenment experience. When placed in the context of their creation and in the life of the man who created them these revealing haiku seem more like the product of an artist engaged in the creative process than an ardent practitioner displaying his insights. Basho is poet more than practitioner. He is a tourist viewing important scenes for their aesthetic quality, rather than their meditative meaning, and he connects with nature as aesthetic and cultural, rather than as the bare container of existence, and, thereby, teacher of Buddhist insights. This is not to say that he is unaware of Zen practice and does not on occasion turn his efforts in that direction, but that practice is secondary to the artistic and cultural traveler trying to view important scenes and to see them as his famous predecessors described them.

To travel halfway across Japan on foot and then to have a famous landscape obscured by bad weather was disappointing to Basho. How would a real practitioner use such as occasion as part of practice? There is little evidence in his journals that Basho regards what he does in such a framework, although his insights are often quite trenchant. When Saigyo, the poet Basho most revered and whose travels he tried to emulate, found a pilgrimage site not up to his expectations, Saigyo used the experience to study the mind state, "disappointment," and see through it.

Famed for its springtime
Naninwa in Tsu, seen today at last:
A field of withered reeds
Bent down by harsh winds—my dream
To see it come false—come true.[89]

Basho began his adventure with a traveling companion and serving man, Sora. Both were dressed as pilgrims. Apparently monks' robes were standard for those whose travels might be regarded as spiritual, although the robes in no way implied that the pilgrim had taken monastic vows.

(The following are notes I took while reading Basho's travel diary; I have left them pretty much as I wrote them so that you can see my gut reactions. The numbers refer to sections.[90])

#1. Basho sees his travel as "the journey itself home."

#3. He was frightened by the thought of the journey and did not think he would survive it, although at the time he was traveling the Japanese countryside was pacified and well worn. Basho avails himself of the all the conveniences offered to travelers. Nevertheless, he walked considerable distances, though never far from way stations or local peasants. It did take considerable effort. In contrast, walking as a means of transportation is almost inconceivable to modern Americans. Basho's "Thin shoulders feeling packs drag," testifies to his exertion.

#8. At one point a farmer offers a horse because it is too hard to describe the route, and the horse knows the way. Basho submits to the convenience. The farmer says, "so better let the Hoosier take you as far as he can and when he stops, just send him back." The horse took them to the next village and from the picture Basho penned, it looks as though he rode and his servant man, Sora, walked.

#10. Of a hermit's quarters:

less than five foot square
thatched abode
a pity to put it up at all
but there is rain.

and while walking: "beckoning others to come along too, mostly younger people, got caught up in such eager chatter, reached mountain unaware." So on occasion he does take note of his mind state but not with the persistence of someone dedicated to meditation practice.

#11. At a hot springs the experience is spoiled by "Noxious fumes of the rock not yet abated and such a pile of dead butterflies, bees and other bugs, sand underneath hard to see." If one were attuned to nature for its own sake or as a teacher, in what other frame might the experience be cast?

#14. "passed a place called Kagenuma, but overcast sky hindered reflection." When asked what came of their goal of crossing the Shirakawa barrier: "what with the aches of so much traveling, with body and mind exhausted," he didn't get much of a chance to make poetry, which was the point of traveling in the first place. If he couldn't make poetry there was no reason to proceed.

#15. They came upon a "priest completely out of things." Basho imagines his state as "in mountain depths gathering chestnuts," which I take to indicate that the priest was in deep eremitic meditation, but Basho offers no specifics.

#17. Tourists vexed locals even then: "the villagers tired of people passing through tearing out their green grain," destroyed a local tourist attraction.

#19. In the face of adversity he strikes a Buddhist pose. Lousy lodgings, "roof leaking, fleas, mosquitoes in droves, no sleep," and diarrhea almost makes him pass out. "[B]ut the night's traces dragged, mind balked." And so Basho, "[h]ired horses" to escape the discomfort. "Future seemed farther off than ever… but what a pilgrimage to far places calls for: willingness to let the world go, its momentariness, to die on the road, human destiny, which lifted spirit a little." He recognizes there is a lesson to be learned from adversity but he does address his own resistance.

#23. The purpose of all the travail is cultural: a "sense of time past. One blessing of such a pilgrimage, one joy coming through, aches of the journey forgotten, shaken into eyes."

#27. Some people he encountered appeared to be engaged in an authentic nature practice: "And there too amongst pines still seen religious recluses, several here and there, by thatched huts where twigs drop off, living quietly." From a safe poetic distance they inspired him: "and though unknown to me, they drew my heart/mind, moon now mirrored in sea, the day's view altered, renewed."

#29. Basho and Sora got lost and wandered through uninspiring scenery: "bypassed a dismal stretch of marshland."

#31. Unlike the Korean Zen master Soen sa Nim, who, during the Cold War, defying advice and political common sense, crossed the border into anti-Buddhist, communist Poland without much difficulty, Basho and Sora drew attention: "so [the border] guards eyed us suspiciously." Because of rain they stayed in a guard hut for three days: "forced to hang on in that dull retreat"

what with fleas and lice
the horse's having a piss
right at the pillow

There is hardly much Zen sentiment in this famous haiku when placed in the context of "forced to hang out in that dull retreat" —a phrase rarely quoted by those who reproduce the haiku as a model of Zen.

#32. When the trail was difficult to follow: "so we hired a man... the mountain was high and thickly wooded, beyond bird cry, in deep forest darkness like groping about at night. Felt as if dirt were tumbling from overloaded clouds, pushed, pushed on through shino bush, waded water, stumbled rock drenched in cold sweat." When they finally emerged and the guide told them that the trip had been easier than usual, the neophyte travelers were even more frightened.

#34. On ascending to a temple he finds some solace: "Climbed along edges of and crept over boulders, worshipped at temples, penetrating scene, profound quietness, heart/mind open clear."

silence itself is
in rock absorbing

cicada sounds

#37. The pilgrims pushed to their limits but to what end? To say they did it? To explore the nature of that pushing? To have an aesthetic experience, as inspiration for poem writing? "Climbed Gassen... walking on ice and snow... each breath a last one, numb, reached the peak," in order to see daybreak from that viewpoint.

#40. "with heat and rain, spirit sore afflicted, taken ill, no way to keep up writing."

#46. When Sora departs because of illness: "Pain for one who goes, emptiness of one left behind." A sentiment which forest renunciants would take as grist for the mill of investigating attachment. [They could take meditation companions but were warned not to become attached to them. In the next chapter we find forest monks traveling together for a while but regularly parting.]

The calligrapher who prepared the manuscript along with Basho wrote a postscript praising the trip and the author concludes with, "A pity only that he turns wearier, and more and more white comes tingeing his brows." Disease, old age, and death, is that not where Zen practice begins?

With an apology for the harshness of my comments, here we have Basho in all his contradictions. He is a prematurely aging aesthete, not in the best health, posing as a recluse who undertakes a rigorous trip. Basho does have a sense of Zen, but he falls short as a practitioner. His dedication is to poetry and sentiment, which he expresses in the language of Zen. For the most part, Basho is collecting experiences. With respect to nature, Basho is sensitive, but it is the sensitivity of an aesthete-tourist of his times not that of a Zen hermit using nature to understand one's relationship to existence. Basho's poetry is beautiful, and it is hard to imagine him writing it without him being present for the events he portrays, but he errs on the side of romanticism. He does not give the reader the full picture of a haiku's natural setting. He distills only that which gives an intended effect: a sense that the writer is at one with his natural subject. In reality, there is much more to the story. While well-meaning and a much better poet, Basho stands in stark contrast to his hero, Saigyo, who lived more deeply what he wrote. Saigyo was not trying to convince the reader of an idea with his poetic skill.

Turning to the scholars who try to place Basho in a more realistic context, I do not want to come across as Basho bashing. Although he might have liked it, Basho is not responsible for people placing him on a Zen pedestal. He was a great nature poet, even if he bent nature to his art. And he did want to convey Buddhist truths, even if he compromises by sentimentalizing them. In the philosophy and aesthetics of the time, reality was equated with emotion. Thus, from one perspective, when Basho conveys his sentiments they stand for the reality of the situation. This is appealing to Westerners who identify strongly with the romantic melancholy of the Japanese hermits. Besides the hardships of travel that Basho often downplays in his haiku poems, his critics observe that nature for Basho often has a friendly face. Under the headnote from a Taoist line, "As we look calmly, we see everything is content with itself," is the poem:

playing in the blossoms
a horsefly... don't eat it,
friendly sparrows!

or

a tiny crab
crawls up my leg...
clear water[91]

Rather than spontaneous utterances which are manifestations of Zen insight, Basho worked over his poems to perfect them. Even in his famous "frog by a lily pond, plop!" the last line was reworked for aesthetic reasons. Basho was also not above making up facts. Weather was changed to fit earlier poetic imagery, days added, and an innkeeper, "Jack, the Buddha" was invented. A disciple quotes him as elevating the "'way of elegance' above that of truth."[92] We can glean this in the following poem:

> *between the waves*
> *mingling small seashells*
> *bush-clover debris*[93]

One might assume this means: "During the short interval between two breaking waves, the poet saw scattered on the beach tiny seashells and mingled with them fallen petals of bush-clover that looked like debris." More likely, however, is the following "aestheticized" scenario: "The poet had probably seen fallen bush-clover in the yard of a Buddhist temple, where he had stopped to rest earlier in the day. Accordingly there is no way in which seashells scattered on the beach could have mingled with flower petals in the temple yard; it was Basho's poetic fiction that brought the two together."[94] And again:

> *first winter shower—*
> *the monkey also seems to want*
> *a small raincoat*[95]

This is based on imagination rather than on detailed acquaintance with the Japanese macaque. Basho is anthropomorphizing, more Disney-ized than naturalized by the wilds which, I argue, is at the heart of eremitic Zen. The only shivering monkeys I have come across are in Jane Goodall's descriptions of wild chimps with fever. Still another Basho poem is suspect:

a wild duck, ill
on a cold night, falls from the sky
and sleeps a while[96]

This poem may refer to the fact that flying birds do sometimes die of cold while in flight, but naturalists have argued about the actuality and the frequency of such occurrences.[97] Basho's interpreters can't decide whether this is something that he really saw or if it is a metaphor for his being sick at the time. It was written in a place famous for wild ducks. Finally we have,

always hateful—
those crows, except in this
morning's snow scene[98]

Crows hateful to a Zen hermit?? Basho could have used practice and nature to explore each other, as did a thirteenth-century aristocrat who was not even a monk. He went to visit a hijiri (holy man) living in a hut near others. "The voice of the mountains, the echoes of the valleys, are all but the sermons of the Buddha... [They read together and discussed practice,] and passed the time in meditation, when I saw that the brushwood fence shone all white... when I pushed open the pine door... it was the moonlight reflecting upon frost... The darkness of my heart cleared up. I stepped out into the garden. In the universe there is nothing as splendid as the ice before my eyes. The cries of the monkeys that could be heard from the mountains were like a rainstorm blowing through the tops of trees... when I looked around, I saw high peaks... when I looked at that scenery this heart... purified itself, attracted to the heart of a... [hijiri]... I again returned [to the hut]... facing the wall, I sat in meditation."[99]

Similarly one might question Basho's cultivation of compassion, a central tenet of Zen as stated in the Bodhisattva vow to save all sentient beings. During his first pilgrimage Basho came upon an abandoned three-year-old child. The title of his journal entry was appropriately called, "The Records of a Weather-exposed Skeleton." The parents, he wrote, "must have thought this child was unable to ride through the stormy waters of life which run as wild as the rapid river itself, and that he was destined to have a life even shorter than that of the morning dew... it was so pitiful that I gave him what little food I had with me."[100]

> *The ancient poet*
> *Who pitied monkeys for their cries*
> *What would he say, if he saw*
> *This child crying in the autumn wind.*

"If [your suffering is the will of fate], you must raise your voice to the heaven and I must pass on, leaving you behind." Now, it is true that the community standards we hold are very different from those which existed in Basho's time. Throughout much of history children have simply been abandoned when there was too little food or social disruption. We should be wary of condemnations of Basho based on our own moral standards fostered by distinct norms and cultural conditions. Nevertheless, there is a contrasting story of the Chan Master who was accused by a local girl of fathering her illegitimate child. When the town's people approached him accusingly and demanded that he care for the child, he responded, "Oh so," and took the child in his care. Sometime later, the girl relented and confessed that the father was actually a fisher lad. The town's people went back to the Chan Master and apologized, taking the child back to his mother. His response was again, "Oh, so."

Robert Aitken Roshi, an American Zen Master, was introduced to Zen while interned by the Japanese during World War II. He has no illusions about the depth of Basho's meditation practice or experiential understanding of Zen. "It would be clearly wrong to claim Basho as a Zen poet." There is "thin evidence for a case to establish Zen as anything more than an element in his environment."[101] Aitken Roshi sets out to interpret Basho through the lens of practice, and although he admits that this view may not present the historical Basho, he believes that it gets to the essence of what it is that Basho was reaching toward. In the spirit of authentic practice, Aitken Roshi turns Basho, with all his talent and faults, into just the living exemplar of Zen that his admirers desired to see in him. "Here lies my conviction that Basho's haiku are to be read from the fundamental standpoint of Zen. He wrote of dusty roads, bird songs, cool breezes; of ideas, emotions, and recollections... playing with these forms and worlds in a way that resonates [with] deepest experience. My task is to make that way clear, to compare it to the way expressed in Zen literature, and to open the door to Zen in the process."[102]

Here are some examples of how Aitken Roshi re-renders Basho,

Now, as soon as eyes,
Of the hawk, too, darken,
Quail chirp.[103]

"This verse reflects Basho's sensitivity to the interplay of life in nature. The quail hides during the day in prudent respect for the hawk. The hawk preys upon quail, the quail upon insects, the insects upon smaller things. Yet each is pursuing its own life quite independently... But this is only an overtone of the verse... As the sun changes to the lamp, zazen [sitting] changes to kinhin [walking meditation], the eyes of the hawk change to the chirping of the quail. Step by minute step, the universe changes. Now light, now dark, now hawk, now quail, now sea, now land. It is at the edge of transition that we find experience."[104] Aitken Roshi sees Basho as grasping the outline of life's processes but points to how much deeper an understanding of it might arise by carefully looking in practice at how life changes from moment to moment.

From his own experience, Aitken Roshi makes the connection between nature and meditation. "In Guam there is a fish that climbs trees... well little bushes anyway. When you walk near them, the little fishes scatter and plunge back into their original element. These first amphibia, far older than the earliest human, yet still at the very point of transition from the sea, evoke the experience of immediacy at the hinge of evolution."[105] This is the foundation of our connection to life. Of Basho's poem,

> *The matsutake!*
> *A leaf from an unknown pine tree*
> *Stuck fast.*[106]

(The matsutake is an edible fungus that grows near pines.) Aitken Roshi comments, "The human mind tends to separate food from its sources, so we can eat brains, tongues, and intestines without qualm. But seeing leaf from the unknown tree stuck fast to the matsutake puts Basho in touch with the natural origins of that fungus in the forest, and with his own natural origins."[107]

The Roshi excuses Basho: "Huang-po and Yu-men take their students to task for their style of wandering, their spirit, their attitude... not for the wandering itself... Basho was compelled to wander all over Japan; Thoreau was compelled to wander in Concord." But what compelled them? For Basho, it seems to have been the image of being a Zen poet; for Thoreau, some combination of transcendental feeling about nature, misanthropy, and finally, a dedication to scientific natural history. Huang-po and Yu-men presumably wanted their students to have their wandering serve meditation. If it didn't it would not have been worthwhile.

The Roshi continues, "A monk asked Yun-men: 'What is

Buddha?' Yun-men said, 'A dried shit stick!' The dried shit stick was a piece of wood used just as our ancestors used a corncob in their outhouses. A dried up old stick used for such a purpose might be the ultimate in useless objects from a worldly point of view."[108] Aitken Roshi illuminates this with his own verse:

> *Little white maggots*
> *In fermenting night soil*
> *Steam with Buddhahood.*[109]

and Basho again:

> *A village where no temple bell sounds—*
> *What do they do?*
> *Twilight in spring.*[110]

"When we have no reminder of our timeless nature, there is no possibility of finding our way."[111] In the Roshi's hands, Basho becomes like Saigyo, a real Zen hermit marrying nature to practice.

In the years after Basho monks continued to wander, but some renowned teachers of the Buddhist establishment discouraged the activity. One of the most famous Japanese Zen masters, Hakuin (1685–1768), criticized quietism, Theravada, and esoteric forms of practice. "Moreover, even should you live in the forests or the wilderness, eat one meal a day, and practice the Way both day and night, it is still difficult to devote yourself to purity in your work... thus words and silence, motion and tranquility are all present in the midst of Zen meditation. When this state is reached, it will be different from that of a person who quietly practices in forests or mountains, and the state to which he attains, as heaven is from earth."[112] While not necessarily following Hakuin, Issa (1763–1827), who took Basho as his master, never strayed from home in his nature imagery. Issa had a miserable childhood. He was rejected by his stepfamily after his mother died. He married three times and all his children died.

Where there are humans
You'll find flies,
and Buddhas.[113]

He was a Shinsu Buddhist, and his tradition held the sacredness of life as in the Vinaya, the earliest Buddhist monastic code. His values would fit well with the ancient forest renunciants. "How can... foolish men dig the ground... ?"[114] Or how can they fell a tree because of the killing that entails?

Issa aspired to the Zen practice he imagined Basho did but was unable to do it because of his commitment to Shinsu and his family. As his translator says, "Issa is best read in a well-trodden backyard, midsummer, filled with flies, fireflies, wasps, mosquitoes and pea-blossoms, cobwebs, moths, and mustard-seeds... At a moment when summer-evening creatures are blasted with insect 'zappers' and dizzied with the stench of poison, he reminds us, over and over, of the individual reality of each life destroyed."[115] I am writing this in a year of the return of the 17-year locust, cicadas. I remember vividly three of their generations ago during my childhood when they covered the trees and sidewalks of the South Side of Chicago. Grotesque, they buzzed incessantly and were crushed under feet and cars. Issa's poem:

First cicada:
life is
cruel, cruel, cruel.[116]

touches upon the unavoidable interrelationships of nature. In his poetry he humorously personifies unpleasant aspects of nature.

Treated shabbily
by fleas, by flies,
day quits.[117]

Issa was attuned to life and death in nature, but, as with Basho, he was unable to address his own suffering.

We now come to the most profound of the Zen hermits, Ryokan (1758–1831). Although one might have expected to find him in an era when the Japanese lived close to a landscape that had not yet been changed so much by human activities, the opposite is true. He lived in a Japan about to open to the West and take on Western economic and bureaucratic values. He lived in a Japan depleted of much of its forest resources, a Japan where wildlife was no longer abundant. In such a setting, Ryokan was able to find enough solitude and nature to support a hermit practice. He grew up in a fishing town in an era of growing, coastal, mercantile transportation. His father was village headman but resigned and later committed suicide. At 17 Ryokan entered a Soto monastery, where he practiced for 12 years. During this period he endured abject poverty. He drew inspiration from Dogen. Toward the end of his studies his teacher attested to his attainments:

> To Ryokan, good as foolish, who walks the broadest way.
> So free and so untrammeled, none can truly fathom him.
> I grant this certificate with a stick of mountain wood.
> Everywhere he will find quiet and rest as inside the walls.[118]

This was prophetic.

After his teacher died he wandered for five years. Little is known about this part of his life. Afterward, he returned to his home village but had no permanent residence for another eight years. Then he moved into a small cottage below a temple halfway up 1,000-feet-high Mt. Kugami, where monkeys and

210

wild deer abounded. There he stayed for 12 years, until at 59 advancing age necessitated a move to the base of the mountain. There he spent 10 years. In 1826, at 69, infirmity forced him into a cottage attached to the house of a benefactor. Ryokan felt claustrophobic, so close to others. In 1827, a 29-year-old nun, Teishen, became his disciple and cared for him until the end. They had a Platonic love affair that has been preserved in the poems they exchanged. He died in 1831 after suffering terrible diarrhea. Ryokan was indeed a *furabo*, a lunatic, that is, an "old monk who wanders about fluttering like a thin piece of fabric in the wind," like a scarecrow with tattered flapping robes.

The practice that Ryokan undertook in his years as a hermit was supported by his training in the monastery.

Many a time in my youth I sat down for long meditation,
Hoping to master by practice the art of quiet breathing.
What virtue I now have in me to foster my heart's peace, I owe to
the hard discipline I underwent in my youth.[119]

And he applied that discipline throughout his life until he could no longer to do it. Practice was an irreplaceable ingredient in his understanding of life.

Since I began to climb this steep path of discipline,
I have lived behind a fast gate and a thousand hills.
Aged trees rise dark about me, fettered by ivy vines.
Rocks look cold on hillsides, half-covered in clouds.[120]

Here we begin to get a sense of Ryokan's practice. Nature teaches him how to meditate and his practice illuminates nature. The poem is a metaphor for the difficulties encountered in meditation. Its symbols come from the nature he observes. While Zen Master Aitken Roshi finds in Basho metaphors for teaching Zen, which he admits Basho may not have known he had,

Ryokan, the Zen master without students, lived the metaphors he offers. His authenticity is reflected in the real feel of the circumstances he pictures rather than a "mere" artistic epiphany. These last few sentences I wrote while steeped in Ryokan's poetry, typing on my computer in my van on the side of Lama Mountain in the dark. Around me were silhouetted ponderosa pines. The night air was clear and black with the stars sparkling as they do at 8,600 feet and no humidity. A nosy moth flew into my beard and I jerked away with a fear still with me from childhood. I felt the fear, and then the moth was gone, but where? The natural setting, the activity, the fear, are all part of being present, all both very real and a passing illusion without regard for aesthetics. I take that to be Ryokan's teaching.

> *In the stillness by the empty window*
> *I sit in formal meditation wearing my monk's surplice,*
> *. . .*
> *Moonlight floods the room;*
> *The rain stops, but the eaves drip and drip.*
> *Perfect this moment —*
> *In the vast emptiness, my understanding deepens.*[121]

While there are difficulties in formal practice, there is also sometimes — clarity. Here it is reflected through the Soto practice of just sitting with whatever is present: "the eaves drip and drip."

Ultimately, one may even have to surrender to the mind's inability to hold the discipline. Although it is rarely discussed by meditation teachers, when the mind begins to break down, practice becomes difficult, if not impossible.[122]

> *I've grown old and tired;*
> *This winter cold is the*
> *Worst I've suffered through.*
> *. . .*

Unable to beg for rice,
How will I survive the chill?
Even meditation helps no longer;
Nothing left to do but compose poems
In memory of deceased friends.[123]

Like the forest renunciants, Ryokan took asceticism seriously. "In general, to remove oneself from the doting pubic, involved with kin and family, to sit up-right in a grass hut, to circle about beneath the trees, to be a friend to the voice of the brook and the hue of the hills... these are the practices adopted by the ancient sages and the model of ages to come."[124] He observed the rule from the Theravada Visuddhimagga of begging from every house, not skipping any. He even begged at the brothel. He was not always successful in his begging but Mahayana allowed the gathering of wild greens.

Foraging became part of his practice:

A solitary trail stretches away through a million trees.
A thousand pinnacles above me are hid in clouds and mist.
Not autumn yet, fallen leaves lie thick upon the ground.
Hardly a rainy day, but all the rocks are dark and grim.
A basket in my hands, I hunt for mushrooms in the woods.
A bucket below my arm, I draw water from a stony spring.
Who can indeed content himself with this manner of life,
Unless he has seen himself altogether lost in the world?[125]

and:

When all thoughts
Are exhausted
I slip into the woods
And gather
A pile of shepherd's purse.

Although he liked society's food much better: "Deep in the mountains the food is tasteless."[126]

He took the ascetic practices to vanquish desire and aversion seriously. He kept his leftovers rotting in a pot and ate them after removing the maggots (a habit that sailors in the nineteenth-century British navy accepted as part of life: they knocked their hardtack against wood to drive the maggots out). He was committed to non-harming, which had been an important part of practice and survival for the forest renunciants. Answering a young monk who complained that Ryokan ate fish, he said, "I eat fish when offered, but I also let the fleas and mosquitoes feed on me."[127] The first part of this is in accord with the ancient Buddhist rule of eating whatever is offered, including, according to one story, a leper's finger which fell into a disciple's bowl! The second part fits well with non-harming as a way of offering yourself up without resistance to whatever happens in the world. This means surrendering to the Darwinian observation that all that eat are likewise eaten. Ryokan carried this out in small ways. He slept with one leg outside a mosquito net, so that the bugs would have food and he would not roll on them in his sleep. He also took his lice out to sun them and then put them back in his robe.

On a retreat in 1977 lead by Dhiravamsa, who was for many years a monk in Thailand, we sat for hours at a time in a Jewish summer camp in New Hampshire. We had to vow before each sitting not to move. We never knew how long we would sit, sometimes thirty minutes, sometimes three hours, and Dhira made us promise neither to wear insect repellent nor kill the mosquitoes. It was more compassionate to let mosquitoes bite you than repel them, and they would bite someone else. At one evening sitting I would observe very closely mosquitoes biting me: at first a tickling of their light tread, then stillness because I couldn't feel their stinger enter my flesh. When the mosquito left there would be a little pause and then I could feel a gradual increase of the itching until I had to restrain from the urge to squirm. I counted 21 bites, desperately holding still until the end of the sitting. Finally, a mosquito landed on my lips and I thought, "Oh no," the final insult. It bit me just as the bell rang. Not only were lice objects of Ryokan's compassion for their Buddha-nature, but plants too. When bamboo growing under his porch floor began to push against it, he tried to cut a hole to let it through and accidentally set the roof on fire. He then held a memorial service for the burnt bamboo and rebuilt the porch with movable floorboards and no roof. He regarded bamboo as his friend and teacher.

> *Now I sing the glory of the bamboo trees around my house.*
> *Several thousands stand together, forming a placid shade.*
> *Young shoots run wild, blocking the roads here and there.*
> *Old branches stretch all the way, cutting across the sky.*
> *...*
> *Their trunks are upright and their knots are far between.*
> *Their hearts are void of stuffing and their roots sturdy.*
> *Bamboo trees, I admire you for your honesty and strength.*
> *Be my friends, and stand about my retreat for eternity.*[128]

In this last poem, Ryokan observes nature closely and does not seem to have Saigyo's concerns about becoming too attached to it. His practice seems so authentic that even his critics do not accuse him of being more devoted to nature than to Buddhism. From nature Ryokan learned many things about life. In contrast to the Darwinian idea that things in nature fit together as a result of meticulous natural selection, Ryokan felt,

> *Flowers have no close designs to lure butterflies to stay,*
> *Nor butterflies any ambition to take advantage of flowers,*
> *But butterflies do not dally far behind when flowers blow,*
> *And flowers bloom all at once as soon as butterflies come.*[129]

Yes, there are ultraviolet patterns on petals, making runways for bees, and pheromone attractants lure butterflies to sweet food. Some orchids even mimic the females of insects to lure males into pollination. But ultimately Ryokan is right: Evolution here is nothing overly complex; it is just flowers and butterflies. Another translator renders the poem differently.

With no-mind, blossoms invite the butterfly;
With no-mind, the butterfly visits the blossoms.[130]

This translation might be construed to mean that the mechanism of natural selection also has Buddha-nature. This is not an anti-scientific sentiment. It is just that the explanations may finally come down to, "It happens. Don't know!"[131]

Beyond insight into causality in nature, Ryokan observes how its power dwarfs human intentions.

Within my garden
I grew autumn bush-clovers,
Along with pampas,
Pansies, golden dandelions,
A tiny silk-tree,
A plantain, morning glories,
Hemp agrimonies,
An aster, moist dayflowers,
And forget-me-nots,
And early and late each day,
Never neglecting,
I fed them with clear water,
Defending them from the sun,
Doing what I could for them.
By common consent
My good plants were exalted
Above the others,

And I believed so too myself,
Yet destiny desired
That one evening in mid-May,
Or more precisely
At dusk on the twenty-fifth,
Came a huge tempest,
Assaulting my garden plants
With mighty anger,
Pulling them down with fury;
And without pity
Poured upon them heavy rain.
And all my flowers
Were ruined, torn to pieces.
For days thereafter
My heart sank in depression,
Yet no help I found,
For it was useless to blame
The wind above our reproach.
My garden flowers
I planted and nursed myself
With genuine love,
I must learn to resign them
To the pleasure of the wind.[132]

Taking in this experience leads to a deeper understanding and acceptance of the Buddha's observation of impermanence. And Ryokan observed how he became as worn as the nature around him, like old butterflies with torn wings and insects missing legs.

Torn and tattered, torn and tattered,
Torn and tattered is this life.
Food? Wild vegetables from the roadside.
The shrubs and bushes advance toward my hut.
Often the moon and I sit together all night,

And more than once I have lost myself among
the wild flowers,
Forgetting to return home.
No wonder I left the community life:
How could such a crazy monk live in a temple?[133]
Finally, he just carefully observed what went on around him.

After long waiting,
When a pine-cricket begins,
How moving it is
To hear a bell-cricket sing
As if in answer,
Waving its wings in the grass,
Alas, wet with autumn dew.[134]

The challenge for the hermit is not merely the interesting observations of all the little things that make up the natural world. It is
to experience the deeper silence in which nature is set.

As a summer night advances into chaste hours of morning,
From bamboo leaves, dewdrops fall to the brushwood gate.
The pounding noise from my west neighbour has long died.
The rank grass of my garden is moist with gathering dew.
Far and near, the frogs of the marsh chant their chorus.
High and low, fireflies fly about, their lamps blinking.
Keenly awake, I cannot possibly seal my eye with sleep.
Slowly rubbing my pillow, I think beyond space and time.[135]

Or as I experienced it:

Sleeping in an old trailer with broken windows in the middle
of the night, in the quiet of winter, at ten or fifteen degrees
below zero, listening to the air crackle as it does on such cold
nights, sleep seems far away and I can hear the silence. At four
thirty in the morning, the meditation hall bell, a half a mile

away, rings crisply through the woods. Sound and stillness intermingle.

Ryokan finds silence all about. It is displayed in nature's uneventfulness.

Utterly devoid of movement, this small house of mine,
All day long, not a single human eye ever glances in.
I sit alone at the window, absorbed in deep thinking,
My ears bent to the quiet falls of scattering leaves.[136]

This was also the experience of a friend on a three-month retreat. He meditated for days on end in the autumn woods of New England where the leaves turn iridescent yellow, orange, red, and brown. He stood for hours staring at one leaf waiting for it to fall. No leaf he watched ever fell, yet all around him leaves fell. Silence and practice suffuse Ryokan's being. Returning home from begging he washes his feet and climbs a rock to meditate. "After all, I wear a monk's robe how could I spend the years doing nothing?"[137]

A single path through a dense forest,
mountains peek out from between the floating mist.
Not yet autumn, the leaves have already disappeared,
and without rain the rocks are always dark.[138]

As with the other hermits and recluses, loneliness and one's moods, highlighted in the silence, are some of the greatest challenges. Some seasons seem to bring these on more strongly. Like Saigyo, Ryokan had difficulty with the monsoons.

Late in October,
When frosty showers drizzle
Yesterday, today,

For many days without cease,
Outside my cottage,
Battering down ample leaves
In such profusion
That every walk by my house
Is deeply buried,
...
No doubt I know well enough
From my yesterdays
That life is merely a dream,
And yet in no way
Can I give ease to my heart
In this sad season.[139]

Winter is harder:

Lifted high above,
Some steps up Mount Kugami,
I live by myself,
Confined by midwinter snow
Falling every day
Over hills and valleys.
Not a single bird
Sings aloud about my house,
...
Thus in complete seclusion,
...
Every day, for days,
Each year, as long as I am,
I live here confined alone.[140]

and:

How many more days

Must I abide before springtide?
Time and time again,
Numbering the days and months,
I look out for the fresh spring.[141]

Pathways through these mind states can be strange. Shamans in hunter-gatherer society use psychotropic substances and ecstatic ritual to explore what Aldous Huxley called the antipodes of the mind, places of great fear, aggression, desire, and joy. The deeper a meditation practice becomes, the more these parts of the human mind may be exposed.[142] Ryokan explains his journey into the dark corners of the mind using images from his natural surroundings.

On the floor of an empty hall I planted myself alone.
But nowhere could I find ease for my oppressed heart.
And so I mounted a horse, traveling far at a gallop,
And climbed a mountain, to command a vast, vast view.
Presently a whirlwind came blowing out of the ground,
And the sun dropped westward, losing its usual light.
The winding river at once surged, its waves mounting,
And the boundless stretch of wilderness lay obscured.
Black monkeys called one another in descending gloom,
And a stray fowl roved southward, flapping its wings.
When I saw this, a hundred thoughts twisted my brows,
And fear a million times sterner froze my inner core.
Groping for a way to retreat, I could nowhere see it.
Like the year at its close, I stood lost unto myself.[143]

The resource that he had to carry him into and through such places was his commitment to meditation practice. And even though he sometimes achieved clarity of mind, the feelings were still there but no longer driving his being. A poem echoes Saigyo's early one on the same theme.

Sometimes I sit quietly,
Listening to the sound of falling leaves.
Peaceful indeed is the life of a monk,
Cut off from all worldly matters.
Then why do I shed these tears?[144]

Although a monk and a hermit for 58 years Ryokan did much of what life offers. He was the town fool with whom the children loved to play ball. He had intimacy in his last years. He lived fully in the silence of the woods in rapport with nature. He had compassion for all things around him. He probed the meaning of life in the spirit of Buddhist meditation. Living 1,200 years after Cold Mountain, Ryokan brought the practice-recluse tradition to a new depth. As if in a reverential bow of understanding to his predecessor, Ryokan wrote:

My home is a cave, without a thing in it—
Pure and marvelously empty,
As bright and clear as the sun.
A dish of mountain vegetables is sufficient,
And a patched coat is plenty of cover for me.
Let a thousand wizards show up to grant me any
wish!
I already have the Supreme Buddha
in my possession![145]

Chapter 5

Forest Monks

Buddhism left India by several routes. At the beginning of the Common Era Buddhism was carried into northwestern India. Then, turning north and east, it passed through Central Asia to China. From there it moved both southward across China, reaching Indochina, and northward into Korea. Crossing the Sea of Japan and the East China Sea, it came to rest in Japan. There this migration remained until the mid-twentieth century, when Buddhism crossed the Pacific to take root anew in the United States. As Buddhism moved it adapted to the new environments it met and influenced them in turn. We know little of the form Buddhism took in Central Asia, but its East Asian adaptations were quite different from each other. Although they are all Buddhists, the orderly, black-robed Japanese monks sitting in their temple in Bodhgaya, India—the place of Buddha's enlightenment—stand in sharp contrast to the ornate red-robed Tibetan or shaved-headed, saffron-robed Theravadan Buddhists in their nearby temples. And none of these Buddhists in their traditional settings would recognize American Buddhism as portrayed by the popular media.

Another route Buddhism took out of India occurred in the third century BCE. During the reign of King Asoka Buddhist missionaries accompanying diplomats and merchants spread Buddhism around the northeast corner of India and across the Bay of Bengal into Burma. Before the first century BCE Buddhism also crossed the straits of South India and took root in Ceylon. From there Ceylon's nineteenth-century imperial rulers carried what has been called Protestant Buddhism, as a curiosity, back to Great Britain. After a period of overlapping traditions the Buddhism which emerged in East Asia was Mahayana

Buddhism, that of South and Southeast Asia, Theravada. During the first millennium of this era Theravada Buddhism filtered back and forth between Sri Lanka and Southeast Asia. The Pali tradition was solidified by Buddhaghosa in Sri Lanka in the fifth century. Based on his translations of the commentaries into Pali and the powerful codification of rules and practice techniques in the *Visuddhimagga*, the Pali texts became the foundation of Buddhism in Burma. In the eleventh century the Sinhalese of Sri Lanka reconquered their island after being overwhelmed by a Hindu Tamil invasion from south India. The victors turned to Burma to renew the Buddhism that the Tamils had suppressed. From Burma and Sri Lanka Theravada spread to the rest of Southeast Asia until it met Chinese-inspired Mahayana in Vietnam. Here it gave a Theravada-like flavor to Vietnamese Zen. Buddhism did not fully come to Thailand until the thirteenth century. It became widespread when the country was under threat of Muslim invasion. The central Thai government adopted an invigorated Theravada Buddhism from Burmese and Sri Lankan sources.

From this simple sketch one can see that Buddhist presence south and east of India was complex. As with the traditions that spread to the north, we find only fragments on how meditation related to nature. As we saw in our discussion of the Elders, meditation, like humility in Christianity, existed more as religious rhetoric than actual practice. What royalty adopted, what peasants believed in, what the temples and monasteries traded in was not meditation but rituals, beliefs, magical promises, theological debates, the training of children, and rudimentary social services. Politics and economic power played a large role in the religion. There were great monasteries owning large estates, which they worked with slaves. Often religious sects allied themselves with competing political forces. It is not that meditation practice was entirely missing. Scholar monks studied both the *Sutra on The Four Foundations of Mindfulness*, the basic text on meditation, and the meditation instructions from the *Visuddhimagga*. Only a few, however, actually undertook the practices these texts recommended. Meditation contributed only fractionally to Buddhism as it existed in these countries.

Moreover, as we noted before, the Theravadan tradition of forest renunciation drops from view after the time of the Buddha, although it may have lingered in obscure forms. One can imagine individuals going off on their own and engaging in forest practice. There may have been lineages that carried on forest practice for several generations. But, true to the spirit of practicing meditation in nature by living aloof from society, they left no record of their activities. There are references to forest monks in Buddhist scholars' chronicles, but these mostly referred to schismatic sects who lost disputes and withdrew from centers of power until they regained influence. They were forest monks only in the sense that they sought refuge away from seats of power. As was noted, the monastic code and the texts, as interpreted by scholar monks, held forest practice in high esteem but also established rules that mitigated against it. Thus, we have little to go on to trace the relationship between nature and meditation in the southeastern sweep of Theravada until, that is, 1892, when a pair of Thai monks began a serious, rigorous, and ultimately, charismatic forest practice.

Called *Thudong Kammathaan* or ascetic meditation monks, the forest monks of Thailand dove into untamed and dangerous forests to practice meditation as the Buddha first recommended it. In so doing they confronted disease, old age, and death as they occurred in the wild, and they endeavored to tame their minds' reactions to them. They lived at the boundaries where village life and, eventually, modern civilization touched the wild. Moving back and forth from village to forest they came across tribals and a few remaining hunter-gatherers. The encounter between meditation practice and aboriginal lifestyle allows for comparisons between how the two perspectives looked upon the natural world. With the forest monks of Thailand the relationship between the wilds and meditation is no longer so clouded. We can almost touch in time the experiences they had, but as we shall see, modern civilization overtook them. War and politics drove them out of the forests, and economic development destroyed the wildlands in which they had wandered.

The landscapes of Southeast Asia were more like early Buddhist India than China or Japan. The geography is dominated by finger-like mountain ranges separated by great river valleys that radiate from the southeastern corner of the Tibetan plateau. The rivers flow to the south and somewhat to the east. One range of mountains runs along the border of Burma and Thailand. A second, beginning in the mountainous north of Thailand, runs south and eastward. The two major rivers are the Chao Phraya River, running out of the northern mountains through central Thailand, by Bangkok, and then into the Gulf of Siam, and the great Mekong River, rising in the Himalayas, running first through China, then dividing Thailand and Laos in the northeast and east before flowing east into Cambodia and Vietnam. Most of Thailand's people live along the Chao Phraya where they grow rice in the floodplains. Until recently the Mekong was remote and forested. The mountains bounding Burma and Thailand to the north and west range above 5,000 feet, gaining height as they head north toward China. The highest peak in Thailand, 8,481 feet, is located near the town of Chengmai in the North. The mountains on the east side of the Chao Phraya plain separate Northeast Thailand from the rest of the country. They range up to 6,000 feet but average only about 2,000 feet. The whole of the Northeast is a low plateau sloping gradually toward the Mekong River. Northeast Thailand is geographically more part of Laos than Thailand.

Thailand's climate is tropical. In May the southwest monsoon brings rain, reaching a maximum downfall in September. Between November and February it is cooler and drier, leaving

March and April stagnant and hot. The average temperatures range from 77° to 84°F, although during the winter the higher elevations in the north and northeast sometimes experience frost. The modern forest tradition arose in the northern corner of Northeast Thailand, called Isan. The monks in this tradition wandered throughout the five northern-most provinces of the Northeast. They crossed the Mekong and walked into the forests of Laos. They also traveled through the mountains of northern Thailand into the Shan plateau of Burma and down into the Mon areas of Burma west of the Thai-Burmese border. Occasionally they strayed as far as Phnom Penh in Central Cambodia and Rangoon, Burma. The landscape and peoples of these regions had an important effect on the monks' lives and practice.

Because of its remoteness from the Central Plain of the Chao Phraya River, sparsely populated Isan maintained much of its aboriginal forest cover until well into the twentieth century. The forests through which monks wandered ranged from seasonal evergreen forests to mixed deciduous forests to dry deciduous forests. The seasonal evergreen forest is not quite so wet, lush, or dense as a tropical rainforest. Single trees tower above the canopy. The bases of these trees are supported by buttressed trunks, giving the trees their distinctive jungle-like character. The mixed deciduous and dry deciduous forests are more common in the Northeast and even less closed in. They sometimes have impenetrable understories of different kinds of bamboo whose names say much about humans' relation to them: pygmy bamboo, thorny bamboo, elephant trail bamboo. During the dry season brown and yellow leaves cover the ground of the dry deciduous forests, keeping down any growth and allowing easy passage. The dry leaves crackled as the monks trod them under foot. Each of these kinds of forest presented particular challenges to forest monks. The dry deciduous forests often burned during the dry season, which the wanderers noted with due appreciation of the risk this implied, and bamboo thickets are extremely dangerous because broken bamboo is very sharp.

The flora of Thailand is one of the most abundant in the world. Even the northern regions are bedecked with gaudy flowers. Thailand has 280 mammal, 925 bird, 500 butterfly, and 10,000 beetle species. The Asian elephant lives in wild packs and ranges over large areas. Elephants were captured and domesticated, as they had been in ancient India. Wild elephants were threatening to forest monks but also played an important symbolic role. Rhinoceroses, tigers, leopards, panthers, and other cats can be found, along with wild dogs, which hunt in packs, wild boar, barking deer, Indian sambur (the largest deer), wild water buffalo, gaur (a form of wild cattle), gibbons, macaques, anteaters, lemurs, bats, and 75 kinds of lizards. There are also 13 poisonous snakes, including cobras, kriats, coral snakes, and vipers.

In the North malaria-bearing mosquitoes thrive, and in the Northeast termites build nests 10 feet high. "Leeches are numerous in the rainforests... the traveler has no rest because one species climbs up from the soil, and another adheres to the passerby from the twigs of the bushes along the side of the path... Leeches will penetrate the smallest opening in a person's clothes... Wounds tend to become infected and to heal very slowly."[1] In the Northeast, ticks from dry grasses cause irritations lasting weeks and occasionally carry tick fever or scrub typhus.

The point of this is not just to list the components of an enchantingly rich biogeography but to understand how wild and dangerous was the environment in which the monks wandered and to see the more remote parts of Thailand in the late nineteenth century as a metaphorical window into what it may have been like in India at the time of Buddha. From this we can better understand what the Buddha intended when he recommended forest practice.

In India when Aryans swept into the Ganges plains they displaced the indigenous Dravidians, who withdrew into the forests. There, living in many culturally distinct groupings, aborigines continued alongside developing Aryan civilizations. In the woods they hunted and gathered, then gradually adopted farming and the technologies and cultural traits of the invaders. Even though Buddhism vanished from India long ago, tribals have managed to survive with varying degrees of autonomy until the present. Similarly, in Thailand, although rice cultivation as well as bronze and, later, iron tools had existed since the end of the second millennium BCE, indigenous peoples continued to occupy much of the country until historic times, when they gradually gave way to ethnic Thais, who were pushed from southern China by the Han. The Thais moved south and settled the river valleys, where they carried on rice cultivation and built societies that occasionally exercised wide political control— although rarely over the indigenous tribal peoples who withdrew to hilly or mountainous retreats.

In the nineteenth century, and continuing but diminishing into the twentieth century, some of Thailand's hunting-gathering populations also grew subsistence crops and took part in some trade. Thais called the hill peoples "holders of the wild" or "the people of the upland fields." Among hill people were the Karen, Miao (or Hmong), Yao, Lahu, and Lisu. Most lived in migratory villages, where they engaged in slash-and-burn cultivation and extracted resources from the forests. A few maintained pure hunter-gatherer lifestyles. Although some were nominally Buddhist or Christian, many retained animistic beliefs.

During the nineteenth and well into the twentieth century Thailand sported neither a unified government exercising power over a defined territory nor an accepted official language. Each tribal group had its own tongue, and among ethnic Thais in areas such as the Northeast either Lao or an older dialect of Thai was spoken. There were two written languages: Tham, a scriptural language that derived from Shan and Mon of Burma, and Thai Noi, which was similar to Lao. Many Thais near the Laotian border considered themselves Lao, and since the borders were ill-defined they traveled back and forth without restraint. Wars and agricultural failure led whole villages to move to unoccupied lands. One forest monk described his family resettling after a string of bad harvests. They "trekked down to the lowlands... crossing several high mountain ranges... and dense jungle tracks."[2] Without pack animals or elephants, they had to carry their belongings for a week. His mother was from a Lao tribe that had been forced out of Laos. "[T]hey blazed a trail... penetrating deep jungles, fording streams and traversing mountain ranges." There were bandits and small pox. Until the twentieth century central governments exercised little control over the hinterlands.

In the nineteenth century the British conquest of Burma and French incursions into Indochina caused alarm among Thailand's rulers. From mid-century on, the central government instituted a process of modernization to counter the increasing threats of Western imperialism. King Chulalongkorn, who ruled Thailand from 1868 to 1910, built railways and a telegraph system and established a modern bureaucracy with courts and a school system. He also began to extend centralized rule into the peripheries of the country. His successor made primary education compulsory and spread the use of a standard Thai language. The kings of the nineteenth century supported ever more organized and powerful Buddhist institutions. Texts were translated, monastic codes clarified, monks given institutional power, and, in the mid-nineteenth century, a king who had been a monk for 26 years established a reform Theravada sect called the *Thammayut Nikaya*.

In the twentieth century central authorities used the clergy to pull the countryside into a more integrated nation state. The *Thammayut Nikaya* was an important vehicle for this. Monks were sent around the country to enforce the monastic code, formally ordain and register rural monks, establish schools, and teach standard Thai. Monks who were not ordained in the *Thammayut*

Nikaya were lumped together and considered part of the older more widespread sect called the *Mahanikai*, which had its own hierarchy.

The areas which the *Thammayut* reformers penetrated were not easily accessible from the capital. Until 1910 fast boats along the rivers and runners in the interior relayed messages between Bangkok and the provinces. Village runners used networks of forest trails that connected to new settlements. "At nighttime nobody dared move outside the settlement for fear of tigers and malevolent spirits."[3] To reach the capital of the Northeast from the far northeastern town of Ubon took 12 days running. Trips of three weeks by oxcart were common. An ordinary monk mentioned a 31-day walk from the edge of the Northeast to Ubon, a provincial center. For officials and their retinues the trip by oxcart was considered more comfortable, but took longer than walking. In 1899 one official monk took three months to return to Bangkok from Laos and then two months to travel to Ubon. When ordered on new tours of inspection he complained of the amount of traveling time required. Like transplanted villagers, travelers had to brave wild animals, bandits, and malaria. In 1900 a rail line was built to the edge of the Northeast. Malaria took the lives of many of the construction workers. Service was extended to Ubon in 1930.

Buddhism came to Southeast Asia in a manner similar to the way it came to China: The royalty and the gentry adopted it in dramatic, documented gestures. They would send to Sri Lanka for ordaining clergy to initiate or rejuvenate Buddhism. For almost two millennia anonymous monks came from India and elsewhere to settle among villagers in Thailand. The locals and their monks would come into conflict with monks from the capital when royal religion was imposed on the countryside or when rural Buddhism rose to challenge a decadent urban clergy. When Buddhism came to villages it either assimilated local beliefs or coexisted with them, as had happened when Buddhism encountered Shinto in Japan. However, local beliefs in Southeast Asia were not unified enough to effectively contest Buddhism.

In the first part of the twentieth century when reform monks came to remote villages they found illiterate local monks doing many things forbidden by the 223-rule monastic code. They participated in celebrations that included playing games, drinking, and promiscuity. Some rode horses, worked in villages, and owned property, even slaves. They ate at irregular hours, smoked opium, gambled, and were reputed to possess knives and swords. Unlike monks from the city local monks tended to blend in with the isolated villages in which they lived.

The two founders of modern forest practice were ordained in the period when reformers were trying to assert control over remote villages. The more famous, Ajaan Mun, was born in a village in the Northeast in 1870.[4] He was ordained in the local *wat* (temple or monastery) as a novice at age 15, studied a bit, and then disrobed. Temporary monkhood was not only acceptable but common in Theravada Buddhism. Even today young men and women, businessmen, or political leaders ordain for periods lasting from only days to years, and it is expected that a young man ordain for a short while prior to marriage.

Four years after his first ordination Mun was reordained at a *Thammayut wat* in Ubon. As a monk he chose to study meditation. He then went off to engage in ascetic practice with his teacher, Ajaan Sao (1859–1941). Fifty years before Mun was ordained Ubon had been the monastic residence of the mid-century king, who while a monk had been instrumental in having Buddhist commentaries translated into Thai. Apparently Ajaan Sao read one of these translations, which included the 13 *dhutanga* (ascetic) rules, and he decided he would try to rigorously practice them. So he and his student went off to become forest monks.

At that time other forest monks wandered about, but it is unclear what they were doing. We have seen that the label "forest monk" had been used in a number of different ways. Historians and Buddhist scholars often note the existence of wandering Buddhist ascetics since the time of the Buddha.[5] We saw in India, China, and Japan, that renunciants, recluses, and hermits had competition from wandering Brahmans, shamans, astrologers, and necromancers. In the Theravada history of Buddhism forest monk had various meanings. It could refer to an ascetic, to someone who merely practiced meditation, to a rural monk, to someone from a dissenting sect, or to a disorderly deviant. In Burma, royalty would sometimes sponsor a monastery in the wilds as a way of colonizing a new area. The "forest monks" residing there were not particularly known for their meditation practice, asceticism, or interest in the forests. And robbers, Robin Hoods, and other forest ne'er do-wells occasionally used monk's garb as disguises. In short, few, perhaps very few, of those known as forest monks practiced according to the Buddha's ideal.

Although we have little evidence concerning what was actually done in the forests, one meditation teacher in nineteenth-century Thailand became famous for teaching *dhutanga* practices, which his disciples apparently undertook in the forests in the midst of the wild animals that then existed near the capital.[6] Though there were other wandering monks at the time, including village monks on tourist-like pilgrimages to holy sites, Sao and Mun seemed to have derived their forest practices from books rather than from living mentors.

The two men traveled for a while together, but Ajaan Sao was unable to advise Mun how to progress in his meditation practice, so Mun went off on his own, spending eight months wandering as far as Rangoon in search of someone to guide him. Sao, the teacher, and Mun, the student, were of different dispositions. Although Sao had a number of students he was rumored to have striven to become a silent Buddha. He "liked doing construction work, planting chili and fruit trees... He was down to earth, calm, compassionate, diligent, and generous in his teaching of the Vinaya. He spoke little... [He] was a loner and had not ambition."[7] Ajaan Mun, on the other hand, passionately strove to plumb the depths of meditation practice and insisted on precise adherence to the *dhutanga* rules. Ajaan Sao retired into relative obscurity, whereas Ajaan Mun, despite years alone in remote forests, became a revered saint with many students and several biographers. Because of those biographers, we have a window into his forest practice: how he used nature as an ingredient in meditation and meditation as a way of seeing nature.

In looking at the practice of the *Thudong Kammathaan* monks it is as if time had been rolled back 2,500 years. The seasonal evergreen and dry deciduous forests of Thailand through which the forest monks walked had not changed much since the Buddha wandered through similar forests in ancient India. The villagers on whom the forest monks depended had slightly more contact with the modern world than ancient Indians did, but villages were still surrounded by forest or jungle. Walking to the nearest town might take several days. By the 1890s villagers had acquired a few metal tools or utensils, as well as kerosene lamps. Scant Western medicine was available. Most of the villagers were tied to the agricultural seasons, growing staples such as dry-land rice and millet using slash-and-burn techniques. Among the villagers were a few who hunted in the forests and others who gathered forest delicacies or medicinals. Village monks worked because there was no surplus labor in the villages to support the building and maintenance of the *wats*. In this milieu two village monks, a 40-year-old and a 22-year-old, using only the *dhutanga* rules from a Thai rendition of the *Visuddhimagga*, went back into the forest and recreated a forest monasticism presumably much like that which existed at the time of the Buddha.

In the *dhutanga* rules one must:

1) Wear clothes made only of discarded cloth.
2) Wear three robes sewn of patches of the cloth.

3) Eat only alms food.
4) Practice gapless wandering, which means collecting from each and every house without preference.
5) Eat one meal per day in an uninterrupted session.
6) Mix lumps of alms food together in one bowl.
7) Refuse any food offered after the meal.
8) Dwell in the forest or,
9) at the root of a tree or,
10) in the open air or,
11) in the charnel ground.
12) Sleep wherever assigned (when in a *wat*).
13) Never lie down, i.e., sleep sitting up.

Ajaans Sao and Mun strictly observed most of these. Ajaan Mun only wore rag robes. This was a necessity in his early wandering days when there were no patrons to offer robes, but he continued the practice even when followers provided for him. He picked up discarded clothes and bits of cloth. He wore the material until it decomposed. Some of his later students were embarrassed by this behavior and gave him new cloth, which he gave away again. In old age he finally accepted cloth left near his meditation path.

Remember, the *Visuddhimagga* allowed observing the *Dhutanga* rules with various degrees of strictness. Rules 3 through 7, about the one meal a day, were upheld, except when illness made them dangerous. And rule 8, dwelling in the forest, was honored except when at urban *wats*. Even when forest monks gathered, they went back to the forest to practice meditation and sleep at night. Meditation in the charnel ground, sleeping in assigned places, and never lying down were practices either engaged in because of circumstance or left up to the individual. As for other ascetic rules, monks carried with them the same equipment that the ancient forest renunciants had. These included their three garments, a begging bowl, a *klot*, which is an umbrella with a mosquito net draped over it, and live coals for a fire. Later on they added a fourth robe, a bathing wrap, and matches.

Daily, or as often as possible, monks would go to nearby villages or dwellings and beg for their one meal, then retreat to the forest to consume it. At night they found a spot to sit, often under a tree, opened their *klot* with its mosquito net, and sat, vowing not to move until morning. During the rains retreat monks settled in one place, sometimes near a *wat* or a large enough group of houses that residents could afford to feed them. There the monks practiced meditation for three months. In the dry seasons, they wandered, stopping at a cave or other suitable place for a while and then moving on.

Ajaan Mun's monastic life can be divided in periods. From 1892 to 1915 he wandered around Isan, into Laos, and from the mountains of northern Thailand into Burma. At one point he walked to Bangkok to visit a childhood friend who had become an important *Thammayut* administrator. In this first period of his life he was purported to have had unshakable insights into Buddhist truths. The rigor of his practice and the power of his presence began to attract students, whom he would instruct but send on their way. The number of students increased during the second period, from 1916 until 1928, when he continued moving about the Northeast, gathering students in his wake. When he stopped in one locale Ajaan Mun insisted his students spread themselves out over a wide area and only come to see him occasionally. He continued his daily practice. In 1928, as teaching responsibilities increased, he decided that his own practice needed more work, so he dropped out of sight. For 11 years he engaged in solitary forest practice in the North. From 1940 to 1949, the last nine years of his life, he returned to the Northeast and began teaching again. During this period his fame grew and he attracted urban admirers, including Thai royalty. Although he continued to teach with the ferocity for which he became famous, his increasing age and doting followers tempered the rigor of his asceticism.

Scholars have argued about the role of forest monastics in the consolidation of the modern Thai state. Some see the forest monks as unwitting agents of the state's use of religion to integrate remote provinces into a modernized Thai society. They regard the *Thammayut Nikaya* (the sect in which most of the forest monks were ordained) as a vehicle for spreading standard spoken Thai, increasing literacy, bringing administrative order to the provinces, and rooting out village magic and other pre-modern social habits. Other scholars argue that the mystique surrounding the forest monks fed into the Thai fondness for spirit healing and fortune-telling. Still others claim that, although they were sometimes swept up in larger social and political currents, the forest monks only cared about their own practice and disavowed any social service, educational, or cultural role.

What is clear is that Thai society changed enormously during the years the forest monks wandered the woods. Changes were environmental, political, and social. These changes eventually undermined forest practice, as I describe later. When Thai politics and world events intruded upon local village life, my focus will be on those forest monks who really did meditation in the wild.

Ajaan Mun and his students worked with simple meditation techniques from the sutras. They began with the establishment of concentration, extended that to contemplation of the body, focused attention on desire and aversion, and finally cultivated insight into the world as it changes. For Ajaan Mun each act of the day was to be done with awareness. In sitting meditation, concentration was established by repeating the mantra "Buddho," a word meaning the essence of Buddha-ness. Attention was focused on this until the mind became stable in its ability to hold one point and became so settled that it would not lose balance. Contemplations of the body came from the *Sutra on The Foundations of Mindfulness* or the *Visuddhimagga*. They included feeling sensations as they occur or contemplations on the decay of the body. Ajaan Mun used strict adherence to the *dhutanga* rules as a device for cutting through desire and aversion as habits of mind. The rules acted as foils. Their restrictions on behavior are fertile ground for the mind's reactions. For example, when mixing food together in a begging bowl the practitioner is instructed to observe how attachment to different tastes and textures influences one's actions. When I do a modified version of this at meals on meditation retreats I sometimes feel the disgust of other meditators eating near me. I actually like lots of kinds of foods mixed together but do not practice the extreme mixing Ajaan Mun would have insisted upon and which the *Visuddhimagga* so vividly describes.

There is nothing very distinctive in these practices. They can be done, as they have been for centuries, by meditators in monasteries. Cenobites claim them as their own. The experiences of Thai forest monks will show more vividly what is so special about the forest as a setting for meditation. As a teenager Ajaan Tate (1902–1996) left this village to follow a couple of magical monks, whom he soon discovered were frauds. After a few days with them he became homesick and returned. Later two disciples of Ajaan Mun came through his village while walking *thudong*. *Thudong* is the Thai word for *dhutanga*, but in Thai culture it usually means to casually "wander for seclusion in the forest," rather than to specifically engage in the rigorous, ascetic, meditation practices there. As authentic *Thudong Kammathaan* (ascetic meditation monks) Ajaan Muns followers taught Tate how to practice meditation using the mantra "Buddho." He accompanied them to help them with their malaria and, at 22, he was ordained. "Most academic monks considered going off on a *thudong* a disgraceful thing to do... In those days *thudong* was uncommon, and some saw it as akin to undisciplined vagrancy."[8]

As Tate wrote of his second rains retreat in 1924, "while living in a cave, I trained my mindfulness in order to give it a constancy throughout the day and night. (I even made sure that however my mind had been established before going to sleep, it would return to the same state on awakening.)" In the intensity of practice things which he could not handle arose: "[S]ome huge, looming black form came forward and seated itself on my chest, so that I couldn't breathe. My heart nearly gave out in the struggle to regain consciousness." At this point in his meditation, he would drop into a trance-like state that he described as "the underlying flux of the subconscious." "I thought that wisdom's only function was to purge the out-wanderings of the heart [when Thai Buddhists use the word heart in this context they also mean mind] and return it to a state of stillness. I therefore did not try to use investigative discernment on an examination of the body and sense impressions and so failed to come to an understanding about body and heart... I was living alone without a competent [meditation] companion to give me advice." So Tate undertook an arduous trip of several years to find Ajaan Mun, who was sequestered in Burma. When he finally found Ajaan Mun the advice he got was to contemplate the loathsomeness of the body and not to stray from that. When Tate did this practice his troublesome states subsided. At the time this advice was given Ajaan Mun had been practicing in the forests for almost 34 years.

Like the forest renunciants before him Ajaan Mun believed that the forest was a place one could find original insight not easily available on the path of scholarship or in a monastery. He thought that forests would support adherence to the monastic code. He felt that those who strayed from its discipline in the wilds would become ill. Unlike the religious establishment during much of Theravada history, which believed enlightenment was a rare occurrence that had mostly taken place during the Buddha's time, Mun's forest experience convinced him that

239

enlightenment was indeed available. For Mun's followers, Ajaan Mun was a living example of what could be achieved with rigorous practice, almost a living Buddha. Like Ajaan Mun many of the forest monks were not Buddhist scholars nor bound by the sentiments that pervaded monasteries. Some had very little Buddhist education. They did not consult the commentaries or use the many concentration exercises of the *Visuddhimagga*. Some forest monks felt the practices of the *Visuddhimagga* could lead practitioners to confuse its complicated mental exercises with reality. They might then act on their thoughts as if they were real or feel that their experiences were merely thought.

In contrast, forest practice fostered groundedness. Ajaan Mun's advice to Ajaan Tate was to pay attention to the components of his experiences. The forest, as a container for them, was meant to bring simple sensation into sharp focus. As Mun's biographer says of his practice, "Staying in the wilds or forest, one is constantly reminded of isolation and seclusion. There is little opportunity for self-complacency to insert itself."[9] "Living in the forest... the senses are not stimulated to any great extent, so sensory deprivation sets in and they [the senses] find themselves becoming tranquil."[10] According to his biographer, Mun's mind was most unfettered "during the night when he was seated under the branches of a lonely tree... [with] no enclosure nor [sic] any kind of protection to be expected."[11] For him "walking the whole day was developing insight meditation the whole day... While the body was ambling through the scorching meadows interspersed with forested areas, the mind was absorbed in the theme of meditation, oblivious to the heat of the noonday sun." "This is, in a sense, a rehearsal or preparation, the mind that has been tamed and trained can hold its own and become detached from the condition of the body." Here, detached means that he was alert to his mind's wandering from the primary point of attention and was able to catch it whenever it resisted the reality of the moment or strayed into distraction.

Years later a forest monk described how he contemplated his skin, bones, breath, and heartbeat while he was walking through the forests. It is not clear how aware he or Mun were of their surroundings while doing this.[12] A central reason for doing forest practice was that dangers of the forests would necessitate being alert, not only to one's state of mind but also to the forests themselves. I have no information of how forest monks actually accomplished this. As we will see shortly, some did not do it successfully.

One of Mun's students who spent many years wandering sums up what the forests meant: "I have come to consider the principles of nature: It's a quiet place where you can observe the influences of the environment."[13] Wild nature is strong, resilient, and ever alert, while domesticated beings easily fall prey. "If we spend all our time wallowing around in companionship," we get stuck. The student goes on to tell a story of how he played dead when he encountered a bear. "No one is interested in a dead person. Since I live in the forest, I should play dead. Whoever praises or attacks me, I'll have to be still... quiet in thought and deed... if I want to survive... When in the woods if you keep your mind still... you are sure to be safe and free from dying... In the forest, vines turn to the right, which reminds one that the Buddha taught you must go to the right in thought and deed keeping above defilements. Just as some trees fold their leaves at night so that the stars are visible, so in sitting only the eyes are closed but you are alert and bright... living in the forest. The mind becomes confident. [The truth of existence] will make itself clear because nature is the teacher... As for [Buddhist under-standing], it's just like science: It exists in nature. When I realized this, I no longer worried about studying the scriptures." The Buddha and his disciples learned directly from nature. The monks' observations of what we would now consider forest biology contain biological gems, whose accuracy is not easy to ascertain. I don't know whether all forest vines turn to the right, but Darwin's experimental pea tendrils did.[14]

As another student of Ajaan Mun put it: "[The Buddha] always spent his time living in the forest."[15] Paraphrasing the sutras, he continued: "Look yonder! There's a mountain! A deep forest! There are the mountainsides! There are the canyons! There are the creeks! Streams! Cliff! Hilltops! Mountain slopes! There are the waterfronts and rivers by the hillsides! These are the places of ease and quietude, free from all forms of entanglement. You should seek this kind of location and strive in these environments... The [Buddha] attained his buddhahood from these settings and surroundings. He did not become enlightened through mingling and socializing. Neither did he become enlightened through indulgence in mirth and gaiety... These places are deserted and quiet, free from confusions and trouble. These places are not wanted by people."[16]

One scholar of the forest tradition summed up their connection to nature as follows:

Being out of the ordinary, these special individuals, able to coexist with the wild and untamed, must have spiritually transcended (through personal conquest) their own mental defilements... the 'disordered regions of the mind'... With the presence of 'worldly renouncers,' the forest habitat becomes sanctified (though still potentially harmful) and its symbolic powers possess... 'an aura of mystery and hint of the existence of the superhuman or of a grace beyond the good as ordinarily conceived.'[17]

Wild nature is both an existentially threatening and a spiritually transcendent setting for taming the mind. The effort at meditation and the absence of distracting human relationships make accessible the recesses of the mind. Meditating on his own Ajaan Tate, like the Chinese recluses and Japanese hermits, wandered into those regions of the mind that are often held in the dark. His intense practice in the cave opened him to these forces, and his arduous trip through the wilds, which we will touch on later, brought him to Ajaan Mun, whose instructions kept him from getting lost. Ajaan Tate's experiences are akin to those of a Native American vision quest.[18] We can touch upon this intersection by comparing the monks' lives to the ways that Thai hunter-gatherers, tribals, and villagers lived in the forests.

Besides its quiet and its metaphorical value nature had very immediate impacts on forest monks. The forests of Thailand were neither accommodating nor safe. Most forest monks grew up in villages, and, according to reports of village life, villagers were not totally comfortable with the wild. Some scholars claim that villagers were terrified of the forest because of the wild animals and the demons they believed resided there. They claim that villagers almost never traveled unaccompanied. This view of villagers' relationship to the woods that surrounded them is widely accepted but is not the whole story.[19] Among the villagers were foragers, who hunted and gathered in the forests. Villagers frequently let their animals browse in the woods. Villagers also undertook migrations. Thus, while villagers told frightening stories of the surrounding forests, some among them possessed intimate knowledge of how forests worked. My guess is that, while there was fear, it has been exaggerated in the telling by scholars and other urbanites for whom the forests were truly intimidating and by Buddhist biographers to make the forest monks seem all the braver. Monks who had been villagers did take to living in the forbidding woods and learned how to survive there. They did not develop these skills from scratch. Before we look at how they did this we need to look again at the role of karma and loving-kindness.

When the original Indian forest renunciants took to the wilds at the time of the Buddha they did so in order to grapple with their craving and aversion and to come to terms with their karma. The idea of karma has two aspects. The first stems from the belief in rebirth and has to do with the totality of one's collective inheritance at any moment in time. Karma may include the shadow of good or bad deeds done in some past birth that somehow influences the present moment. Or it may be one's genes or childhood trauma that affects the present. Another interpretation of karma has to do with the intention with which a person does something. If one acts with "don't know mind" or "beginner's mind," that is a mind without defilement, then the action does not carry a kick from the past, a harmful karma that infects the future. By framing how they acted in the wilds, monks tried not to make damaging karma. The tools that the forest monks took with them into the wilds were the discipline of *dhutanga* and the intention not to harm. Discipline kept the monks' minds and behaviors in check, while non-harming affected their relationship with the nature in which they were engulfed. The two are ultimately interwoven. Meditation and discipline keep discontent from flowering into unwise acts, while the best a monk could do to prevent intentional, and even accidental, bad karma from being initiated was to adopt a non-harming stance. By stepping out of the village life that so completely supported them the monks immersed themselves in untempered nature. As they did this they tried to create as little harmful karma as possible.

The first place that this became an issue was eating. In Theravada, unlike Mahayana, monks and nuns are not allowed productive labor with its unavoidable, if unintended, bad karma. The food they consumed must be freely given to them. While there is a complex Buddhist ideology of how laypeople can store up merit for a better rebirth when they feed and house monastics, what interests us here is the monks' side of the equation: what it means for them to accept such support. There are two elements from the receivers' standpoint. The first is that by accepting contributions Buddhist monastics incur the reciprocal obligation to practice. Support makes it possible for them to dedicate their time to trying to gain enlightenment. It is a kind of spiritual division of labor: The donors give food and the recipients give their effort at practice and return to the donors the fruits thereof, such as teachings and the example of pure living. Ajaan Mun and his students took this obligation seriously. "I was very much aware that being a monk my existence rested in the hands of the villagers, and I therefore continued my meditation practice to repay my debt to them."[20] By not tilling the soil, by not killing or accepting flesh of animals specifically killed for them, by not even picking wild plants, monks and nuns do not accrue the karma of such acts. (Worse for the butcher but also bad for the tiller, who perforce must kill bugs and vermin.) This also gives monks a kind of space to unravel dependent origination with more ease than they might have if they were mired in the necessity of reproducing daily life. So, while forest monks could not stray too far from the people who fed them, they also could wander into a natural landscape dominated by the red rule of tooth and claw with the intention to take part in that order as little as possible.

Although forest monks mostly stayed within a day or so walk from a village, on numerous occasions monks crossing forests either became lost or did not come upon a village. They then went without food for four or five days. The villagers they begged from were mostly Buddhist, so understood the ritual, but sometimes could not afford to feed the monks or did not want to. In fifth-century Sri Lanka, Buddhaghosa reported the hostile response, "Go away, old baldpate." We saw that some villages were so poor that village monks had to work because there was no surplus food on which they could live, even if there were good will. Going off into the forests meant taking on the risk of starving. Once Ajaan Tate and a companion walked for three days across a large tract of virgin forest without food. At another time, when no one in the nearby village offered food, he vowed that he would not eat until invited. He kept walking until a woman in a further village ran out and offered him a meal.

In Burma in 1921 another forest monk was given so little food that he had to return to Thailand. In distress monks were not above stretching the rules. "We thought to ask straight out for something to eat but were afraid that this was something blameworthy. So instead we tried to explain indirectly by mentioning that we had not eaten anything, and that as I had an injured foot it wouldn't be possible to go on alms round."[21] When the villagers did not produce food for him and a companion, he traded his two boxes of matches with some boys for rice, chili, and bean paste.

There were also rules that allowed a forest monk to pick up fallen wild or domestic fruit if it was clear that either the owner of the fruit would not use it or animals nearby did not need it. My guess is that this happened more than was reported, although most ascetic monks claimed to have strictly adhered to the rules of only taking what was offered, eating only once a day, and never carrying food for later consumption.

On occasion forest monks encountered hostility. Villagers often did not make a distinction between authentic forest practitioners and rogue monks, that is, nefarious persons who traveled the countryside in the guise of monks. The latter were treated with fear and rejection, as hobos or the homeless now are. Also, established village monks often felt competition from the wanderers and so received them coolly. Because of political discord between the reform *Thammayut Nikaya* and the *Mahanikai*, the followers of Ajaan Mun, who, like him, were ordained Thammayut, were sometimes threatened, stoned, or denied food. It was said that someone even tried to poison one of them. In 1930 Mun's senior student and his followers were chased away from some villages. But on the whole indifference and hostility were less frequent than support. Although, as we will see later, in remote places forest monks had to teach non-Buddhist tribals to feed them; obtaining food was not so difficult that forest monks emphasized the difficulty. The greatest risks continued to come from the environment itself.

At times the monks wandered in the Northeast among villages spread out across the dry deciduous forests. These forests were not too dense and were crisscrossed by paths on which the villagers moved by foot or ox cart. Other places were less traveled. Often, "the wandering monks' journeys were uncharted. They had no maps, or guides, no specific idea of where they were actually going. For them, it did not matter how long it took to get from one place to another. It was the process, the wandering that counted, not the destination. They got lost many times... A wandering monk could walk past a hamlet hidden in a thick forest and not know it was there... At worst he missed a meal."[22] This was all part of forest practice. "[H]e accepted the discomforts he encountered and learned to recognize... [suffering] when it arose and let it go."

Some forest monks took special pleasure in wandering where things were difficult. In Laos in the early days one monk crossed the Mekong using elephant trails in an otherwise pathless forest. "Much of the terrain was virgin forest. Underneath the giant trees, the forest floor was open and easy to walk through. But after walking through this forest of tall trees [we] came to a dense jungle. It was impossible to walk through the thickets. [We] had to follow wild elephant tracks. The trails are the main thoroughfares [of the tribal peoples] and provide the easiest access to find food or forest products. Wild elephants usually travel in herds numbering in the dozens. Practically all good paths in mountain country have been made by elephants walking in file from one seasonal feeding ground to another."[23] A geographer observed that, "Rhinoceros are poor path-makers, preferring to burrow under tangled vegetation rather than walk over it."[24]

While searching for Ajaan Mun in Burma Ajaan Tate encountered harrowing circumstances. He and his traveling companion got lost. "For about ten hours we were forced to pick our way along the rocky stream bed, for the steep mountain slopes rising on both sides forced the path down from the bank. As the climb progressed, it became so narrow and the jungle so thick that no sunlight could penetrate... As there was no longer any path forward we had to turn back and almost straight away I mis-stepped on a rock and fell so that the sole of my foot was deeply gashed... We reached the summit around seven in the evening and saw a rather distinct footpath winding its way along the summit ridge-line... Suddenly nearby, 'Aak, Aak!'... a stag... had cried out and stamped the ground in alarm. This startled us so much that my heart seemed to miss beats... After seeing the flattened sleeping place of this wild deer so close to the path, it became obvious that we were still a long way from human habitation... [Spending the night there,] we were unable to get any sleep. The wind was too strong to hang the mosquito nets from our *klot*s [umbrella-tent], while on the ground it wasn't just termites attacking us, swarms of ants came, attracted by the blood from my wound and the sweat of our bodies. We had to wrap cloths around our eyes to prevent the ants from getting to drink from our tears."[25] The next day they finally reached a village.

The popular image of forest monks is that they led charmed lives in the face of these dangers. This has been reinforced both by monks themselves in their reminiscences and scholarly commentators.[26] It is not unusual to hear a "Dharma talk" at a meditation center which relates the monks' miraculous calming of wild beasts. In contrast, there is abundant evidence that some did not survive the rigors of their practice. The greatest cause of mortality seems to have been disease. Malaria struck almost everyone. Many of the monks either died or had to leave the forests because of their illness. Snakebites were probably the second most dangerous risk. Monks' garb and bones were telltale signs. While lost in the mountains, two monks came across bones, alms bowls, and robes. In Laos, "There was a stone pathway... [88 yards] long bordering an abyss. Below the bridge, he saw corpses and bowls scattered. Those were *thudong* monks who had fallen... Of the five monks traveling together, some fell into the abyss and others died from stomach flu."[27] Monks sometimes had to watch their companions die. As with everything else that happened to them, the monks tried to use these hardships as their teacher.

Both Ajaan Mun and his biographer, when he in turn became a teacher, insisted that proper practice was a prophylactic against disease and the fear that accompanied it: If one died trying to conquer suffering, then that was the proper way to have lived. One of Mun's followers wrote: "Walking [I] recite *Buddho*. We don't speak unless it is necessary... Eat only one meal a day, only from the bowl. Even given up smoking cigarettes since the beginning of the rain season... will not drink water... unless absolutely necessary... these days I have been constipated."[28] When another forest monk had fever and a storm blew up he prayed to live long enough to be released from suffering. He asked that the rain go elsewhere because it was not proper to ask that it desist. He did loving-kindness meditation for the spirits of the rain and wind. "Woke up late at night and found the whole body wet. Didn't know whether it was because of mosquito bites or over sweating. The fever went down and I felt lighter."[29] On Ajaan Mun's advice one forest monk used so much concentration that it was reported that the disease infecting him leapt out of his body and went crashing away through the jungle. After that he was apparently healed. Siddhartha's second of the four signs, disease, was to be met in nature, using only the power of meditation. Ajaan Mun felt that survival, particularly from malaria, was an indication of the strength of a monk's practice. Being overcome implied the opposite.

In the primeval forests of Thailand death came from the Darwinian struggle for existence. The monks recognized the reality of what poet Alfred Tennyson called "nature red in tooth and claw" but conducted themselves so as to contribute as little as possible to aggravating or exacerbating nature's aggressive side. Although many wild things are dangerous to humans, our civilization has so beaten them back as to make them almost irrelevant. The forest monks, armed only with concentration and non-harming, put themselves in situations where they faced these dangers. Unlike villagers who traversed the forests from one safe haven to another, or who harvested trees and hunted animals, and unlike hunter-gatherers who subsisted directly off of nature, forest monks simply walked through the forests or sat quietly in meditation.

By not producing or gathering food for themselves forest monks tried to understand and temper the process of eating and being eaten. Making less karma implied suffering its effects less. Ajaan Mun instructed his students to sit still in the face of great danger and study how their minds reacted. To face one's fear and to probe its nature was one of the first lessons learned by forest monks. Mun felt that fear was a great teacher. Referring to a monk who faced a tiger, Mun's biographer says, "It is very difficult to train a mind without any pressure or force to tame it. A moment of danger is often helpful in making it retire into seclusion within split seconds."[30] Mun's students had ample opportunity to test this claim.

The forests of Thailand sheltered many beasts that the monks had reason to fear. At the top of the list were wild buffalo with great horn racks, elephants, tigers, clouded leopards, black panthers, bears, wild cattle, which gather in harems, banteng (wild red ox), boars, and snakes. Ajaan Mun's prescription for fear of tigers was to do walking meditation for three to five hours and then do sitting meditation for several hours alone on a raised platform too high for tigers to leap on. Fear was to be used to drive concentration to insight. This was much easier to prescribe than it was for his followers to actually do.

I lived in a forest about half a kilometer from the village. One day I heard the calls of two elephants fighting, one a wild elephant and the other a domesticated elephant in rut. They battled for three days running, until the wild elephant could no longer put up a fight and died. With that, the elephant in rut went insane, running wild through the forest where I was staying, chasing people and goring them with his tusks... I decided to depend upon my powers of endurance and my belief in the power of loving-kindness... Hearing his call I stuck my head out and saw [the elephant] standing there in a frightening stance with his ears back and his tusks gleaming white... I lost my nerve. I jumped out of the hut and ran [to climb a tree]. [As I] had taken my first step up the trunk, a sound like a person whispering came to my ears: "You're not for real. You're afraid to die. Whoever's afraid to die will have to die again." Hearing this I let go of the tree and hurried back to the hut. I got into half-lotus position and, with my eyes open, sat facing the elephant and meditating, spreading thoughts of good will... finally the elephant flapped its ears up and down a few times, turned around and walked back in the forest.[31]

Another monk "heard a tiger roar and became so terrified... that I began to tremble and shake so much that I couldn't sleep and my meditation wouldn't settle down." At first he did not realize what was going on inside of him. Then he recognized it as fear, "[So] I sat up and established mindfulness, settling the mind in stillness on a single object and ready to sacrifice my life. Hadn't I already accepted death? Wasn't that the reason for my coming to live here? Aren't tiger and human both a fabrication of the same four elements? After death won't both end in the same condition? Who eats who [sic]... who is the one who dies and who is the one that doesn't die? When I was willing to relinquish and investigate in this dauntless, single-minded way, I could no longer hear the noise of the tiger." The monk then realized that his fears were "latent defilements laying submerged in the depths of the heart that are so extremely difficult to dispose of. To conquer the defilement is absolutely impossible without a willingness to relinquish one's attachment and grasping for these conditioned things."[32] In this case, the monk had the Buddhist insight that both eater and eaten were illusory so that the outcome of the interaction was ultimately unimportant. What counted was overcoming the suffering that lodged in one's clinging to an identity as if it were something permanent. This is an example of what Ajaan Mun meant by fear driving concentration to insight.

The strategy and behavior of the forest monks reveal something important about human nature. The design of the human brain is the result of evolution. Buried in its interior are response mechanisms that were and are crucial to the survival of our animal species during its evolution. Many of these mechanisms were in place eons before the cerebral cortex evolved thought, speech, and human suffering, as we now know them. Fear as a survival mechanism is centered in a part of the brain called the amygdala. Responses among the senses, the amygdala, and the brain stem that initiate immediate action are often automatic and instinctual; they do not reach the cortex until after a person has reacted to circumstances that threaten survival. For example, you may drop an iron frying pan only to realize a brief time later that the handle was very hot. Whether or not it might be better to think before leaping away from a surprise attack of a tiger is irrelevant, we were wired to leap first and ask questions later. Asking questions later helps us plan for survival but sometimes also undermines it, making things more difficult. Anxiety is a common ailment of modern society treated by such drugs as Xanax. Terror can be immobilizing, hence, self-destructive. American sailors in World War II had nervous breakdowns waiting for the repeated Japanese kamikaze attacks they knew would come.[33]

Forest monks purposely played with fire. Using meditation practice forest monks put themselves in danger's way. They went into a primal setting and observed both their automatic responses and the added mental factors. They refused to flee and confronted their fear with the Zen, koan-like inquiry: "Who eats whom... who is the one who dies and who is the one that doesn't die?" They did not defend themselves in nature's competition but surrendered to fate. They used nature's own forces, humans' animal fear of pain and humans' ability to concentrate, to overcome some of nature's negative evolutionary effects, that is, anxiety and obsessive fear, both of which make human life more difficult. They are important sources of suffering. The forest monks seemed truly able to live the Buddha's ideal: to "relinquish one's attachment and grasping for these conditioned things."

In Isan as late as the 1950s there were still dangerous animals. At 3:00 a.m., a forest monk was awakened by a wild elephant coming toward his hut. It stopped a few meters away: "It must be the captain of the herd... It's gigantic, like a huge wall in front of my hut... I was scared almost without... [mindfulness]... the body was shining as if possessed by a spirit." The monk went outside with a torch to scare it away and then reasoned with himself: '[T]he elephant is an animal and it's not afraid of you. If you're afraid you're worse than an elephant.'... Taking refuge in the Buddha... he reentered his hut and meditated on death." His mind calmed down. "No longer afraid of the elephant or death... [I] felt grateful to the elephant who taught [me] to face death... I thought about the elephant with compassion and pity... the focused mind must have a very strong power. Within seconds the elephant trumpeted as if it had been hit by something, an explosive sound that vibrated throughout the whole forest. It then walked away into the forest ripping off trees as it went."[34]

Concentration and insight turn meditation inward toward the

mind and emotions. Compassion adds a dimension by turning practice outward. We have seen that the early Buddhists viewed animals as lesser than humans. They viewed animals as violent, victimized, hungry, and dirty. Animals were locked into a cycle of suffering with less chance for redemption. Even though the forest monks lived for years in direct contact with wild animals they continued to express this view. What they saw, which may have led them to believe differently, rarely found a voice. According to one monk, "The animals, though they possess nothing but what they have on themselves, are discontented just like humans; they, however, are ridden by 'fear' which is not man's natural condition."[35] He continues, "The animals differ from human beings in that they do not possess an all-round wisdom and are thus guided solely by the instinct of self-preservation, with only thoughts of finding food and shelter each day."[36] "The bear," for example, "is one mass of suffering. It is hungry, it is thirsty, it wanders around all day and night looking for food and water. It is afraid of everything that moves. And its fur is filled with ticks, some the size of a thumbnail, and however much it scratches, it will never be rid of them." He "[taught] his pupils to view the animals... as fellow sufferers... of... uncertain temperament and prey to sudden rage or fear... therefore to be neither afraid nor aggressive toward them."[37] Forest monks often cultivated loving-kindness both because of concern for animals' pitiful karma and because a forest monk had no other protection.

They did this by reciting two mantras. One applied to all the animals they might meet, and humans as well, is: "May all sentient beings be happy. May all sentient beings be peaceful. May all sentient beings be free from suffering." The other is a specific remedy for a monk feeling threatened by an animal: "If I have not harmed you in a past life, please do not harm me now!" The first may have been inspired by genuine compassion, while the latter seems more fear driven. Both mantras were thought to be effective. Ajaan Mun claimed animals draw back from a mind focused on loving-kindness because they can sense it. According to Mun's biographer, "An aspirant must cultivate the live-with-[truth] and die-with-[truth] attitude of mind... From such a mind the attacker will draw back, be it a tiger, snake or elephant... [A monk's] attitude toward them is based on loving-kindness which has a mysterious but real and profound influence."[38] The mind imbued with Buddhist truths is powerful. "It is true that animals do not know this but they can feel and sense it." There were miraculous stories of animals abiding peacefully in the presence of Ajaan Mun because of his powers of meditation and compassion.

Loving-kindness and the ability to contain fear did seem to give the forest monks a special relationship to wild things. In the sutras the Buddha asked Tissa whether the noise of wild beasts frightened him. Tissa replied that, "a feeling of love for the forest arose within him." In the same vein is a story from Sri Lanka: "when Pannananda went out early in the morning to pace back and forth on his meditation walkway, a leopard would be stretched out dozing in the sand. Pannananda would then shoo the leopard away and calmly begin his meditation." The anthropologist reporting this continues, "This may seem an unlikely story, but I have seen monks deal in a similarly firm way with both wild boar and elephants, so I have no hesitation in accepting the tale... as... not very strange in the life of a monk in the jungles. But to a villager who goes in mortal terror of the forest animals it is quite a different matter."[39] Villagers, he heard, were often harmed. At another rural hermitage, the monks said, "Animals which frequent the hermitage... bear, leopard, wild boar, buffalo, elephant... are 'our friends'... their presence effectively keeps away casual visitors." Here the Buddhist forest monks mirror the role of shamans and medicine men in a variety of cultures. One might speculate that the nature-based understanding of human nature hunter-gatherers possessed was reconstructed by ascetics or recluses in traditions devoted to exploring the ultimate meaning of life.[40] It may be a conscious articulation of how survival-based emotional states interact among mammals. Lessons from observations of interactions with other species are internalized in successful meditation practice.

A Mun follower, when doing walking meditation, became aware of a tiger "only a couple of meters away from" his walking track. "It was sitting very much like a house dog sits... It looked more like a big, stuffed doll than a live thing. [The monk] felt no fear, nor was there any harmful intent on the part of the tiger."[41] Out of compassion he thought that the tiger might be better off hunting food than sitting there. It roared, so he then quickly thought it is fine if the tiger wants to sit and guard me, so much the better. After the monk sat and chanted for a while, he looked up and the tiger was gone but he heard it roaring for the next few days. He later told Mun that the roar had made his hair stand on end and his head feel numb but he was unaware of conscious fear, although he conjectured there may have been fear in the depths of his unconscious. This might be an example of the forest monk's ability to observe and uncouple the automatic processes of the brain. He was aware of the more visceral, uncontrollable fear going on but his powers of meditation kept it from ramifying in the thinking parts of the brain.

Although the mode by which loving-kindness works is unclear, there are accounts of it acting as a direct protection. Staying overnight in an overgrown cemetery in order to conquer his fear of ghosts, a forest monk vowed not to leave.

After a moment or so there was a rustling sound up in the top of the tree. I looked up and saw that a large nest of red ants had broken open. This was because there was a vine wrapped around the nest. I had sat down on the base of the vine, so now red ants were spilling out onto my mat, swarming all over, biting in earnest. I sat upright. They were all over my legs. I made up my mind to spread thoughts of good will, dedicating the merit to all living beings and making a vow: "Since being ordained, I've never even thought of killing or harming a living being. If in a previous lifetime, I've ever eaten or harmed any of you all, then go ahead and bite me until you've had your fill. But if I've never harmed you, then let's call an end to this. Don't bite me at all."[42]

He sat in meditation and the ants did not bite him.

Another monk may not have had such a good past relationship with ants. A third generation monk in the forest tradition told how his teacher had set up his *klot* in a place which he thought safe and reiterated a vow not to move for the night. He was sitting in meditation when ants, which were crawling over the surface of his *klot*, found entry at the pole that held it up and began dropping in on his head. He did the loving-kindness chant, suggesting that if he had not harmed them in another life, would they please not harm him now. Apparently unmoved, the ants bit him. It was painful but they eventually went away. He remained still, living up to his vow. The student himself, in more civilized circumstances, once had a cobra crawl underneath his platform while he sat quietly.

Although several scholars feel that the monks' non-harming protected them against violence from large animals in contrast to the fearful villagers who were often injured, forest monks did have unpleasant encounters with animals, and monks who survived in the wilds did take precautions. In Cambodia in 1934 a wild buffalo charged a monk and two disciples from behind. The disciples climbed a tree. The monk was knocked over but not hurt. Wild water buffalo are particularly dangerous. As the areas along rivers where they prefer to live have been converted to rice paddies, they have sought refuge in swamps. Like Eskimos who stake out their bitches in heat to mate with wolves in order to keep wild pulling-energy in their dog teams, Thai villagers mate their female domesticated water buffalo with wild males, but kill the male offspring because they are too dangerous.[43] The monk was lucky, and his companions took a wise course of action.

When wandering Ajaan Mun feared bears most and so, as advised in National Parks, he whistled while he walked to alert them to his presence. Monks reported that bears they encountered, unlike tigers, may suddenly attack rather than run. The sun bear of the western Thai mountains is mostly herbivorous and insectivorous. They attack without provocation, biting and scratching but not eating their victim. So both Mun and the Sri Lankan monk cited above, who saw bears as being subject to sudden and irrational rage or fear, were accurate in their observations of nature, even though the Sri Lankan explanation of their behavior (the result of a miserable life) may be wrong. And most wild great cats, it seems, avoid humans. Leopards only attack when provoked. Tigers have poor eyesight. Only the old and injured are reputed to attack humans in Thailand, but monks related that in Laos, where the locals did not bury their dead, tigers developed a taste for humans. It was also said that although Vietnamese tigers were man-eaters the Vietnamese were not frightened of them and thought the Thai and Lao cowardly because they feared their local cats which were not interested in people.[44]

Although some students of forest monks may have taken to the woods with careless daring teachers' instructions for forest practice were tempered with words of warning. According to one third-generation monk in the forest tradition, when one picks a place for sitting and sets up a *klot* the vow not to move for the night makes it important to pick a place that is out of harm's way. Once, to see what would happen, Ajaan Cha (1919–1992) went against the advice of not sleeping on an old trail. When a tiger approached him that night he focused on the thought that if he were meant to be eaten then so be it. The tiger went off. After that incident he was not afraid to die but also did not sleep on old trails again. Another forest monk, "used to recite [protective chants] for hours in the forest."[45] And a number of forest monks insisted that their students learn the precise Pali pronunciation of these chants so that they would be effective. As was mentioned, the Buddha gave special chants for snakes.

Another of Ajaan Mun's followers, Ajaan Khao Analayo (1888–1983), made a distinction between domesticated and truly wild elephants. With the former, which were sent to browse in the woods, he felt communication was easier because they understood humans, while the latter presented a greater danger because they were unfamiliar with monks' practices. The descriptions of Khao's encounters with wild animals were written by the same monk who wrote Ajaan Mun's biography. The writer uses almost the same language to describe the role of fear and how animals perceive it as he does for Ajaan Mun. One wild elephant rushed "towards [Khao], getting closer every minute, and there was no time for him to run away from it. Then he remembered how forest elephants are usually afraid of fire. So he quickly left the [meditation] path and went to get all his remaining candles from the place where he was staying. He then stuck them into the ground all along the sides of his... path and lit them as fast as he could... pacing back and forth as if he was not concerned about the elephant at all although in fact he was so afraid of it that he could hardly breathe. When he first saw it charging towards him, so strong and aggressive, he focused his attention solely on 'Buddho.' It acted as though it intended to crush him to death—but when it reached him it just stood there like a lifeless dummy... [He] lost all fear. In fact, he felt positively bold and daring, confident that he could have walked right up to the elephant without the least feeling of fear. Having thought about it, he realized that to walk right up to such a wild jungle animal would be an act of carelessness based on conceit, which he shouldn't do... The elephant must have stood there for about an hour, by which time the candles were almost finished. Some had already gone out and the rest would not last much longer when the elephant backed away, turned round and walked off by the way it had come. It then went looking for food in the forest around that area, where it could be heard breaking branches and treading on dead wood, making a lot of noise. He was faced with a critical situation without any way to escape or hide, so there was no alternative but to face up to it using these methods—if he died it would be only because there was no way to avoid it... nothing could possibly do any harm to him."[46]

As Khao related, "[Another elephant] came walking straight towards me of its own free will. With its eyes wide open, it came right up close, well within the light of the candles that I had set in place. But it did not squash me or tear me to pieces; nor was it startled and frightened by the fire of the candles, for it did not run away into the forest to save itself from the fire. Instead, after walking up to me in a bold, imposing manner, like it was the 'boss', it just stood there for over an hour, appearing neither aggressive nor afraid. After that, it simply went away. This is what made me think about that animal with amazement, so much so that I have not forgotten it to this day."[47]

There was also a survival rule of not stepping outside of one's *klot* to investigate noises at night. It was said that to do so was to risk death. This made sense because at night the jungle unleashes its full fury. "One night a tiger came and pounced on and began to eat a water buffalo close by my [Ajaan Tate's] hut. I tried to drive it away by striking a bamboo and shouting but the tiger would have none of it. It refused to let go of its prey and succeeded in dragging it away to eat. This time I was not afraid, but I didn't dare to leave my hut and go over to aid the water buffalo in case the tiger decided to gobble up a man as well."[48] This action was well advised because animals are most dangerous when protecting their kill. On encountering a dead moose surrounded by grizzly scat, hiking friends made a wide detour. In any case, would compassion for the water buffalo have been compassion for the tiger, who needs to kill in order to live?

The karma of interfering in nature with such a sense of compassion is unclear.

If one believes in the eye-for-an-eye conception of karma in the mantra, "If I have not harmed you in a past life, etc.," then one has to accept its consequences. My karma with bears is mixed. I was walking back to my van at Lama Foundation at 8,600 feet in the Sangre de Cristo Mountains of New Mexico. It was the first night of a meditation retreat led by Jack Kornfield. The visiting meditators had been cautioned about an errant bear on the land. The bear had already broken into the larder and slashed a tent. I was managing the retreat, and I had thought about giving a little talk to the meditators about how the monks of the forest tradition did loving-kindness meditations when in the presence of dangerous animals. While walking in the dark down an overgrown old road to where my van was parked in the Lama graveyard I became a bit frightened by the possibility of running into the bear. The night was very dark, only occasionally illuminated by distant lightning. As is my wont I was walking at night without a flashlight. I wondered what I would do if I encountered a bear I could not see.

So I began the mantra: "If I have not harmed you in a previous life, please do not harm me now!" Then I remembered the mama bear with two cubs I ran into on the trail at Middle Creek one evening 20 years before while walking to dinner at Pete and Cindy's teepee where we were homesteading in the empty coastal mountains of British Columbia 900 miles north of Vancouver. As I was coming up an incline on the path through the woods, I heard the sound of bear cubs scurrying up trees, a sound I had heard before. Then, a few feet ahead of me on the trail, the mother bear rose above me, her paws extended above her head as she roared at me. She towered over me. I stepped back completely unafraid, knowing all that I had to do was retreat. I called to my brother who was walking some yards behind with his wife and child. He was carrying a rifle as we usually did in the back country, a large bore 30-ought-six. He came up quickly, put the rifle over my shoulder and, at quite close range, blew off the side of the bear's head with one and then a second shot.

My feeling was, "No! It is not necessary." It all happened very quickly. I don't know what went on in his mind, but I sensed that he was more interested in obtaining meat, which we hadn't had for months, than in protecting us. Certainly, I felt in no danger even though the raging bear was standing over me. My brother went back to fetch the dogs and their packs and his wife went to get Pete. The cubs watched me from the trees they had scrambled up. Standing alone next to the dead bear, I talked to the cubs, telling them that it might be wiser if they made themselves scarce. At the time I thought that since the cubs had been weaned, they would survive on their own. I have since learned that cubs are poor hunters and risk starvation. Even when they know how to hunt, survival is precarious because younger bears have to compete with more skilled older bears who will drive them out of feeding territories when food is scarce.

As we were skinning the bear, I could see why some indigenous people have been reluctant to eat bear. The skin carefully separated from the exposed chest revealed a musculature very like a human's. The bear's pectoral muscles resembled those of a perfectly formed, immensely strong athlete. It was exquisite. From up the tree the cubs watched us. While skinning the bear in the twilight, which extends way into night that far north, one of us leaned forward onto the bear's chest. Out of the mouth of the half blown away head came a terrible roar. We leapt up in fright, only to break out laughing when we realized that it was just air being expelled from the lungs. We continued our work, and that evening we dined on fresh bear liver. On our return home we saw that the cubs were gone. I wished them well.

Walking down the trail at Lama in the dark more than 20 years later, I was not sure I qualified for the saving grace of the mantra.

The bear at Lama was a desperate young bear pushed out of higher altitudes because the gambel oaks had a poor acorn crop on which bears depended. It was suffering a fate similar to that the cubs without a mother may have encountered. Indeed, in this life I have the karma of harming bears. Or, at least, it would be up to a bear to decide what I deserve for my past acts, knowing in its bear nature and its individual bear karma whatever it knows. So I had to be concerned about this karmic heir to the cubs I helped orphan. Although the thought was frightening, it was also freeing to know that I indeed might have to face a wild beast as the arbiter of my fate and that the killing I have done in my life would stand as a weight on some ineffable scale. I understood a bit more of how far away I am from passing the test of the forest monks to face one's fear in the midst of wild beasts with a vow of non-harming and no protections from industrial society. But the test itself now feels more real and reasonable.

Three or four days later the Lama bear finally visited. I was meditating in my van just before sunrise. I had just achieved some degree of concentration, emerging out of the blurriness that occurs on waking. I was observing: "rising, falling, rising, falling" of my abdomen. I heard a noise: "Banging: a squirrel in the engine compartment? Banging: sheet metal? On the roof?" I opened my eyes to see a bear out the back window, which was slanted open at the bottom. The bear was sniffing not five inches away from my face. It was a beautiful beast with gold flecks in its fur and claws that were long and bright yellow. Because it couldn't see inside it was trying to sniff things out and there was curiosity in its face and nose. My heart did not skip a beat. Later I realized I had failed to notice its ears in order to tell its age. (Like a dog's paws they look relatively smaller as the animal's head grows). I moved a bit and it pulled back, unsure what was inside. It stood up and put its front paws on the spare tire mounted outside the rear door. Standing on its back legs it was my height and more than matched my weight. My heart jumped, and I thought it was not wise to let it try to probe more forcefully, so I banged on the metal van roof and said, "Go away." It turned around and fled. I knew immediately that I had reacted too quickly. I had much more time to just be with it before there was any danger. I dug my camera out and then followed it into the woods. I wanted to see if the bear was interested in my shit buried nearby and maybe get a picture. It was not interested in the former. Then I realized that my heart was pounding because I knew well the risks of following an unskilled, hungry, young bear into the bush just to get a snapshot.

It was pretty clear to me that had I assumed the posture of a forest monk meditating in the midst of wild beasts and intoned the mantra, "If I have not harmed you in a past life, do not harm me now," I would have been on very shaky ground. That is, I would have endangered myself. And yet I am tempted to try if given another chance, although the naturalist in me may again outweigh the forest monk. What I know about bear behavior might save the meditator from his due encounter with karma. Each evening after this encounter I would walk as quietly as I could back from the meditation hall to my van parked in the cemetery. I wanted to meet my teacher again. A couple of days later I learned that the bear had been trapped by Fish and Game and removed to a place with less people. The woods felt much lonelier after that.

Although monks succumbed to malaria, other diseases, and poisonous snakes, I have only one verified account of a monk being killed by a large wild animal. That event occurred after most of the forest monks had settled and the forests were vanishing. The victim was a troubled New Yorker with a compulsively noisy mind who came to Thailand and ended up in Ajaan Cha's monastery. The initiate had difficulty doing the practice and living with his own mind. At one point Ajaan Cha sent him away, and he later relinquished ordination. After a while at home he went to Sri Lanka and was preordained. Encountering more difficulties in a monastery, he went off to live alone in the jungle. There, "He was trampled by elephants and his bones were found."[49] There is no explanation of his fate, although the forest monks might have attributed it to his inability to cultivate loving-kindness for himself or wild beings. When told of his death Ajaan Cha's comment was, "Now he can be at peace."

In addition to learning how to survive in non-harming ways with wild animals the forest monks had to handle encounters with the spirits that the Thais believed lived in forests. In Buddhism there are six realms of being. Close to human beings are the devas and the hungry ghosts (nagas) who are incorporeal yet capable of discerning wisdom. When Buddhism came into contact with local beliefs it was easy to identify local spirits with the devas and nagas. Although in more rationalistic Buddhism (like the meditation taught in the West), the idea of devas and nagas has been downplayed, historical Buddhism is syncretic, mixed with the villagers' and gentry's preexistent beliefs. The forest monks not only believed in devas and hungry ghosts but also had to come to terms with village spirit worship. His monk biographer states as gospel truth that on many occasions Ajaan Mun was visited in the forests by devas and nagas. They interrupted his meditation with constant requests for him to teach them. Acknowledging not only Buddhist but local spirits, Mun instructed some followers to engage with them directly as proving grounds for the monks' meditation practice.

One of Mun's students was a kind of spelunker of spirits. While meditating one day he was told by voices to go to a mountain where there was an old abandoned temple. It was a frightening place. "I stayed for two nights... The second night... a tiger came... I sat in meditation, scared stiff, while the tiger walked around my umbrella tent. My body felt frozen and numb. I started chanting... All the old chants I had forgotten now came back to me... I sat like this from 2:00 a.m. to 5:00 a.m., when the tiger finally left."[50] The next day the monk learned that the tiger had eaten a farmer's ox. He then climbed to the top of the mountain where Mun had said there was a spirit. He had nothing to eat. "That night I felt faint... the whole mountain seemed to be swaying like a boat in the middle of a choppy sea... but my mind was in good shape, not the least bit afraid."

He vowed to stay until someone came to feed him. The next day an old woman arrived with food. After these experiences he visited a series of caves because Ajaan Mun said they were filled with spirits. At Golden Gourd Cave, where another monk had supposedly been kept up all night by ghosts, he spent an uneventful night. This monk liked the challenge of checking out haunted caves. Although we may regard these stories as myth, they were accepted as reality by the monks who told them and the people among whom they lived.

In its mission of spreading reform Buddhism and modern Thai nationalism the *Thammayut Nikaya* tried to root out village spirit belief and also unsightly habits among the monks, such as chewing betel, a mild stimulant that inhibits intestinal parasites. Regular usage stains gums and teeth a deep red and can cause damage to them. The forest monks assisted the *Thammayut Nikaya* in combating village spirit belief because it demonstrated the superiority of Buddhism, but they also resisted modernization. Ajaan Mun smoked tobacco, chewed betel nut, and ate meat. This a jarring image for those who imagine the forest tradition as a kind of pure asceticism according to our standards. Western meditators are not comfortable with pictures of red-toothed monks using spittoons or dangling cigarettes. When Thai and Burmese monks visiting the Insight Meditation Society in the late 1970s expected to be served meat the vegetarian staff members were shocked, and strategies for cooking meat outside of the main building had to be concocted. With little interest in the modern rationalism that was being promoted by the government and church, the monks combated spirit worship on their own. They used their lack of fear of the wilds to convince the villagers that Buddhism was more powerful than local spirits. Challenging local demons, they would set up their *klots* next to potent village shrines in the forests and spend nights there. The monks' courage, their uncorrupted asceticism (by Thai village standards), and their teaching of loving-kindness were said to have overcome the villagers' paganism. In one place a forest monk had the audacity to order all ancestral spirit shrines burned. In 1929 the central government outlawed spirit worship. In the same year, another forest monk upset villagers by dwelling in a shrine in the forest. He then taught them to use the mantra "Buddho" as a way of preventing the spirits from entering their bodies. The monks advocated their observation-based meditation standpoint: that fears were a source of suffering to be carefully examined. This was a central tenet of ancient Buddhism, and they in no way thought of it as part of rationalistic modernism.

A report of questionable veracity from a popular magazine illustrates this. Ajaan Mun and a follower were staying in a wood where the villagers believed there was a creature who had killed a woman. They sat in the forest at night amidst screams, and a dead owl fell out of the trees. "Both monks then proceeded to meditate. Around 2:00 a.m. they heard a cry in the distance. It grew louder as it came closer and stopped behind a big tree. Then, something jumped down, and the monks saw that it was a large monkey, an extraordinary one with red eyes and shining hair. It bared its teeth, jumped up into a tree and disappeared as the monks looked on. Shortly afterwards the dead body of a squirrel fell down with a thud from the branches of the tree... When the villagers came to give alms in the morning, the monks showed them the dead owl and squirrel... [The follower] explained to the villagers that what they believed to be a demon was, in fact, a monkey-like animal that killed and ate other animals."[51] When the villagers wanted to kill the animal the monk told them, "Your beliefs should have a basis in reason.

Don't believe blindly. What you call [a demon] is most likely a forest monkey. We cannot say what type of monkey it is because we did not see it clearly," but it has unusual power so be careful.

Whether one gives credence to these stories or not is a matter of belief. Computer animated films, which so realistically present dreamlike materials as fictional portraits of possible experience, touch on the aspects of the human mind that are akin to those brought out in forest monks' confrontation with spirits. In Haitian Voodoo and other belief systems people experience spirits, and believers take those experiences to be real.[52] For the monks the night was a special challenge. I used to do walking meditation in the country all night long. I paced back and forth along a short stretch of road as the night deepened; after midnight it would almost be as if there were other things out there with me. About 1:00 or 2:00 a.m. the hair on the back of my neck would stand up. It was frightening. Since forest monks, like the villagers, believed there actually were spirits, the challenge was to embrace one's fear and release it as just another insubstantial state of mind. In the middle of the night in the forests of Thailand this was no mean feat.

The forest monks had contact with non-Thai, tribal groups, including some of the few surviving hunter-gatherers. It seems likely that the forest renunciants of Buddha's India interacted with the hunter-gatherers, who were prevalent in the forests of their time. We have no evidence what those contacts were like. Hunter-gatherers have a special relationship to nature because of their intimate involvement with life and death in nature. Both the silent concentration they use to hunt and some of their spiritual practices overlapped meditation. Vision quests, initiation rituals, and shamanistic voyages into fear and ecstasy have their counterparts in meditation. For hunter-gatherers these activities arise out of their contact with nature. Their use of them may have reduced the degree to which their minds spun out of control and caused them discontent.[53]

An important way that meditation differs from hunter-gatherer practices is the centrality of the cultivation of wisdom and compassion. The point of meditation is not only the conquest of fear to better deal with survival but to live non-harmingly with wisdom. What was it like when mendicant forest monks traveling the wilds encountered peoples whose lives were centered there? To answer this question we have the monks' descriptions of their contact with tribals and one account of a meeting with a genuine hunter-gatherer group.

We begin with the former. The tribals in Thailand and Burma were mostly agricultural peoples. Historically, some were forced out of the fertile valley floors by wet-land, rice growing Thais and Burmans arriving from the north. Other tribals were later migrants who made their way down the mountain ridges. Tribals grew dry-land rice, millet, or taro. As the dominant racial groups built civilizations, the tribals continued living by slash-and-burn gardening, raising animals, and hunting and foraging wild plants in the forests. Most retained their animistic beliefs until some Burmese tribals became Christian during the British occupation. Although tribals had contact with Buddhist believers, most were not Buddhists and often would resist attempts to convert them. The greatest problem that the forest monks had, when they wandered among the hilltribes, was obtaining food. Because the tribals were not familiar with the tradition of begging the monks had to convince them to offer food. For this monks used various tricks but were not always successful.

The simplest of techniques ranged from boldly hinting to outright asking: "To get food from the forest dwellers... we have to do it the old way... stand in front of their huts and make noises by coughing or clearing our throats... sometimes [we] have to tell them to bring rice."[54] The monks would also sometimes impress the tribals with the purity of their behavior or their courage in confronting unfriendly spirits. One story about Ajaan Mun and another monk has them wandering deep in the woods among a tribal people who had been warned by their headman that the monks were tigers in disguise. The tribal people knew nothing of alms giving, and the monks were given only rice, for which they had to ask.

Using telepathy, a skill his biographer attributes to him, Ajaan Mun figured out what was going on. He knew that the tribals would suffer a bad karmic effect for refusing to feed the monks. They would be reborn as tigers. He took pity on them and stayed around. To leave would have condemned them to such a fate. The tribals offered the monks inadequate amounts of rice and neither shade nor water. Living there without support was miserable for the monks, but they stayed out of compassion. After months the tribals could find no fault with monks and asked them about what they were doing. Ajaan Mun answered that he was looking for his "buddho" and set them to looking also. In this manner he tricked them into meditating. After winning their hearts, he moved on despite their pleas that he stay.[55]

Although Thai villagers had disdain for hilltribes this judgment was not always shared by the forest monks. During Ajaan Mun's last 11 years of wandering between 1929 and 1940 he was mostly alone, living among the hill peoples in the north of Thailand and in Burma. "To those not acquainted with these people, the term 'hilltribes' usually meant dirtiness and ugliness, as well as a primitive or barbarous way of life. But his experiences with them were all to the contrary. He found that they had beautiful features with white skin, and they were not at all dirty."[56] They were cultured and had "no crimes of greed and violence."

Another forest monk lived six years in the mountains of Burma and learned the local language. He spent the rains retreats near the hilltribes and in between wandered from mountain to mountain, staying in caves from six days to a month at a time. He and Mun found the people to be well behaved. In fact, Mun felt that because they lived closer to nature they were less corrupted and more receptive to his teaching. "These hilltribes people were by nature honest and docile. There followed amazing results to such an extent that their minds became brilliant and enabled them to know the minds of others." They overcame their fear of ghosts.[57]

One might suspect that Ajaan Mun's biographer idealized these interactions and that some of the contacts with tribals were not so smooth. While wandering among the Moo-Ser hilltribe a forest monk who was gawked at thought, "They were dirty and smelled. It was too much for me and made me feel quite dizzy."[58] And often monks had to leave an area because no one would feed them. Yet it is surprising how generous the tribals, who were sometimes in want themselves, actually were. "Whenever I was walking through these mountain ranges and one or two isolated houses I could immediately surmise that I wouldn't be able to stay with so few people."] There had been poor harvests, yet the people were generous. They were living off wild yams, taros, and other potato-like tubers, which they regarded as starvation food, but this monk actually liked to eat these, and so they happily supported him. Ajaan Mun joined him with this hilltribe for a rains retreat. Later, this same monk tried to woo another hilltribe from their spirit worship but was unsuccessful.

By the beginning of the twentieth century there were probably very few pure hunter-gatherers left in Thailand. After all, thousands of years before the Burmans or the Thais arrived agriculture was evident. Unlike North America, where agricultural advance from Mexico northward was stopped by the inability of corn and other domesticated crops to adapt to colder climates, Southeast Asia had no such barrier except in the most mountainous terrains. Thus, any group which survived as hunter-gatherers did so by strongly resisting either the influence or domination of agriculturists. It also may be that the hunter-gatherers of the last century were at times agriculturists and for unknown reasons returned to subsistence foraging. Tracing such lifestyle changes is quite difficult because they are happening to non-sedentary peoples whose oral histories are unreliable. Of the few Thai aboriginal groups in recent times who lived very close to nature only one seems to have sustained itself solely by foraging.

The Mlabri or Phi Thong Luang (Spirits of the Yellow Leaves) live in hilly forested areas between 2,100 and 3,000 feet. The first known contact by Europeans was in 1963. They moved about within a roughly 30-kilometer radius. In the 1980s they lived in bands of 10 to 15, but there were groups twice that size in the 1960s. On arriving at a new place the women foraged for wild yams, medicinals, and other plants and hunted small animals. The men traveled in wider arcs searching for boar, deer, monkey, rattans (building palms), and honey. They moved on by the time the leaves they used to construct their windbreaks turned yellow (hence their name). Their foraging areas were bounded by farm clearings with whose residents they traded. The edges of farm clearings were favorable hunting habitats. They exchanged forest products for iron and manufactured goods. They also worked for farmers and helped in land clearance. As farm clearings encroached on the woods their foraging became limited to the little remaining game and herbs.[59] Less than 300 of them survive, half now settled.

One forest monk came across the Spirits of the Yellow Leaves long before European anthropologists heard of them. One might assume that they lived more freely in the forest then. In 1936, when Ajaan Tate came across them, they hunted with poison spears, which spoiled the meat when the spears penetrated the kill too deeply. Because this group was so wary of authorities and open spaces Tate surmised they might have been fugitive slaves. He also felt they were racially Thai. Tate "felt sympathy and pity" for them and wanted "to help them to become established in some stable livelihood."[60] When he suggested that they plant rice and taro, "they immediately started to protest that they were forest people and they couldn't do such a thing." So he gave up trying to convince them. "What a shame [he thought]. Even though these people were endowed with priceless humanity, they were unable to take full advantage of it because of their birth in an unsuitable environment."

In this sentiment we may have an ironic contradiction in the lives of the forest monks that reaches back to the time of the Buddha. The forest monks turned their backs on cenobitic existence to seek an unmediated experience of life and death in wild nature. In doing this they learned a great deal about the forests and survival. Among their numbers were monks famous for their wide knowledge of healing herbs found in the forests. Ajaan Mun and Ajaan Cha both had their bags of mysterious plants which they used to treat monks and laypersons. On the one hand, the monks felt that tribals had an innocence that allowed them to understand Buddhist truths easily. Yet the monks still regarded them as living more crudely than Thai peasants. Their lack of more productive agriculture and its amenities led them to take the life of wild animals unnecessarily. This put them lower on the hierarchy of rebirth, closer to animals, than were agriculturists. The irony is that although the monks depended on tribals for survival, ate the tribals' meat and roots, and witnessed their great knowledge of and courage within the woods, the forest monks never gave the tribals full credit.

On balance, the forest monks' ambivalent attitudes about the hill peoples tilted toward civilization. They were poised to take them into the, then, slightly more modern Thai village world. If the monks had succeeded, I am not sure whether it would have been done more to save the forest peoples from the suffering of animal-like incarnations or because the monks regarded the way out of the woods as a path to wisdom. As it was, both the forest tradition and the hilltribes were swallowed by an expanding, modern society, and the monks went docilely along with the changes.

Before we turn to the domestication of the forest tradition I need to say a few words about its style of teaching. In all, one might say that there were three generations of forest monks. Ajaan Mun and Sao constituted the first generation. They had students dating from the second decade of this century until 1949. While still wandering, many of those students also had students, who likewise became *Thudong Kammathaan*. Most of the students who came after the second and third generation of monks settled into *wats* and were taught in the style of the wanderers without themselves ever wandering. Ajaan Mun's teaching was fashioned to the need of the individual student. According to students' testimony he showed different faces to different students. Overriding his variable manner was an insistence on the conscientious observance of the *dhutanga* rules.

In some locales where monks gathered to be instructed by Ajaan Mun, they each had a narrow bamboo bed off the ground (just high enough so a tiger would not leap onto it) and a walking path often cleared and smoothed by laypersons. The woody plants around them were left undisturbed so they could not see each other. Ajaan Mun put the fearful ones on the outer edges so they could face their fears. When it rained at night, "Every [monk] had to sit in the dark within his *klot* trembling with cold, being more like a destitute blind man."[61] Everyone got malaria. Some died. Ajaan Mun was skilled at answering the questioner rather than the question. Students were frightened, often terrified, of him because he was believed to be able to detect vagrant thoughts and then would chastise their owner.

In the early 1940s Ajaan Mun established himself in Isan in a valley surrounded by mountains. A number of followers lived in the caves and other places within a 30 kilometer radius. "Usually one [monk] would stay alone, or sometimes two together... the pathways from one village to another in the forests... were merely trails... winding deep into the forests and around or up mountains... [A missed turn] would lead the unwary traveler away from a nearby village, taking him deeper and deeper into the forest... the traveler who lost his way would have to spend a night in the middle of the forest or find himself starving there. Only a hunter who sometimes had been off the beaten track would be able to save that lost traveler."[62] These were the hardships his students would endure for his teaching.

Between 1945 and 1949 Ajaan Mun settled in the village of Ban Naung Phue, "located in the midst of a dense forest... about seventy-five households... self-sufficient... The Un River... was the lifeline of villagers. The people had plenty to eat. Their lives were peaceful. It was quite far from a gravel road reachable in 3 to 4 hours on foot or 8 by oxcart... Because of the thick vegetation, the air circulation was not good. Every year, many inhabitants had malaria attacks and died... Many monks who came to visit Phra Ajaan Mun were stricken with jungle fever and died here."[63] Monks came and went. Approximately 15 were there at any one time.

Ajaan Mun taught by forcing his students to be observant without instructing them directly. Students sometimes felt that they were being punished by Mun because he assigned them tasks without their knowing what was really expected. Students learned how to watch and then to do things to his satisfaction. One monk even peeped through the rattan slats of Mun's hut to see how he did things. In his old age his students took care of his needs, including attending to his clothes, cleaning his quarters, massaging him, and removing his feces from the collecting bowl under his hut. He was exacting in keeping the schedule and in requiring cleanliness. The monks worked hard maintaining the *wat*. Although attending to Ajaan Mun's needs exposed a student to his criticisms, it also gave the student greater opportunity to learn from him. Some students experienced him as ferocious, others found him gentle.

When the students became teachers in their own right they reconstructed the style they had learned from Mun. Ajaan Cha, one of his most celebrated students, spent only a few days in Mun's presence. He was a *Mahanikai* monk who had become an ascetic meditation monk. He wandered into Ajaan Mun's encampment in the last years of Mun's life. Since, according to the monastic rules, he could not stay for more than seven days without being ordained in the *Thammayut Nikaya*, he left. Because Ajaan Mun felt that there needed to be ascetic meditation monks in the other sect he recommended that Ajaan Cha not reordain. In the few days that Ajaan Cha was with Ajaan Mun he absorbed aspects of Mun's teaching style. As will be related below, when Ajaan Cha settled in his own *wat* he replicated them.

Although some of the forest monks settled down in *wats* a number continued to wander after Ajaan Mun's death in 1949. By that time he had become the center of national attention. Many important monks from the *Thammayut* hierarchy in Bangkok attended his funeral. Because of the increasing fame of the tradition forest monks found themselves sought after and the recipients of patronage. Beginning in the 1930s the central authorities tried to lure the monks closer to towns by setting up *wats* for them. Some of the forest monks began to stay in these for the rains retreats. Mun apparently criticized two for doing so. Nonetheless, monks did begin to settle. In 1937 the forest monks were formally incorporated into the *Thammayut Nikaya*. The authorities imposed restrictions supposedly to protect the monks, but in reality the rules were instituted to keep track of them.

Forest monks were required to travel in pairs and carry a letter of permission from the authorities indicating their affiliation. Every monk had to be affiliated with a *wat* and was required to return there for the rains retreat. They also had to notify their *wat* of their whereabouts if they were unable to make it back. My sense is that most of the forest monks ignored these regulations. Nevertheless, with the onset of World War II, Thailand's alliance with Japan, the British reoccupation of Burma, Burmese independence, and the two Indochina wars the world in which the monks wandered began to change.

During World War II Thai monks wandering in Burma had to avoid British soldiers, who they feared would execute them because of the Thai government's relationship with Japan. It is odd that I found no mention of forest monks coming across Japanese soldiers, who used Thailand as a way station or who occupied the rest of Southeast Asia. Did the monks continue to wander as if the War did not exist? After the War the battle between communism and capitalism began to affect the monks' lives. Between 1951 and 1971 the United States spent more than $3 billion in Thailand financing military and strategic rural development. A goal of American aid was to change Thai village subsistence farming to commercial agricultural production. This was accompanied by greater extraction of timber. The percentage of forests in Thailand went from 51% in 1961 to 19% in 1988. The acreage in farming exploded. Thirty large dams were built, flooding thousands of acres. A number of golf complexes were built on forestland. In the Northeast development proceeded apace. Most of the hardwood forests in the Northeast were cut down. The Northeast was 41% forested in 1961 as compared to 14% in 1988. The first paved road to the Northeast was finished in 1957. Then followed gravel roads into the interior. In the late 1960s the Friendship Highway was completed to the far reaches of the Northeast, tying the entire area together by a network of paved roads.

In spite of this development, during the 1950s and the early 1960s monks continued to wander and find wild nature. As late as 1969 three monks wandered about a place called Pink Forest, but the trend was toward settling down. Three social factors began the process, until, finally, politics allowed no choice. As we noted, by the time of Ajaan Mun's death forest monks were receiving more notice and patronage, and the *Thammayut Nikaya*, while recognizing the monks' contributions to Buddhist practice, wanted to control their activities. In addition, some of the monks were growing older. Ajaan Mun made his last pilgrimage to visit a pagoda when he was 74. After that he no longer wandered but lived in *wats* for the remaining six years of his life.

It was not uncommon that when a forest monk came to a locale the villagers would erect a *wat* and invite the monk to stay. Some stayed for a while then moved on, sometimes leaving a student in charge. As the outside world invaded Isan during the 1950s, the monks retreated into more inhospitable resting places. "[M]any forest monasteries were established in places where few ordinary folk were willing to visit... malevolent spirits and ghosts... malarial fevers and wild animals... the former began to be controlled in some areas with DDT in the 1950s with the expansion of rice production... as simultaneously the latter were driven out of cleared gardens and rice fields to the receding surrounding forests."[64]

It was still possible to find forest life. "In those days herds of wild elephants roamed the forested area. Around the forest hermitage there were several wild... [Indian gooseberry] trees, whose fruits were medicinal. Wild animals such as porcupines, wild boar, barking deer... came to feed on these fruits. While picking the... fruit that fell on the ground, the monks and novices would sometimes run into a wild animal and jump back startled. In those days there was no clear division of space between man and beasts."[65] One monk saw wild elephant herds playing. The last of Mun's disciples to establish a forest *wat* did so from 1953 to 1958. He and 14 disciples spent the rains retreats in a remote place. One night one of them shouted at the tigers to quiet down because the monks were reciting the monastic rules. While squatting to defecate, another monk had a tiger leap over him. "One day a wild elephant got into the area and walked to [an initiate's] hut. Using its trunk, it picked up the man's slippers and threw them into the forest. The disciple didn't notice until the elephant shook the hut and then he fled in fear."[66] The teacher said, "The forest is the wild animals' home territory. We human beings are visitors. We must respect their rights."

But the forest monks gave in to the changes. One of them in the late 1930s found wandering less compelling and his students' needs changing. So he began to mix chanting and study into his teaching. Would-be patrons tracked the monks down in places that were no longer so inaccessible, contributed to the monks' upkeep, and financed the construction of permanent *wats*. One monk settled down after 19 years of wandering. The presence of this well-known monk supported by patrons led to rural development. Immigrants were drawn to the areas by easier access and cleared ever more land. Elsewhere, monks began to return to their hometowns. It was not unusual for a monk to settle in the forest near an aging mother in order to see to her care. The villagers would erect a *wat* around the monk, and the monk would remain. The mother would wear white robes, be supported, and cook or sew. Similarly, the religious establishment in Bangkok began to demand the monks' presence. They wanted to check on them and to introduce them to admirers. The members of the hierarchy also wanted the forest monks to attend to their spiritual needs. Later, although with very mixed feelings, monks would visit towns for medical care. After treatment monks stayed for a while and then returned to their *wats* or to forest practice.

While all these factors eroded forest wandering it was the Cold War and the United States war against the Vietnamese that ended the tradition. In 1958 there was a military coup in Thailand, followed by repression of dissidents and alleged communists. Wandering monks were not trusted. In villages of questionable loyalty forest monks were detained for long periods as suspected communists. A prominent meditation teacher was arrested because meditation was viewed by the government as an impediment to modernization. Some of Mun's older disciples settled because of the danger of wandering.

In 1958 a follower found an isolated rocky forest near a two-household hamlet. He set up his *klot* near a cave in which there was a tiger den. On finding him sitting there, the tigress moved her cubs farther away. He did not go on alms round for four days, after which he followed an elephant trail and oxcart track to a village. Without knowing the local language he persuaded the tribal families to give him rice. Three other monks joined him, including a woman, but he sent them away because of lack of food. He decided to subsist on wild vegetables and water. The monk taught the families about alms. Then families from farther away came to support him and his disciples. He taught the locals not to worry about forest spirits, so even more people came to settle and expand their fields. As a result he received plenty of food. Finally, the lack of isolation and quiet made the place unsuitable for meditation. So he left, to the villagers' disappointment. He had made it safe for the village to expand their fields, and so the population grew. While there he was accused of being an insurgent. In 1962, because he knew the jungle well, he evaded a border officer who had orders to kill him. On another occasion he was questioned in his mountain retreat. Yet another monk's retreat with surrounding fruit trees was burned so the communists would not use it.

As the war in Vietnam intensified the monks found themselves affected by it. American bombers were stationed at Thai air bases. On their way back to base from bombing missions in Vietnam, Laos, and Cambodia, they would jettison their extra bombs into the Thai jungles to minimize the risk of explosion on landing. The forest monk just mentioned and his disciples remained in the forests despite this risk. In 1968 he was ordered to leave the forest by the religious authorities. During the late 1960s the Thai government carried out large search-and-destroy missions in the jungles against a growing communist insurgency.

This made the forests unsafe for wandering. Leaving the forest, this monk had villagers clear space in the forests for a *wat*, which then attracted even more settlers. The population went from 10 to 200 households, overwhelming the local Lao population. In 1961 another monk and his students, settling in a roadless area, built a road seven kilometers long to the nearby villages so they could preach to the residents. The monks were fired on one night by village soldiers who later apologized. From the late 1960s on only a few monks, who dodged bullets and the authorities, continued to wander.

The changes that were taking place in the 1960s are exemplified in the life of Ajaan Jumnien who stood somewhere between the second and the third generation of forest tradition.[67] Jumnien was born in a village in southern Thailand in 1936. His father was a fisherman and the local village herbalist. Before marrying his father had been a monk for 13 years and had spent time as a forest practitioner. At age 20 Jumnien ordained as a *Mahanikai* monk. His father was his first teacher, instructing him in concentration practice for many years and then insight meditation. His first seven years as a monk were spent in a *wat* in the South. There, he said he practiced in a cemetery. For the first 18 years after he ordained he went on a three month *thudong* every year. Jumnien wandered part of each year from 1958 until 1974. He experienced the last years of the tradition, but the circumstances in which he walked and the way he did it had changed from the early days.

Before he settled down Ajaan Jumnien had many different teachers. Although ordained as a *Mahanikai* monk, he also studied with *Thammayut* monks who had been early students of Ajaan Mun. Among forest practitioners allegiance did not seem to be important. His father had studied with *Mahanikai* forest practitioners, and some of Jumnien's teachers were famous *Mahanikai* forest monks. This indicates that there was a forest tradition separate from that founded by Ajaan Mun, but I have little information on its history and manner of practice.[68] As we will see, Ajaan Jumnien's practice in the forest differed from his predecessors, who wandered the trackless wilderness, often without a goal, and who settled with tribals for rains retreats. They had little contact with the monastic hierarchy. Although there were still wild forests the countryside in which Jumnien traveled was becoming progressively more developed. On *thudong* Ajaan Jumnien always walked on laid out paths going to a preselected destination. He asked the way of villagers and other monks whom he met. While he occasionally used the sun and vines to indicate direction he was not wandering about. He sometimes took buses or trains to a destination and then walked the return trip. He claims to have never gone to the same place twice. Jumnien was lost only once. It was for four days between Chengkong and Chenglai in the North. He went the wrong way and ended up in Burma. He had no food and tried to use the sun to guide him but it was too foggy and cold. He was not frightened, but he felt that if he had not found a village within two more days it would have probably been the end of his life. He was thirsty but could not find a running stream. He said that it was difficult to find fruits in the jungle, and, in any case, he would not have gathered them. He would only eat offered food.

Ajaan Jumnien loved life in the forests. He found himself bored in town. He never wanted to leave the forests, yet he spent each rains retreat in a *wat*. He said that he was not good at concentration in meditation but that his mind was not occupied, and he never worried. Early in the mornings on top of mountains, he felt bliss. In the forests he was at home with the animals. "He thought all the wild animals were his friends." Once a snake stopped on his lap while he was sitting, and then it continued on its way. Another time there was a snake next to him when he woke, but it did not harm him. He did loving-kindness meditation and did not think animals would harm him. He heard that many monks were harmed by wild animals, usually from stepping on snakes that had young with them. He felt that animals would not bother a monk who vowed to die if necessary.

In his travels Jumnien met snakes, tigers, wild elephants, and many birds. "If you meet snakes, don't go close; just stay away. They won't do you any harm except if [snakes have babies, then the snake will attack]." Poison snakes move slowly. Non-poisonous ones move quickly. He saw bears but never at close range. He was not frightened of bears. "If you stay calm... they will never bother you if you never bother them." Although other forest monks vowed not to move after taking their seat for the night underneath their *klot*, Jumnien never made that pledge. He felt to do so was to put oneself in jeopardy, particularly when there were herds of wild elephants around. Monks who did not move were trampled. At night, he would move out of harm's way. Jumnien also carried what he called his first aid kit for dealing with wild animals. It consisted of a tin can, kerosene, and a rag or paper. "When he met the elephant or something like that, he just lit this thing here and threw it toward the animal. Because the animals were scared of fire, he used this many times so he could get away. A young mama snake would just play with the fire and he could then get away. He did this when he met elephants who would come to look at the fire and he could get away."

Jumnien was not in complete accord with fellow monks who saw animal life as worse than human existence. For him humans suffered more than animals because humans have more needs and more greed. Animals find food when they are hungry and that is it. But humans, even when satiated with food, want more and more. "Animals when they get food by themselves they never bother anybody. Humans have to plan, have to step on somebody to be up on top. He liked to stay with animals better than with human beings." In the woods the only predation he saw was snakes killing snakes. He liked birds the best because of their beauty. He observed that they fought with each other less than other animals. He said that he knew the names of the more prominent birds like peacocks, turkeys, and macaws but did not know the names of many others. Birds and other small animals were his messengers of danger. By noticing their flying away and noise making he would be alerted to potential danger.

Besides the healing herbs that his father taught him to collect in the forest, Jumnien used modern medicines. He took antimalarial medicine every six days and he carried an allergy medicine with him. When he ran out of the latter, he would stop in a village and have the villagers fetch a new supply for him. He also carried sugar with him as a water purity tester. He would dissolve some sugar in questionable water and see if ants would drink it. If they drank and died he would then consider the water undrinkable. His father also taught him other jungle survival skills, such as not drinking water in which wild mushrooms grew. He would also examine mosquitoes. If malarial mosquitoes were present, then he would either meditate under his mosquito net or leave the area. He never contracted malaria while he wandered, but was infected while staying in a *wat* in Laos. The only other illness he had was colds.

During Jumnien's travels in Burma and the North of Thailand, he met many hilltribes. All, except those who were Christians, offered him alms. He liked tribals because they believed in spirits. He felt he could help them more. When they were harmed and attributed it to spirits, he said he could give them medicine to heal their pain. He gave them medication for their ailments and explained what was happening to them with Buddhist homilies. When they got diarrhea from bad water they thought they had offended the spirit of the water. He gave them medication and taught them to do loving-kindness. He convinced them to ask the spirit to please let them have the water that belongs to human beings, but then they must also boil the water first. "Everything raw belongs to the spirit, everything cooked belongs to human beings." So they should also cook food before eating it.

Because his precautions and medication healed them the hill peoples believed he possessed magical powers. His strategy was to get the hill peoples to trust him so that they would be open to his message about meditation and non-harming. Although he had heard of the "Spirits of the Yellow Leaves," the remaining hunter-gatherers, he never encountered them. By Jumnien's time they had become very cautious. If they met monks by accident they would not wait until the leaves of their shelters yellowed. They would move right away. They were afraid the monks would divulge their whereabouts. They did not to want to meet anyone. Indeed, he said, the reason they were called "spirits" was because, like spirits, once you met them, they disappeared.

Jumnien's forest *thudongs* came to an end around 1974. During the Vietnam War he experienced difficulties like other forest monks. Both the Thai communists and the government "took out contracts" on him because he was for peace. He felt that local Thai authorities liked to drum up fear of the communists because that was a way of getting money from the Americans. *Thudong* became dangerous because of what he felt were threats to his life by both sides. He finally stopped doing *thudong* for reasons of health.

Ajaan Jumnien's experiences illustrate how the changing circumstances had affected the way wandering was done. The forests in which Jumnien walked had become tamer. He availed himself, more than did his predecessors, of the products of modern civilization that had become widespread. He had no doubts about disseminating public health information in his contact with hilltribes. These were real differences from the life of the first generation of forest monks. It is difficult to know what differences there were between him and his predecessors with respect to his understanding of the nature in which he traveled. It is clear that he hedged his bets around the risks of wilderness more than they did. I have no evidence about how the students of Ajaan Mun felt about malarial medicines when they first became available after World War II and then more prevalent in the 1950s. Even though a monk's ability to endure malaria was thought to be an indication of the depth of his practice, my guess is that many of them took the new medicines. Jumnien accepted them without reservation. He also used a greater understanding of the risks of nature from the perspective of modern medicine. He did not simply offer himself up to the elements, relying only on his powers of meditation, as Ajaan Mun seemed to advocate.

Ajaan Jumnien's understanding of natural history is hard to ascertain. He could identify the *Anopheles* mosquitoes that carry malaria, and he knew the herbs that he collected. His stories about snakes are charming. I do not know whether fast or slow is adequate to distinguish between poisonous and non-poisonous snakes. Certainly rattlesnakes where I live do not flee on seeing someone. I asked one of the world's experts on snakes about mother snakes and their young. He responded, "My general impression from working in various cultures (including my mom's folks in rural East Texas) is that folk natural history is a mosaic of accurate and insightful knowledge and wild rumor or mythology. In this case there is an underlying element of known fact: We now know of several dozen species of snakes worldwide, including some boas and pythons, many pit vipers, at least some cobras and their relatives, and a few colubrids [mostly nonvenomous snakes] in which the female remains with her eggs throughout incubation or with her young for a short time after birth. What might also be relevant re your monks is that King Cobras build a nest of vegetation (e.g., bamboo trash) in which they remain with the clutch. Whether the female actively defends the eggs or young is uncertain. I don't know of any evidence for any snakes herding or otherwise traveling with their offspring."[69]

Although certainly less equipped than modern backpackers, in order to avoid injury Jumnien had to know more than they about the woods in which he traveled. Whether the generations of forest monks before him had a deeper knowledge for survival and learned more through their own observations is difficult to say. Jumnien was a villager who learned specialized knowledge of the forest from his father, whose role was village forager. This was a considerable amount of knowledge but limited in comparison to peoples who live intimately with the forest as a matter of survival. Rather than shun technology as a means of protection, Jumnien took some of the improvements civilization offered with him on his return to nature and these mediated his relationship with it.

How any of these changes in his relationship to the forests altered the depths of his meditation is hard to say. While talking with Ajaan Jumnien I had the impression of a man of easy disposition for whom walking in the moderate wild fit his personality. The calm of the forest and his naturally quiet mind supported each other. From him one does not feel the ferocity of Ajaan Mun and some of his disciples, for whom sitting with tigers was a way of subduing fear and craving. Ajaan Jumnien took the circumstances of forest practice as he found them, used them as a support for his insight and wisdom, and then moved on without hesitation as the world changed. He took the qualities of wisdom, which had been nurtured in the forest, and carried them back into the civilized world with ease.

When I spoke to him it was in the living room of a ranch-style house in the Central Valley of California. All the amenities of modern life were present. It was at the end of a long day. Earlier in the evening I had waited while he performed ritual blessings for the local Thai women and children. When I left after midnight I expressed how tired I was. He looked at me with a smile and said that he felt very alert. As I walked out the door he laid back on a couch to watch the television set, which someone had turned on for him. The words were in a language he did not understand. It looked to me like the beginning of what would be an even longer evening. At the end of it he would sleep under his *klot* that was set up in the bedroom. Although he had not taken the vow of not-moving at night as other forest monks had, he did vow to sleep under his tent-umbrella for the rest of his life. And so he did in suburban California that evening.

In addition to the political impact of the war in Vietnam that made wandering in Thailand impossible, the forests themselves began to vanish at an exponential rate and with them the wildlife that lived there. By 1970 wild boar had vanished. Tigers were last seen at a forest hermitage in 1972. Between 1958 and 1988, 88% of the forests of Thailand were destroyed. Pictures of where forests stood now show mile after mile of farms. In 1988 there were huge floods and then student protests about environmental destruction. These led the government to cancel all forest concessions. Despite this, logging continued, either because of government corruption or small time illegal cutting. Since the mid-1970s, the forest monks have become so popular that patrons began to protect the woods around their *wats*. These woods remain some of the only unaffected forests in Thailand, although they too are subject to illegal harvesting.

Even if forest monks wanted to be *Thudong Kammathaan* there would be little way to do it. According to Ajaan Mun's biographer, Mun stayed for a long time in the Dong Phya Yen forest. Then it was wild, with widely separated villages, each with a few houses whose inhabitants grew rice and hunted. "Now this forest has been cleared... Bald-headed mountains can be seen all over this area. Gone with the malaria and the wild beasts are the forests, the fertility, the humidity, and the beauty of the mountain scenery."[70] By 1956 one forest monk found himself offered rides while walking along roadways, and many of his students were not hardy enough to keep up with him. When forest monks wandered during the dry season the shade of the trees was an important protection. With large trees harvested from those forests which still existed and trees removed from rice fields, exposure to the sun made wandering more arduous, if not impossible. Also walking down roads with speeding vehicles became downright dangerous.

Ajaan Cha settled near his home village and a *wat* grew up around him. He taught in the spirit of Ajaan Mun, replacing wandering in the forests with meticulous observation of the monastic code, work, and practice in a monastery. He seemed to have Mun's uncanny ability to know what students were thinking, but unlike Ajaan Mun, Ajaan Cha delivered his reminders with humor. While students were sometimes terrified by his knowledge of their mental states, they were also reassured by the loving humor with which he seemed to embrace them. During the retreat which I sat with him on his one visit to America I was standing near him after the retreat was over when a woman came to inquire about a male friend who had ordained in Ajaan Cha's monastery. With a twinkle in his eye he said, "His mind was confused, so I sent him into the woods until it settled down." It seemed clear that Ajaan Cha had picked what was most challenging for the new monk and with great compassion sent him off to tackle it. Whether it took a few months or many years made little difference to Ajaan Cha. Teachers like Ajaan Cha, who embodied Ajaan Mun's ability to see students clearly, can be intimidating. I both wanted to ask what he saw in me and was terrified to do so.

At his *wat* Ajaan Cha told very few tales of his life as a wanderer and trained none of his students in the tradition. In the late 1960s a number of Westerners who wanted to learn meditation were drawn to him. Perhaps he talked little about his past to his Western students because he felt that they were not suited for life in the forests. Ajaan Cha thought Westerners talked too much and they had "stupid feet," i.e., were clumsy in the forest, because they were always getting bruises and cuts from hitting their feet on stones and roots. These would take a long time to heal.[71] Nevertheless, his Western students spread his teaching style. From his *wat* has grown a series of monasteries around the world. The Westerners who run them carry on his version of ascetic meditation without the practice of wandering in wild forests.

An American who first came to be a monk in the early 1970s noted how much the changes taking place in Thailand affected Ajaan Cha's monastery. In the early 1980s the young man returned after five years absence to a monastery that he remembered as being far from village noises. Now the disturbances had become "pretty common almost everywhere... because electric lines have spread out closer to the *wats*... [The meditation huts] in the best caves are falling apart, those remaining have been poisoned with DDT... Illegal loggers trespass with chain saws, as they do in the forests all over the country, gunshots are heard occasionally as hunters chase small game; sometimes they try to smoke the animals out of the woods, then flee and leave the forest to burn when the monks apprehend them."[72]

These days Thai monks who would like to go on *thudong* come to stay in the Ajaan Cha-inspired monasteries in England, where they can walk around the gentle countryside. It is by no means wild, but at least there are woods and intrusive development is not omnipresent. Though such trips have their challenges, they are not equivalent to the wanderings of the forest monks who once walked the wilds free of the trappings of modern civilization. While it is rumored that some forest-dwelling monks showed up at Ajaan Tate's funeral in 1996, it appears that, after 2,500 years of episodic history, this form of spiritual quest has all but vanished.

Chapter 6

Conclusion

When I began writing this book in the mid-1990s only a few forest monks who had been students of Ajaan Mun were still living. A few were teaching, but most were infirm. Many of the forest monks lived and died, having experienced only bits of modern society. One actually made his way to India in the late 1930s and flew in an airplane. In his late 70s he traveled by air to Australia and other places but was not impressed with life lived so globally. For the forest monks who did not survive into the 1970s a train ride from the edge of the Northeast to Bangkok was the extent of their participation in civilization. And while modern medicine did begin to touch them, some had doubts about it. One escaped from treatment in a Bangkok hospital, returning back to the Northeast where he recovered on his own. "To the old forest monks, much of modern Thai society was beyond their comprehension."[1]

When Ajaan Cha slipped into a coma around 1980 he was kept alive for many years by modern medicine. Another of Ajaan Mun's monks objected to this, knowing that it was neither wanted by Ajaan Cha nor countenanced by the ideals of forest practice. Although many forest monks did not live to see the effects of modern civilization on the human mind, those who did voiced grave reservations about the bad influences material prosperity might have on human suffering. Ajaan Cha observed that in the Thai countryside people were getting darker inside as the lights of civilization spread. A forest monk who died in 1985 at age 97 felt that, "[Although] technologically society has progressed 100%, ethically it has deteriorated by 200%... This is the dark age."

Lying in the sun under the redwood trees in my yard, slowed

by a head cold, I listen to the sounds around me. In the background are the ever-present rumble of cars, a man hammering, and from the woods the quiet chattering of a winter wren and the raucous conversation of acorn woodpeckers in their colonial tree, a dead, old Douglas fir, up the hill from me. I become still, observe again how much more the noises of civilization grab my attention than even the nesting woodpeckers. To the civilized human mind the routine sounds of nature are almost too subtle. If I could erase all the mechanical sounds I would have to listen with different ears to hear what was going on in nature, and even then it would be less interesting. While natural catastrophes can outdo any human effort and nature creates a constant pressure on each creature because of the necessity of sustenance, most of the time little is going on out there that engages the civilized mind. Except for the occasional deer and even rarer coyote or mountain lion, my exurban yard is a quiet place. Until, that is, I spend a lot of quiet time there and look and listen more carefully.

The other day while walking in the woods nearby with an amateur naturalist we noticed an inch-long black spider wasp dragging a paralyzed spider along the ground. The wasp grasped hold of the spider with its front legs and walked backwards, fluttering its wings with each step. The spider was as big as the wasp. Occasionally the wasp would let go of the spider and fly around as if looking for a hole in which to deposit the spider and then lay eggs on it. After a brief sojourn the wasp returned and began dragging the spider again. The wasp wedged itself under a rock, emerged, checked out the spider, then went back under the rock. This was repeated several times. Then the wasp flew off for a bit. When the wasp was away we picked up the spider with a pair of tweezers to see if we could identify it, but the paralytic sting had contorted the spider's front legs over its face. We placed the spider down a foot or so from where the wasp had left it. The wasp returned, not seeming to notice the spider's displacement, and began dragging it again. We then lifted the rock under which the wasp had crawled to see why the wasp did not use it as a burying place. To our surprise, deeper down under the rock was an even larger, quite live spider, waiting, we surmised, for the wasp to descend deeply enough. Spiders and wasps are ancient enemies. Each eats the other. Their encounters have uncertain outcomes.

This is nature. The Buddha and his forest followers went forth into nature to soothe the discontent of the human mind. In the woods they met with unmediated life and death and they learned to live with the endless boredom of nature, with its slight offerings of stimulation to the civilized mind. My friend and I watched the wasp and spider for about 20 minutes and then hurried off to catch up to the people with whom we were surveying native plants. We had become a little impatient because the wasp seemed in no hurry to satisfy our curiosity about what it would eventually do with the spider. Nature had more time than our restless, experience-accumulating minds. If I had redefined the situation as meditation rather than a field trip, I might have relaxed and sat for hours with wasp and spider. How I reacted to the situation—whether or not I saw the outcome of their encounter—would have simply been more material for observation about how minds work. And the spider-wasp interaction would have been another reminder of the way nature works. Life, as it did for the forest monks, would have continued to go on at its own pace. I would not have tracked down events to witness their conclusion. I would have let what is "interesting" come and go as was its wont. I would have sat still and observed my being's reaction to life's processes. But later when I related the incident to a third amateur naturalist who had studied spiders she responded: "Why don't I ever get to see neat things like that?"

If the forest monks had been naturalists rather than villagers going off into the forests to practice meditation they would perhaps have had their Buddhist ideas confirmed beyond their greatest expectations. Nature does have a beauty to it, especially in first impressions, and the forest monks were very aware of this. They, like the early renunciants, the Chinese recluses, and Zen hermits, waxed eloquent about nature. On the other hand, the aspects of nature that were not pretty, that were uncomfortable, were more profound teachers for them. Living beings are born and die; life feeds on life. The wasp and the spider are locked in a dance of death not to be taken lightly. When a spider-hunting wasp gets stuck in a spider's web, both creatures react with a nervousness that seems to reflect an ancient awareness of how even-pitted their species have been during eons of their evolution. If one wants to practice meditation with the help of nature, then settling down and observing how the mind reacts while nature presents its harsh realities is crucial. The spirit of the meditator attuned to nature is that of the Zen poem: "Sitting quietly, doing nothing/Spring comes and the grass grows by itself."

With somewhat differing emphases the practitioners we have discussed saw life as hierarchical. Being born as an animal was thought to be worse karma than to be born human, although this might not always be the case. It is possible to live a very destructive human existence, causing much harm, and presumably an animal could live relatively non-harmingly. There is indeed altruism in the animal world, and some species are more destructive than others.[2] When forest practitioners saw altruism in nature they regarded it as meritorious. And in some kinds of Mahayana, living one's being totally and completely without malice or gratuitous harming, no matter what life offers, is thought to contribute to a higher rebirth. Zen Master Soen sa Nim told the story of a butcher becoming enlightened while killing a cow. So, even if the life unfolds according to the red rule of tooth and claw, if done without malice, it provides the next step up. In general, Buddhists felt humans needed to overcome any animal-like tendencies. The reason forest practitioners lived outside of the comforts of civilization was to look as directly as possible at these crudities and to study the response of the mind to them. That animals possessed feelings like humans, the meditators in nature saw firsthand. That humans were animals too was clear from the direct impact that nature had on the meditators. Although they would never have characterized it this way, the forest practitioners' job was, in a way, to study their own natural history.

Looking back over 2,500 years of forest practice we began with an original tradition established by the forest renunciants of India. It antedated the Buddha and was carried on by some of his followers. The renunciants took to the woods and endured all kinds of discomfort. Their experience and their realizations lent them a kind of charisma. Living at a time when nature was not so remote they easily moved in and out of society, but they also lived in a period of rapid societal expansion. The Buddhist religion which was flourishing by the time of the Asokan Empire in the third century BCE acknowledged forest practice but also hemmed it in. So, as Buddhism spread the cenobitic or monastery asceticism of the *Visuddhimagga*, which fit nicely into civilized life, dominated. This left the eremites, if they existed, living outside our purview. One credit owed to the *Visuddhimagga* is that although it omitted wildness, its asceticism of the spirit pointed one's attention to how nature existed within civilization. It emphasized rather than hid that which is usually "disgusting to civilized people." It might be hard to say whether cenobites who observed nature within society have a practice from which they learned as much as the forest renunciants about humanity's place in existence and the ending of human suffering.

But cenobitic Buddhist religion in which meditation played only a minor role predominated, and forest practice, if it existed, was invisible for more than 500 years. Then the Chinese and Japanese elaborated their own versions of meditation in the wilds. The Chinese engaged in some authentic forest practice, but much of what was claimed as meditation in the wilds was the posturing of aesthetes who fit more or less comfortably within Chinese civilization, which was at odds with nature. What China contributed to forest practice is the marriage of Taoism, Buddha-nature, and the aesthetic of the Yangtze gorges. These, together with the iconoclasm of the Cold Mountain poets, give greater breadth to meditation in nature. The aversion toward nature which marked the original forest renunciants is replaced by a larger embrace but also a less detailed focus. The Buddha-nature of animals, streams, rocks, trees, and mountains are celebrated, but the nasty details of nature's processes are either not seen or, in any case, not accounted for. And while the Chinese aesthetes created beautiful images of nature from the comfort of their estates, they often failed at practice. In contrast, Cold Mountain and the practice-recluses who emulated him met nature more directly, and that deepened their meditation.

The Japanese expanded on this and, while they too enshrined nature as a cultural construct, their landscape and closer material connection to nature helped generate more actual forest practice. From Saigyo to Ryokan, Zen hermits went off into the woods and left a record of their struggles with nature. Ryokan, with whom we ended the chapter on Zen, could easily stand as a model of how one can pursue meditation in nature today. Even in a world of diminished wilderness, by really living in the woods and paying attention to his surroundings, nature became Ryokan's teacher in the marginal wastelands of his society.

Finally, the forest monks of Thailand recreated forest renunciation as it might have been in the Buddha's day. From them we get many of the details missing from the historical records of early Buddhism. In what may have been the first time in several thousand years they tried to emulate the Buddha's forest practice. They undertook a strict ascetic life in the jungles of Southeast Asia until the Vietnam War and modern world drove them out of the forests and destroyed the wilderness in which they had wandered. With their demise the forest tradition seems to have vanished from the world again. Although there are reports of the continued existence of a few forest monks it is unclear if there is enough undisturbed nature remaining to sustain forest practice. It is also not clear that those of us so dependent on the protections of post-industrial society would be inclined to meet nature unarmed by modern technologies. When it came to modern medicine it was even hard for Ajaan Mun's students to resist. It is certainly possible to sustain oneself in the wastes of Siberia or the mountains of North America and avoid authorities. And there are meditators who have gone off for a week or longer, but such endeavors are quite different from those of the renunciants, recluses, hermits, and forest monks.

Because of time and historical evidence there are many missing pieces to our picture of forest practitioners. One element lacking is a fine-grain image of how much they knew about the woods and how they acted on that knowledge. One gets the sense that those who spent years in the forests knew much more about the wild than they conveyed in their poetry and stories. Society at the time of the Buddha was in the process of erasing its pre-agricultural past. The goal of the early Buddhists was transcendence. This interest is what scholar monks recorded for posterity, not the details of forest life. The retreats of the Chinese practice-recluses and the Zen hermits were much less wild than those that came both before and after them. They also addressed cultured audiences whose interests where likewise slanted away from nature, and so, again, many details of survival are not recorded. Finally, Thai forest monks were speaking to remote villagers. Their audiences were acquainted with heat, cold, insects, and death. The monks never anticipated modern urban admirers who no longer experienced these in their daily lives. As in the case of Ajaan Jumnien, teachers taught survival skills to students, or neophytes had to learn about nature if they were to survive on their own. If the old forest monks still lived, we might learn more about how their practice fit within our understanding of nature.

In forest practice nature teaches. The chattering human mind with its desires and aversions is also a part of nature. Among other practices the Buddha prescribed steadfast, silent observation as a remedy for our discontent. There is no claim that this cannot be done well by cenobites in their temples, yet there is something compelling in the reality of the eremites. Listening each morning to the waxing and waning of bird calls, meeting changes in weather with little protection, knowing hunger and biting insects, and living with other animals teach us how much our understanding of disease, old age, and death has become limited by the civilizations we maintain. The alertness that forest practitioners needed to survive was like that of wild animals. This alertness infused into their practice. It kept them tuned to the subtle tricks of the mind. It reminded them that their bodies were part and parcel of the environment in which they lived. It kept them from resting back into the illusion that civilization and society will exempt us from life's processes. Stepping into wild nature armed only with meditation is a strategy that has been used for the last 2,500 years to grapple with the meaning of life.

Epilogue

Meditation in Nature

I have been encouraged to distill from the history of forest meditators suggestions for how people in the modern world might practice in the wild. The cynic in me is reminded of the beginning of a book on self-psychoanalysis by Karen Horney, a famous Freudian psychotherapist of generations past. Her first suggestion for self-analysis is, "don't try." I have met three forest monks in my life. They belonged to the Thai forest tradition. Two were on in years, and neither shared details of his life in the jungles. The third was quite willing to talk in private about his experiences in the woods, but the more modern Thailand in which he wandered had lost its wild edge and his attitude was more of a perambulator than of a person who threw himself on the mercies of the wilds. I have not met a modern meditator whose practice had the intensity or existential risk of the people mentioned in this book. Gary Snyder, Nanao Sakaki, Red Pine, and I have touched the edges of forest practice but still spend most of our lives protected by industrial society. Forest meditators may be out there, but I have not encountered them. Some people we associate with living in the woods are frequently "off." They may claim some "spiritual" purpose but have the feel of psychological imbalance.[1]

I begin with an anecdote. This morning I awoke, intending to join my friend Bob Stewart on a field trip looking at spring wildflowers and birds.[2] Bob is the best teacher of natural history I have encountered. He is patient with a passion for things of nature, having at times favored birds, flowers, lichens, nudibranchs (naked sea slugs), and now butterflies. He has the rare talent of being able to teach beginners while keeping experts also engaged. A decade ago he was the naturalist for the Open

Space District of Marin County where I live. He returns once a year to take mostly old friends on a few trips around the county. These field trips he leads in California and the Southwest inaugurate spring and summer. Today's trip was to be at Old St. Hilary's Preserve in Tiburon, a very wealthy suburb of San Francisco. Old St. Hilary's is a small seafarer's chapel overlooking Richardson Bay, an alcove of San Francisco Bay. Fishermen once worked out of the harbor, and the chapel supported their Catholic souls. I have taken part in native plant censuses on the hills above St. Hilary's accompanied by wealthy local horse people who graze their horses there and are politically astute, sweet talking environmentalists in order to maintain their privileges.

I got to St. Hilary's, but no Bob. So I made my way to the top to scope for him and his group. On the way up the hill I knew that I would not find them. Plans must have changed. My time was free so why not meditate? It was a beautiful day, clear with a prevailing, cool, spring wind out of the northwest. As I was climbing I paid attention to the wildflowers. We had had a particularly dry winter with cold evenings. Only recently have there been the kind of rains which are so necessary to maintain our Mediterranean ecosystem. So, spring wildflowers have been slow in coming. I wondered if Bob had checked out St. Hilary's and decided there was more he could show people elsewhere. Climbing at a rate to keep my heart pumping but not so much that I couldn't observe what was around me I noticed how few flowers were blooming: a few crushed sun cups, some closed California buttercups, an occasional non-native cranesbill, and the bright yellow-green beginnings of footsteps of spring. At the top of the hill I used my binoculars to look around. Belvedere Cove lay below me calm and peaceful. So I sat down to look and meditate.

Why all the detail? If you remember my discussion, the difference between the practices of the eremites (forest monks) and cenobites (monastery monks) lay in the objects of their attention, not in their orientation toward existence. Forest monks committed themselves to an asceticism of lifestyle. Eremites observed their minds and bodies in the context of the wilds which surrounded them, while cenobites undertook an asceticism of attitude. In a container supportive of their meditation cenobites paid particular attention to the execution of the precepts. In both cases careful attention was crucial. My hillside was hardly wild, but it does offer enough of the untamed to contrast greatly to a meditation center or our daily lives.

I sat closed-eyed for a while and settled into being on an open hillside. I faced directly southeast into the sun which was traveling toward mid-morning. My back was to the wind and I was a little below the top of the hill, so I was protected. The sun was warm. For the next hour or so I was acutely aware of the changes around and thoughts arising and passing through my mind. Because it had occurred to me that I could use my experience for this section of the book there was a subtle tug between my silently experiencing and my mind turning that experience into a narrative for my book. Recluses and hermits emphasized the importance of rigorous monastic training as a prerequisite for forest practice because such training gave them the ability to attend in a concentrated way, crucial for maintaining practice among the distractions of nature. There are no monastery bells, no Zen *jiggy jitsu* to whack you when you begin to nod, no teacher, master, or guru to come to your aid when you find yourself in difficult mental spaces. So I sat with a slight tension between my narrating mind and silent obser-vation. It is something that would have upset me years ago, but I am now not much bothered by the background chatter. When it becomes too loud, I resort to more disciplined concentration to bring it back into bounds.

As I sat quietly, sometimes with closed eyes, sometimes looking, I heard the ever-present noises of civilization: planes, ferries, sightseeing boats, and the beeping of work vehicles. It was as quiet as our world gets. Looking up once I saw a turkey vulture climb a thermal above Angel Island. Closer observation with my binoculars revealed it to be a red-tailed hawk. One tree or violet green swallow swooped by. One bird called. Across the Bay, Berkeley began to emerge as the sun swung more to the west. At one point I lay back on the ground with my eyes closed feeling the sun. A few people walked by on the trail above: a dog walker, then a bark just above my head. My chest tightened in fear before my mind came into play. The walker shouted, "Jackson!" I have little fear of dogs, having trained and mock battled with them over the years. I used to take pride in my ability to calm a snapping dog, so I knew I was OK even though my body had reacted with fright. I opened my eyes and one dog was at my feet. "Jackson, Jackson," the walker whined. I offered my hand to the dog. Was this Jackson? It didn't seem so. It came over, licked my hand, and went off. Jackson was still above my head barking: He couldn't figure out the prone person. But then Jackson calmed and came to lick my hand too. Still the whine: "Jackson, Jackson!" I nonverbally indicated to Jackson that he should return to his caretaker, which he did. But still, "Jackson, Jackson!" My critical thought was that if the dog walker wanted obedience, she should have come over and grabbed Jackson's collar and given him a good shake. Her whining was just another game for Jackson and an irritant to the walker and her wider audience. It was interesting how long the physical traces of the fear remained in my body. It lasted minutes after I knew there was no cause for fear. I observed its slow dissolution.

Again, why the boring detail? As noted in my book, *Dismantling Discontent*, if you are really interested in nature you have to be prepared for the fact that not much happens most of the time, or rather, what is happening is subtle and repetitive. I was just about to leave because I had to pee when a young woman stopped at the top of the hill 20 feet above me. She started to chat on her cell phone. Out of curiosity I put in my hearing aids. The world came alive in a way I hadn't been aware of while sitting without the aids. Her conversation was not interesting, and I couldn't help wondering why one would want to talk on the phone in such a beautiful place. But then I have a friend who calls me on his walks. It is when he feels like he has free time to talk. I find it strange and unsatisfactory communication because of the poor audio of cell phones, the surrounding noises, and the quality of his attention. People believe they can multitask. While things do get done, most studies show that the doing of them is inefficient or sloppy. Despite our illusions and advertising, we are not capable of true multitasking. The next person who passed above was looking down at her Smartphone and had earphones. I guess she was experiencing nature, but I am not sure how.

The coast was clear, so maybe I could pee in the bushes. But as I turned my back to the sun to push myself up I saw the belly-flowers around me. They were opening into the rising sun. There were cranesbills like little sunflowers all pointing toward the sun. I had never noticed that phenomenon before. And English plantain, the "white man's footsteps" which heralded for the Indians the presence of Europeans, and sun cups and a little pink bud I could not identify. When I arose and wandered back the way I had come the sun was at my back. The flowers all seemed to face me. The pink buds turned out to be checkerblooms, and I saw death camas, which made me wonder whether the natives who lived on this hill before the Spanish missions corralled them ate camas lily, the nutritious relative of the death camas.

Within 15 minutes I was back to my car, but not without hesitating at a Y in the trail that I hadn't noticed going up. I am less aware of the way I have come, so I make errors returning, leaving me with extra-long walks and self-critical feelings about my abilities in the woods. Emerging from the conservation land I was immediately conscious of the non-native plants in the yards of the multimillion-dollar houses along the road. Although these wealthy people are politically liberal and live on the borders of conservation land, yet they grew non-native ornamentals, including pride of Madeira, calla lilies, and pampas grass, which are noxious weeds of native habitat. Back in my car I tried to keep my mind as quiet as possible as I drove home.

Is this the best of forest practice that my suburban surroundings can offer? It would not have sufficed for forest practitioners. First of all, my thoughts would have been seen as much a hindrance as any craving. The natural historical and political economic concepts that so framed the way I experienced my surroundings would have had little relevance to forest monks, although they also commented on such factors without seeing their observations as concepts. As I have mentioned elsewhere, when I first started meditating I walked down the road in front of the meditation center in rural Massachusetts and struggled with my mind, which would label each plant that I passed. My mind so tortured me then (and sometimes still does) that I wanted it to shut up. Now my noting of the character of my surroundings is part of my observation. I could reduce it to the dharmas (basic categories of experience) of Theravadan Buddhism, like qualities of sensation and incursion of objects of mind, and I do that when my mind is intrusive. But as a part of the plenum of my whole experience the conceptually based observations make for an aspect of the whole. Sitting silently on the hill, the plants, birds, dogs, fear, dog walker, sun, the contrast between real estate and conserved land, noise of ferries, etc. say something about who I am or am not and where I am. When later in life Henry David Thoreau became an accomplished ecologist working for Louis Agassiz, the famous Harvard professor, Thoreau worried that he had lost the wonder of his earlier transcendental feelings about nature. Yet, reading his detailed descriptions of the day-to-day changes in nature, I cannot help but think his finer attunement to nature enhanced his appreciation of what nature was. It was a much more complete comprehension of his surroundings, losing nothing of the wonder. Like the traditional Inuit, whose discrimination of the many kinds of snow may or may not be accompanied by a conceptual super-structure, knowing what is going on in the nature around you makes for a deeper connectedness. Conceptual understanding need not be an impediment to what meditators call awareness. In my experience it enhances it.

The edge of nature is where we have to do this. And while abiding there may not meet the standards of forest monks, practicing there can be informed by the sentiments of forest practice and may, in fact, be all that civilized citizens are now willing to undertake. Surely, most modern people, like those I passed on the hill, are uninterested.

But where else might we find aspects of forest practice? And here am I am on unsure ground. Vision quests and so-called shamanic practices are offered as workshops led by various guides. Derived from Native American and other indigenous rituals, vision quests may or may not be based on authentic pre-contact practices. When I hung out at Lama Foundation in the Sangre de Cristo Mountains north of Taos in the 1980s friends would go on vision quests with teachers from the Taos Pueblo or go off to do them at Sun Dances in the plains states. I only know what happened from their descriptions. A student would be given a four foot by four foot square somewhere outside, away from houses. The quester was instructed to stay in that space for three or four days without tent, food, or water. He or she was instructed not to meditate but just be there come rain or shine and maybe chant from time to time. For most of my friends these experiences were deeply moving. They emerged with some new understanding of what to do with their lives or how to relate to problems they had. Besides the physical difficulties of staying put, not eating, and being uncomfortable the greatest challenge was fear. Urban questers who had never slept out of doors by themselves before had to face the terror of the dark with its noises. For some the experience was liberating not only of the fear of the out of doors but of fear controlling other aspects of their lives. This, of course, was at the heart of forest practice. Whether or not this practice met the Buddhist standard of understanding, fear as a hindrance could be explored. I don't know if it did meet the standard. I am sure the question is complicated and would take an examination of the different experiences of a number of questers. Whatever the outcome of such a query, it seems to me this aspect of vision questing offers analogies to aspects of forest practice. Other aspects may contradict the spirit of forest practice, particularly an emphasis on ritual, about which early Buddhism was quite ambivalent. Despite the Buddha's criticisms of Brahmanical ritual, ritual became an important ingredient of many Buddhist sects.

I interviewed three people for whom Buddhist-oriented outdoors practice is important in their lives. Two lead meditation retreats in nature, while the third practices in wild places by herself. Each of their practice is quite different, and their experiences illuminate how forest meditation may be done in our current world. Two are old dharma friends, while the third is a student of another old friend. I have drawn from the experience of each different aspect to illuminate how nature meditation may be done, not to compare the relative merits of their practices. For two I present their practice while alone, and for the other his leading of groups. They have much in common. They are dedicated practitioners. Like hermits and forest monks they have spent time sitting regular retreats, so they possess a foundation of monastery practice that hermits and forest monks found essential to maintaining practice in the wilds. They possessed the disposition the Buddha required of forest practitioners so that the forest would not whirl away their minds. They are teachers. I won't cover everything they told about their individual experiences but only what illuminates how to engage in nature practice today.

Carla Brennan teaches meditation near Santa Cruz, California.[3] She has been meditating for almost 40 years, beginning with Zen and then Vipassana or insight meditation. Her feelings of connection to nature began when she was very young. In the 1970s she began practicing Buddhist meditation and took part in a three-month Vipassana retreat in 1979. While on retreat she would go out to meditate in the forests near the meditation center. In the early 1990s she did two month-long, solo, out-of-doors retreats in the mountains under the guidance of a teacher. After a week of being instructed she and a half dozen others were assigned separate areas in which to pitch tents, practice, and remain by themselves for a month. The practices included sitting, chi gung, Tibetan meditations like Tzogchen or Tong lin, and some ritual. An underlying emphasis was on being present, relaxing, and opening one's heart. Without going into the details of these various forms of meditation or ritual, I want to address here the connections of practice with nature. Daily life at her spot would include rising, a ceremony to the eleven directions, doing the medicine wheel, and formally meditating. On and off during the day Carla would engage in some of these practices, but mostly she would relax and just be. "Nature teaches you to be, because it is not thinking about things." After about three days there is a transition: "Nature forces you to be more in your senses, more connected to your body. You are taken out from your routines. It forces you to be in more harmony with your senses—when it is dark, it is dark. Animals treat you differently. You become much more attuned and open. Animals allow you to be a part of their community. They are at ease and approach you. A squirrel came up and sat on my leg. The rabbits come. While doing chi gung a big buck was watching me."

When I asked Carla about fear she related several incidents. "Once I was meditating under a tree with my eyes closed. I heard something and I opened my eyes and I was face to face with a cinnamon black bear, which caused me to be instantaneously on my feet. The bear ran off. I had an incredible sense of belonging, part of Being and energy. We forget completely that all of this is going on in nature. That is part of our dis-ease. But it also reminds you how much you don't belong." At another time a bear threw her food canisters down a ravine. "My view of nature is not romantic. It could have killed me at any moment. Bears are a reminder of our vulnerability. I was afraid in the moment but not afterwards. You have to take bears very seriously. That bear was gorgeous. It was a wake-up call, different from daily life, respect and mystery. Animals don't scare me much." Carla's biggest fear is weather. Once during a windstorm, "the wind rolled my tent with me in it. That kind of freaked me out. I moved my tent after that. I like being that close to the elements, feeling the power of the universe. I both like and fear it. It is opening and enlivening. It gets me out of my illusion of OK-ness." Using established meditation methods she tried to watch fear with awareness. "What dharmically am I learning? What is it showing about me? Being rolled brought up a lot fear, the mind says: I am out of here." Most frightening for her is lightning. During one intense storm the ground was shaking: "I was almost scared out of my mind. I tried to get as much insulation underneath me as I could. I tried to stay with my breath, notice my anxiety level, watch what my mind wanted to do, and stay with the fear: 'This is fear of death. This is good.' With the next kaboom I would be startled and adrenaline would be running. I used to be afraid of flying, afraid of death. Sitting with lightning helped. I would sit through waves of anxiety. I miss lightning now." She also now flies without fear.

For Carla boredom was a sign she was not paying attention. She didn't get bored. "I am an introvert." Being out of doors was endlessly engaging. "Nowhere to go, no place to be, no one to be; I am very good at doing nothing. Being spaced out wasn't a problem. Just being feels very alive, clear, connected. Real doing nothing was often quite joyful." Although hiking around was not allowed, sometimes when Carla's mind closed in on her she took off: "feeling disconnected, inadequate, expelled from Eden. 'I didn't have what it takes for enlightenment, not good enough.' Doubt. I wanted to hike away from myself. That passed. It mysteriously dissolved. It took a lot to not believe this story about myself."

Before she occupied her spot, returning retreatants told her how they had heard the mountain. She was quite skeptical. "A week into the retreat, it started. It wasn't like inner songs. It sounded like it was coming from the landscape, like new age ambient music. There were chords shifting and moving. It was not melodic but quite beautiful. It got louder and softer. I heard other things, like Native American chanting and drumming, bagpipes. Nothing was familiar." Then on four days of prescribed asceticism during the retreat she heard singing and harmonies when she put her head on the ground: "Like something from the old miners who had been there. Quite wonderful. Very real: 'Go tell it on the mountain.' The music turned into patriotic songs, folk songs repeating, driving me crazy. It sounded so real, I thought it was coming from the town. 'No I don't know what this is. This was not in harmony like the prior music.' My self-doubt snowballed, so I went hiking to get away. One tormented night filled with self-negation, I was sleeping outside and woke to someone singing beautiful songs to me from the sky and everything melted. The repetitive music went away and the old sounds came back. This had never happened on a regular retreat. The sound is always there. But our ability to perceive or understand is so much vaster than we know from daily life. Being in nature gets people beyond their small identification... Being alone in nature cuts through conditioning and identification so much more quickly than on a retreat, where you can maintain your habits. The silence is so profound, not just the quiet. A palpable silence, presence. I call it the slipstream of the present.

"On retreats people are thinking the teachings rather than experiencing them. People hold on to a lot more ideas about what the retreat should be like. It results in a lot of doing, more striving. People are identified with conventional views of reality. You need to cut through both of those... engage in a true confrontation with death."

Johann Robbins also grew up in the suburbs. By age sixteen he was going on backpacking trips alone and with friends. When in college he and a friend backpacked up a mountain in Vermont where they met a spiritual hippie who advised them to meditate, and so Johann took up Transcendental Meditation. For many years after college he went backpacking alone or with others. He was a seeker. He meditated using TM and open awareness. On occasion he became elated or filled with fear and loneliness, sometimes weeping. In the 1990s he began doing vision quests and trained to lead them. In the late 1990s he discovered Vipassana and met a teacher who led wilderness Vipassana retreats. These brought together the two sides of his practice: formal sitting and nature. After a few years he began assisting this teacher and when his teacher started to slow down he trained Johann to teach, and Johann began teaching meditation and leading retreats on his own.[4]

I asked Johann about fear. He recalled camping one night above tree line in a storm and getting very afraid. "You don't get that in a meditation hall, the vulnerability. It was scary but useful, a good teaching. Fear of being alone, fear of impermanence, fear of dying. I just sat with it. I didn't run away, in truth I couldn't have. I hung out with it; asked myself what is happening here. On my third desert retreat with my teacher there was a wild sandstorm for about three days. I really freaked out. I sat with it doing *metta*. I couldn't sleep, the sand kept blowing in my tent and the wind was like jet engines, but the fear concentrated me. When dawn of the third day arrived, I emerged from the tent concentrated, happy, and peaceful. Everything inside of me had changed. Now it was just wind. I don't often get scared of conditions like that anymore. When guiding I get triggered a bit if I think the retreatants are at risk, but I am usually happy. If you ask me how the weather is during difficult conditions I usually say it's perfect."

For Johann there is a communal dimension to nature retreats. "When at a meditation center other people there are not such a big part of your experience. On a wilderness retreat [which are conducted mostly in silence] we are all the retreat center, the retreat staff. Everybody is dependent on each other. Everyone works to create everything, paddle the boats together, put up the tents together, cooking, cleaning, etc. It is a cooperative community. We all fall in love with each other. We are often the only humans we see. This huge beautiful challenging landscape; this huge river with a couple of little canoes. It is the same on backpacking retreats."

Although Carla Brennan was trained in formal Vipassana practice, on her retreats she emphasizes what has been called open awareness, just being. Johann incorporates more formal techniques. Although there is usually a stationary solo for a couple of days during the retreat, unlike Carla, Johann and his students are traveling. So he teaches them to do walking meditation. "Not the slow walking of a meditation hall [rising, lifting, placing] that wouldn't work with a backpack. But to focus on one's body, stepping, breath, and seeing. When you are seeing, know that you are seeing, know you are feeling the trail, hearing the birds, all in a very conscious way." They do paddling meditation, using the touch point of one's hands on the paddle, listening to its rhythmic sound, seeing scenery, reading the river. The words "know that you are seeing" come out of the fundamental Buddhist sutra, *The Foundations of Mindfulness*: "When walking a bhikkhu understands, 'I am walking;' when standing, he understands, 'I am standing.'"

Although Johann has little experience with Zen practice his words are like those of a Zen hermit. "Nature is the Dharma, it is the truth, not mediated by words. It is what is... As soon as we convert it into words, we distort it." He urges people to just experience. "Nature is always manifesting not-self, impermanence, and unreliability. There is nothing selfing out there except us. The river is not selfing. If the river gets whipped up by the wind and dumps you over it is impersonal. It is not like the river got mad at you. It just happened. It is such a direct teaching of no-self to watch nature, not humans and institutions, which are themselves selfing, but with nature, which is no-self. A lot of civilization—buildings, etc.—is designed to make the world we live in more predictable, more reliable, more self-like, and more unchanging. That is what culture and technology do... nature is fundamentally unreliable, mostly uncomfortable. Nature is too cold, too hot, too windy. It opens ourselves to what is. That is the Dharma. We work with that."

Like Carla, loving kindness is an important part of his teaching. He encourages students to do *metta*, loving-kindness, for whatever shows up. "Bird, may you be happy. May the mountain be happy. If you have a self-referential thought then you send your self *metta*—oh I am cold, may I be happy. Wherever attention naturally goes, you send metta without directing attention. People feel love for everything that is happening. When an airplane goes overhead, rather than arrgh [because it is disrupting your experience of the wild] you say, 'may they be safe.'" People are encouraged to practice non-harming, even for insects, but repellent is allowed. "We are not taking on the care and feeding of mosquitoes."

"Dangerous animals are usually not a problem because they don't want to encounter us." He teaches how to avoid sneaking up on rattlesnakes or scorpions. Most of his own encounters with bears took place before he had begun Vipassana practice. On his current trips weather and rivers are the greatest challenges. On one occasion a wind suddenly whipped down a river canyon blowing away some tents. Leaders and participants ran down the beach and into the river to retrieve them. It stirred so much adrenalin that afterward they had a sharing circle [no interchanges, each person speaks his or her piece when holding a speaking stick], something they do each morning, breaking the mandated silence of the retreat. Because the travelers are so dependent on each other the circles give a sense of who the participants are and how they are doing. These facilitate bonding.

I asked Johann about how he deals with the technical knowledge that is necessary for survival. Being able to read the river, particularly for a neophyte, seems very different from paying attention to the touch of a paddle. My interest has to do with the description of sitting at St. Hilary's with which I began this epilogue. There are three aspects of mind which play a role in practice. They have been mentioned in the body of this book and are explored in detail in *Dismantling Discontent*. Primary to Vipassana practice is a one-pointed attention on raw experience. Paddling practice may be seen as a kind of one-pointedness. Then there is knowing without articulating the knowing, such as when one simply takes in the scenery. You know what is around you without giving it a name. Finally, there is the knowing which Buddhists call objects of mind, like chattering away to yourself. Johann's response to my question was spontaneous. He might answer with more detail were we to have an extended dialogue.

At the beginning of his river retreats is a day of teaching. A huge amount of information is imparted: how to read currents, load and unload boats, wash dishes, how to recognize dehydration, read how cold your body is, etc. And he reminds people during the trip when needed. He tries to teach retreatants to be alert to the needs of the moment but to rest back in simpler practice at other times. Because of his responsibility, he has to stay alert. "I don't want to get so into the moment to moment experience so much that I pass a camp site, or miss something easy for me but difficult for others." When he recognizes a landmark then he goes back to paying attention to his steps until the next one is encountered. "If I start to think about it worryingly, then I remind myself that I don't have to think about it yet." But he avoids, almost makes fun of, what he calls "science mind." It is the mind that runs on but with facts about the surroundings: 'here is a certain kind of landform; there is a such and such bird.' "Does the bird know it is a Steller's jay? It is not a Steller's jay, or even a bird. It is just what it is. But when I make speaking out of it, [I adulterate the experience of it]. [For communication purposes], it is easier to call it a blue spruce but that is not what it is!"

As Carla's practice has its emphasis, so Johann has his. What for him is distracting science mind is for me a part of the plenum of experience. This is analogous to the difference in perception of their surroundings between forest monks and indigenous people who hunted and gathered in the woods in which the monks wandered. Theravadan Forest monks used learned information to survive wandering, like Johann's paddlers, but they forsook the larger survival skills needed by forest peoples. Much of how they related to their surroundings was done automatically, so they didn't invoke concepts.[5] That could be also true for experienced paddlers, but the question might be, is it possible for cognitive learned knowledge to be so completely owned that it becomes another part of awareness of the environment without the impediments of "science mind"? Johann's response to this query was, "I think it can be. It seems that it has become so for me in many contexts, like reading the river, but most of the retreatants are new to the experience and have to think a lot more." Such issues are a challenge of modern nature meditation.

Laurel Houghton is a yoga teacher in Fairfax, California. She also runs a place where retreats can be held near Mt. Shasta.[6] Laurel knows a great deal about yoga and the theory of yoga. She is also a teacher in the tradition of the Vietnamese Zen master Thich Nhat Hanh. Laurel and I have spent hours rambling through the local landscape, talking about meditation and nature. Like Carla and Johann, Laurel was drawn to the out-of-doors when she was young. In a manner somewhat different from the others, she sees herself as a forest yogi and spends much time on her own in retreat in National Parks and Forests. Although there is a great deal of overlap, Laurel's challenges come from being a woman, without protection, alone in nature. Her concerns have rarely occurred to me or seemingly to Johann, and Carla has done most of her solo retreats under the protective umbrella of a teacher or nearby friends' land. We all recognize that other humans may be the most dangerous thing we might encounter in nature. Again I am bringing up the differences not to evaluate their merit but to illustrate how different practices and situations can be.

When I introduced Laurel to the Thai forest monks' image of sitting with tigers she took to it immediately. She uses a Sanskrit term from yoga to characterize her own tiger nature. Laurel goes off by herself in the desert or mountains for days or weeks. She spends mornings practicing and hikes afterward. Mornings include yoga, pranayama, and meditation. Unlike Carla, Johann, or me, Laurel does concentration practice. It is a kind of focused concentration which leads the mind into states of absorption. In the text above when I described these practices I used the word concentration. The Theravadan technical word for Laurel's states of absorption is *Jhana*.[7] Usually such practices are done in the most protective of settings, where one-pointedness can be honed without any distraction. For Laurel it is otherwise. "I have never found that I have meditated as deeply in a group meditation hall as I do outside. I think our nervous system is interacting with trees, etc., and that has a calming effect on our mind. When I am in deep enough, my sensory system shuts down.

Once I was sitting under a juniper tree doing intense concentration practice, and I felt myself pulled into the tree's root system. It was a very deep state of absorption. Then I think my witness was still operating. Only a few times has my witness shut off... Sometimes I get absorbed into total silence. There is no mind or ecstatic experience. Sometimes the witness is very dim. I get so sensitized because there aren't any people around to pull my armor back up." Absorption and the effort that comes when hiking are interrelated. "*Jhana* practice is developed by the intense focus it takes to climb a hill with a backpack. Climbing a pass is like when doing Jhana practice. It is like an arrow. I will do focused willful absorption practice from sunrise until one, sitting in the same place."

Besides the intense energy it takes to do absorption, sitting like a tiger is manifest by facing the fears that arise for women alone in the woods. It is a gender issue. "Women have very powerful instructions not to be alone anywhere at night and not to be alone in the woods ever. It was taught to us from the time we were little. For women there are tigers everywhere in the woods and wilderness, particularly at night. It can be particularly frightening. At night you get those night terrors. It is really like sitting with tigers. It takes skill to know how to stay safe. I have to work with my own mind. I have pledged to always tell the truth, yet on a trail alone I lie. I let no one know I am alone. I set up camp after dark so it can't be spotted. I often subliminally wonder about even nice people I have encountered during the day and so won't be able to sleep. I don't see girls on trails. Bears rubbing against my tent do not produce a fear even close to the fear of a human male. I take good care of the fear by allowing myself to lie. I reassure myself that no one can find me. I occasionally move camp. I honor those fears. I think those fears are intelligent. Taking care is an expression of Thich Nhat Hanh for discriminating between what is reasonable and what is not."

Laurel handles her fear of harmful humans by "taking care," but she also attends to it other ways. "I have written death notes multiple times. Because I was convinced a mountain lion was going to attack. I sat up all night with a stick and a rock. [Meditating:] 'just fear, just fear. Night fear, I am just in it.' Sitting like a samurai I fell over at 2:30 a.m. and didn't care whether I died. I crashed. Letting go, I gave my life to god. It was the first time in my life I felt the real worth of the power of the wilderness. Then dawn came and there was no fear whatsoever." Although almost everyone has self-doubt at one time or another, for women, especially of Laurel's generation, physical challenges can be intimidating. "Women were encouraged to be weak and dependent. Just walking a path being tested to your limits is valuable to develop will and discipline, the sheer act of will carrying a pack over a pass. It is not so different from meditation practice. You watch your mind talk about being tired. It is just like focusing on your breath, because you're pushing your body physically I think it develops discipline better than sitting practice." Women are tuned to the emotional qualities of interactions with others and that is something that they are occupied with a great deal of the time. "We are hooked into other humans. When you stand up in the meditation hall and you see somebody doing something and you are annoyed with them or fall in love with them... [In the wilderness] you don't have any of those issues so you can focus on practice... Being alone in the wilderness without others requires self-motivation—there is no group; you meditate out of your own will; no surrendering to some form. You yourself are creating the form."

I do not think that going off into the woods with the intention of most of the renunciants, recluses, hermits, and forest monks I have described happens in our society. My sojourns in nature have involved spending lots of time out of doors meditating. I do it as part of my style of life. And, unlike many people, I have access to places where wolves and bears still roam. But taking months, as I did in the past, to sit silently out of doors is probably over, as it was for my progenitors when they aged. For those so drawn, you can climb into the high Sierras and sit for a week. Try the woods of New England, the muskrat marshes of the prairies, the Everglades away from the motorboats, a mosquito-ridden cypress swamp of Louisiana, a remote one of Minnesota's thousand lakes, the deserts of the Southwest. It is not so hard. Carla, Johann, and Laurel offer ways of interweaving meditation with nature. The experiences of the men and women of this book can guide you. Doing so may give you a very different slant on the world in which we live. It may, as the Buddha thought, ease your discontent.

Appendix

Korea and Tibet

Korea and Tibet are Mahayana cultures that seem likely candidates to have produced forest practitioners. Korea stands halfway between China and Japan in East Asian Buddhist history. Like the Korean people, Korean Chan is grounded and earthy. Compared to the whole of China, Korea has a harsh climate whose people are rooted in the less productive soils they tilled. It would seem a good place to connect nature and meditation. That may be the case. There is less written on Korean Buddhism in English than on China and Japan, and I have found few references to how Korean practitioners related to nature. Yet it seems clear they must have. Even the recently deceased Zen Master, Soen sa Nim, spent time alone on a mountain reportedly eating nothing but pine needles. Soen sa Nim appears not to have talked about the details of his experiences. Others have done that before and after him, but I have come across few descriptions. One currently living nun spent years of her childhood, during the Japanese occupation, living in the woods and returned there during the Korean War after she had become a Buddhist nun. She describes both extreme deprivation and great rapport with living beings, especially snakes, but she did not seem to have connected with a tradition that uses nature as a conscious part of practice.[1] So Korean meditators' relationship to nature remains a question mark.

Tibet has one of the most extraordinary geographies in the world. Fertile valleys are surrounded by the world's tallest mountains. Some of its regions are almost inaccessible to each other. There are descriptions of abundant wildlife in Tibet. Besides the famous snow leopard, early twentieth-century Western visitors mention antelope and wild ass roaming in large herds and wolves, foxes, yellow bears, lynx, and tigers, marmots, weasels, badgers, otters, and porcupines.[2] Pre-Buddhist Tibetans practiced a number of animistic beliefs, some of which were called Bon Po. Tibet's access to the Silk Road left it open to larger cultural influences. When Buddhism arrived in Tibet, from the seventh century CE on, Bon Po absorbed some of it and a separate tradition of Lamaistic Buddhism emerged. Lamaistic Buddhism developed a number of sects which often competed with each other and with Bon Po for theological and political dominance.[3] Although both nomadic herders and groups claiming to have antedated the arrival of the now dominant Tibetans must have hunted, Lamaistic proscriptions against killing and eating wildlife made it relatively unafraid of humans and often seen.[4] One would assume from the landscape and wildlife of Tibet and its animism that contact with wild nature would play an important role in the meditation practices elaborated by Tibetan Buddhists.[5] As in the case of Korea, this may be true. But like Korea, I found little evidence of it. And I must admit that though I have done some Korean Zen and taken part in numerous Tibetan teachings, I have not delved deeply into Tibetan practices and literature. Thirteen hundred years of Lamaistic Buddhism created an immense number of religious texts, only a small portion of which have been translated. Also, much of what was not carried out by Lamas fleeing the Chinese was destroyed. In my survey of writings in English, I have found little about meditation's relationship to concrete wild nature and what I have found puts the two in a kind of opposition.

Avalokitesvara is the Bodhisattva of compassion mentioned in the *Heart Sutra*. He is a central figure in Mahayana. "Avalokitesvara's function through history (as reincarnated in successive Tibetan Lamas) is to tame the Tibetans, and this conversion from hunting and gathering to agriculture can be seen as the initial stage of the process."[6] Padmasambhava, the first Tibetan reincarnation of Avalokitesvara and the founder of

Lamaistic Buddhism, civilized Tibet by means of tantric ritual. Taming of the wild focused on malevolent spirits which resided in nature. "It is easy to find correlates for 'tame' versus 'wild' at the social level (peasants on a large central Tibetan estate versus nomadic Golog pastoralists) and at the religious level (monks in a large central Tibetan monastery versus wandering Tantric yogins)... the key element here is the business of 'taming.' Taming is the work of the lama... the lama tames demons and hostile forces, and he also tames his disciples.

"Padmasambhava... performed the original taming of the deities of Tibet and bound them to the services of Buddhist teachings... this act enabled both Buddhism and civilized life to be established in Tibet."[7] Bon Po also addressed the destruction done by the spirits of nature that ran wild in the harsh and capricious physical conditions under which Tibetans lived. The Lamas promoted Buddhism with the claim that they were better shamans and that the civilized society they built was superior to the wild one they subdued. One of Padmasambhava's mythic achievements was the domestication of barley, which gave the Tibetans a stable agricultural life and, along with trade, a sufficient surplus to be able to support a theocratic society with huge monasteries and, maybe, 20 percent of the population living as monks and nuns.

In Lamaistic Buddhist practice there are many references to wildness and taming the wild parts of the mind. Like Padmasambhava, practitioners' work is to address this wildness in themselves and bring it under control. The wild landscape with its powerful spirits is a metaphor for the mind. The head Lama at the Rongbuk Monastery (the highest monastery in the world), where British climbers made their last civilized stop before attempting Everest in the 1920s, describes his own practice: "[T]hen I started Chod practice... I change [sic]... from one dangerous place to another, and the visions and dreams became very wrathful, but I recognize [sic] everything into the magical play of deluded mind."[8] He does not describe what the dangerous places were like, the nature that surrounded them, or the experience of living in them.

I have found a few Tibetan references connecting meditation to real, rather than metaphorical, wild nature. In a classic meditation text, one is instructed on how the environment may affect practice. The student is told to meditate in places conducive to the season. In summer one should meditate in cool places: "huts made of reeds or bamboo or fragrant grass near glaciers or mountain peaks."[9] In autumn dense forests, mountain slopes, and rock-hewn dens are to be sought. Winter meditation should take place in warm, low-lying places, such as dense forests, mountain caves, and earthen houses. And in spring the preferred places are the mountains, forests, and islets or houses that balance heat and cold. "You must resort to secluded and enjoyable places that are pleasing to the mind: Since on mountain peaks the cognitive capacity clears and expands, they are places to dispel depression... on glaciers holistic feeling becomes irradiating and lucent and intrinsic awareness even more clear... in dense forest the cognitive capacity becomes settled in itself and stabilization of mind takes place. They are the places to cultivate inner calm."

After reading this I spent the afternoon climbing 2,000 feet to the top of a hill 11,000 feet above sea level in central Nevada. All around were mountains and sagebrush desert. The hill had pine trees on it. The wind was blowing at about 40 to 50 mph. There were jeep roads all over the hillsides, and I passed several cars on four-wheeled drive jaunts. The inhabitants looked at me strangely, as if it were odd to be walking up the hills. I sat to meditate in the wind and sun. The wind was penetrating and sometimes hurt. Finally, I got out of the wind by sitting in a hollow behind some boulders and trees. I could warm myself. The view and the wind certainly did lift my spirit, yet in the exhilaration of hiking my mind continued to chatter along.

Although I was having an enjoyable time, it was not a place I would want to be if the weather worsened. There would be no protection from the howling wind or rain or cold. The autumn wind was a clear sign that it was time to find a more enclosed habitat for winter meditation, as the text prescribed.

The text also recommends natural things that are useful in cultivating Buddhist understandings and other things to be avoided. Its suggestions are reminiscent of Visuddhimagga's on the influences of different places:

> Rocks remind one of impermanence and disgust with that which does not last,
> River Banks remind not to hold on to the present.
> Houses, markets, solitary trees, people and goblins may be upsetting for beginners, but are good for the experienced.
> Caverns with languorous atmosphere are places where lust is born, but also depression and elation.
> Solitary trees are associated with afflatus, and dangerous rocks and mountains with giddiness
> Places with lovely flowers, at first are pleasing, but later create obstacles.[10]

The text goes on to describe how places can support qualities of mind. The analogies are not very specific: high localities, e.g., mountains, for gaining wider perspective, etc. It is interesting that the last line above warns about the obstacles created by the very things which now draw people to nature.

In other Tibetan texts, such as the *Narrative of Joyfulness in the Forest*, the forest is endowed with majestic trees, fruits, flowers' smells, stars; "birds and deer move about in peace." There are singing honeybees, dancing trees, lotus covered ponds and excellent rain showers.[11] "In the forest the peace of absorption grows naturally." One is instructed how to meditate in a hut, cave or at the foot of tree, surviving on water and fruit:

In the forest, by the example of dead leaves
Come to realize that the body, youth, senses
Change gradually and do not possess any true essence, and
that all types of prosperity are certain to decline.
By the example of the separation of leaves and trees
Come to realize that friends, enemies, as well as one's own
body,
... are bound to separate.
Having realized phenomena in that way,
On a wide seat sit straight and comfortably.
With the attitude of benefiting living beings, meditate on the
mind of enlightenment.

This text goes on to say that one should contemplate with ease the intrinsic nature of the mind. Things in nature teach Buddhist lessons. Empty lotus ponds show that there is no true essence in objects of desire. Change of time and season demonstrate that "the lord of death is certain." Fall of ripened fruit indicate that "all are subject to die, that the time of death is uncertain."

These connections between nature and meditation are not very detailed. Like other Westerners I shared the fantasy of Tibet as Shangri La. In the spirit of this book I feel there must be a mountain tradition in which Lamas faced the elements and lived among snow leopards. I know they did it as metaphor in their practice, but the best can I do is to guess from the hints given above that there may have been a complex relationship between meditation and nature in Lamaistic Buddhism. A deeper understanding of Tibetan Buddhism's relationship to the wild awaits a true scholar of Vajrajana.

Chapter Notes

Chapter 1

1. Although, as Barcelona Museum of Science Director Jorge Wagensberg points out, the footprints in Tanzania on which this diorama is based do not show a couple walking hand-in-hand with a child but rather an australopithecine walking ahead, a female walking behind, and a child weaving in and out between them—a possibly less idyllic but more realistic scene.
2. Fisher, C., 2007, *Dismantling Discontent*.

Chapter 2

1. Buddha, G., 1995, *The Middle Length Discourses of the Buddha*, pp. 145 ff.
2. Caras, R., 1975, *Dangerous to Man*.
3. Geertz, C., 1940, *Agricultural Involution*.
4. Chowdhury, KA, 1978, *Ancient Agriculture and Forestry in North India*.
5. Sharma, R., 1983, "Material Culture and Social Formations in Early India."
6. Sarao, K. 1990, *Urban Centres and Urbanisation as Reflected in the Pali Vinaya and Sutta Pitakas*, p. 169.
7. See the companion volume to this book, *Dismantling Discontent*, for a more complete development of these ideas and references.
8. Gombrich, R., 1988, *Theravada Buddhism*, p. 37.
9. Schultes, R., 1976, *Hallucinogenic Plants*.
10. Heinrich, C., 2002, *Magic Mushrooms in Religion and Alchemy*.
11. Gokhale, B., 1980, "Early Buddhism and the Brahmanas."
12. Dutt, S., 1960, *Early Buddhist Monachism*, p. 42.
13. Randhawa, M., 1980, *A History of Agriculture in India*, p. 303; Olivelle, P., 1996, *Upanisads*, p. xli.
14. Grover, U., 1987, *Symbolism in the Aranyakas and Their Impact*

on the Upanisads, p. 43; Lipner, J., 1994, *Hindus*, pp. 36–37.

15. Especially Gombrich, R., 1996, *How Buddhism Began*, arguing for Buddhism as response to Brahmanism, and Norman, KR, 1997, *A Philological Approach to Buddhism*, questioning that. See also, Williams, P., 2000, *Buddhist Thought*.

16. Gombrich, R., 1988, *Theravada Buddhism*, p. 32.

17. Ibid.

18. Ibid., p. 34.

19. Ray, R., 1994, *Buddhist Saints in India*, p. 9. A quite detailed discussion of the historiography of the existence of the Buddha is found in Penner, H., 2009, *Rediscovering the Buddha*. In Chapter 17 Penner examines the logical inconsistencies of scholars trying to find a historical Buddha. They disavow myth and unreliable texts but usually come around to conclude there must have been a Buddha, since these sources say there was.

20. Williams, P., 1989, *Mahayana Buddhism*.

21. Ling, T., 1973, *The Buddha*. The biographies are found in the Sanskrit *Mahavatsu* and Ashvagosa's *Buddhacarita*.

22. Kosambi, D., 1965, *Ancient India*, p. 123.

23. Dutt, S., 1960, *Early Buddhist Monachism*, p. 48.

24. Mahasi Sayadaw, 1981, *The Wheel of Dhamma*; Khantipalo, B. (n.d.), *The Splendour of Enlightenment: A Life of the Buddha*.

25. Hanh, TN, 1991, *Old Path, White Clouds*, pp. 102–103.

26. Retold very romantically in Mitchell, R., 1989, *The Buddha*. This story is based on commentaries which came hundreds of year after the Buddha's time. See also, Penner, H., 2009, *Rediscovering the Buddha*, p. 35, for a slightly different version: vanquishing doubt with the sincerity of the compassion of one of the Buddha's earlier births.

27. Buddha, G., 1995, *The Middle Length Discourses of the Buddha*, p. 145.

28. Dhirasekara, J., 1982, *Buddhist Monastic Discipline*, p. 7.

29. Ibid. p. 71.

30. Ibid.
31. The word used is "a Brahmana." Dutt, S., 1960, *Early Buddhist Monachism*, pp. 91–93. By the word *Brahmin* and its various forms, the Buddha often meant a person of meditative attainments rather than a person from the Brahmin caste.
32. Chalmers, L., 1932, *Suttanipata*, p. 13, which is inaccurate because bamboo spreads vegetatively, growing in extensive clumps.
33. Norman, KR, 1985, *The Rhinoceros Horn*, pp. 7–8.
34. Dutt, S., 1960. *Early Buddhist Monachism*, pp. 91–93.
35. Norman, KR, 1985, *The Rhinoceros Horn*, p. 7–8, translation slightly modified. The characterization of rhinos as solitary is true for adult males and nonbreeding females. Subadults are highly social animals.
36. Ibid., p. 10.
37. Ibid., pp. 7, 10.
38. Chalmers, L., 1932, *Suttanipata*, p. 11.
39. Zysk, K., 1991, *Asceticism and Healing in Ancient India*, p. 102.
40. Norman, KR, 1985, *The Rhinoceros Horn*, p. 8.
41. Ibid., p. 7.
42. Chalmers, L., 1932, *Suttanipata*, p. 21.
43. Norman, KR, 1997, *A Philological Approach to Buddhism*, p. 84 (Nidd I 89, 17–29).
44. Murcott, S., 1991, *The First Buddhist Women*, pp. 6, 11.
45. Ray, R., 1994, *Buddhist Saints in India*, p. 83.
46. Ibid., p. 84.
47. Ibid.
48. Ibid., pp. 84–87.
49. Norman, KR, 1969–1971, *The Elders' Verses*.
50. Rhys-Davids, C., 1941, *Poems of Cloister and Jungle: A Buddhist Anthology*, p. 39, quoted in Bloom, A., 1972, "Buddhism, Nature and the Environment," p. 117.
51. Rhys-Davids, C., 1941, *Poems of Cloister and Jungle: A*

Buddhist Anthology, p. 22.

52. Ibid., pp. 31, 40.

53. Ibid., p. 41.

54. Basham, A., 1980, "The Background to the Rise of Buddhism," p. 16. E.g., the Mbuti and !Kung.

55. Wagle, N., 1966, Society at the Time of the Buddha, p. 15.

56. Rhys-Davids, C., 1941, Poems of Cloister and Jungle: A Buddhist Anthology, p. 49.

57. Murcott, S., 1991, The First Buddhist Women, p. 48.

58. Rawat, A. (Ed.), 1991, History of Forestry in India, p. 130.

59. Ramayana book 1, Chapter 2, Verse 10 ff.

60. Gadgil, M. & Guha, R., 1992, This Fissured Land, pp. 80–81.

61. Randhawa, M., 1980, A History of Agriculture in India, pp. 336, 377.

62. Ibid., p. 371.

63. Norman, KR, 1997, A Philological Approach to Buddhism, p. 117.

64. Sharma, R., 1983, Perspectives in Social and Economic History of Early India, p. 136.

65. Cf., Freeman, C., 2003, The Closing of the Western Mind.

66. Auboyer, J., 1961, Daily Life in Ancient India: From 200 BC to 700 AD, p. 73.

67. Norman, KR, 1983, "The Pratyeka-Buddha in Buddhism and Jainism.".

68. Ray, R. 1994, Buddhist Saints in India.

69. Ibid., p. 114.

70. Ibid.

71. Cone, M. & Gombrich, R., 1977, The Perfect Generosity of Prince Vessantara.

72. Harza, K., 1994, Pali Language and Literature

73. From conversations with Thanissaro Bhikku. The versions here are my responsibility. I don't completely understand what is known about these changes.

74. Gombrich, R., 1988, Theravada Buddhism, p. 13.

75. Basham, A., 1980, "The Background to the Rise of Buddhism," p. 22.
76. Collins, S., 1990, "On the Very Idea of the Pali Canon."
77. Puri, B., 1987, *Buddhism in Central Asia.*
78. Williams, P., 1989, *Mahayana Buddhism,* pp. 7–8; see also, Williams, P., 2000, *Buddhist Thought.*
79. Gombrich, R., 1996, *How Buddhism Began.*
80. Ray, R., 1994, *Buddhist Saints in India,* p. 26.
81. Ibid.
82. Buddhaghosa, 1976, *Visuddhimagga,* Chap. II.
83. Ibid.
84. Ibid.
85. Ibid.
86. Collins, S., 1990, "On the Very Idea of the Pali Canon."
87. Upatissa, 1961, *Vimuttimagga;* Bapat, P., 1937, *Vimuttimagga and Visuddhimagga, A Comparative Study.*
88. Buddhaghosa, 1976, *Visuddhimagga,* Chap. II.
89. Rathje, W., 1992, *Rubbish!*
90. Buddhaghosa, 1976, *Visuddhimagga,* p. 376.
91. Ibid.
92. Ibid., p. 203.
93. Zysk, K. 1991, *Asceticism and Healing in Ancient India,* p. 38.
94. Stonehouse, 1999, *The Zen Works of Stonehouse,* p. 20.
95. Zysk, K., 1991, *Asceticism and Healing in Ancient India.* This is the source for most of this paragraph.
96. Schmithausen, L., 1991, "Buddhism and Nature," p. 12. Much of what follows comes from his careful analysis.
97. Ibid., p. 101.
98. Cf., *Dismantling Discontent* for more detail on this topic.
99. Boowa ÑāAasampanno, AM, 2006, *Venerable Ajaan Khao Analayo.*
100. Schmithausen, L., 1991, "Buddhism and Nature."
101. Ibid., quoted from the Sutra AN IV 246.
102. Ibid., p. 40.

103. Rhys-Davids, C., 1979, *The Book of the Kindred Sayings*, p. 252.
104. Ray, R., 1994, *Buddhist Saints in India*, p. 114 and elsewhere.
105. Strong, J., 1992, *The Legend and Cult of Upagupta*.
106. Schmithausen, L., 1991, "Buddhism and Nature."

Chapter 3

1. Puri, B., 1987, *Buddhism in Central Asia*.
2. Ibid.
3. Ji, Z., 1990, *The Natural History of China*, pp. 42–43; Menzies, N., 1996, "Forestry," p. 557.
4. Wang, C.W., 1961, *The Forests of China*.
5. Bodde, D., 1978, "Marshes in Mencius and Elsewhere," pp. 158–159.
6. Tuan, YF, 1970, *China*, p. 38.
7. Stonehouse, 1999, *The Zen Works of Stonehouse*, pp. 20, 22–23.
8. Loewe, M., 1982, *Chinese Ideas of Life and Death*, p. 45.
9. Martin, C., 1992, *In the Spirit of the Earth*, p. 75.
10. Lee, J., 1978, Migration and Expansion in Chinese History, p. 21.
11. Schafer, E., 1967, *The Vermilion Bird*, p. 14.
12. Ibid., p. 119.
13. Ji, Z., 1990, *The Natural History of China*.
14. Bynner, W., 1944, *The Way of Life According to Lao Tzu*, no. 23.
15. Mitchell, S., 1988, *Tao te Ching*, pp. 28, 29, 59.
16. Chuang Tzu, 1968, *The Complete Works of Chuang Tzu*, p. 16.
17. Ibid., p. 117.
18. Shaw, M., 1988, "Buddhist and Taoist Influences on Chinese Landscape Painting," pp. 185–186.
19. Schafer, E., 1967, *The Vermilion Bird*, p. 145.
20. The first date comes from *The Zen Works of Stonehouse*, and the second from Porter, B., 1993, *Road to Heaven*.
21. Porter, B., 1993, *Road to Heaven*, p. 66.
22. A modern Mahayana criticism of Theravada can be found in Sangharakshita, 1993, *A Survey of Buddhism*.

23. I am not competent to follow these differences. I have seen references to a literature in Japanese analyzing the complex Mahayana philosophic attitudes toward nature.

24. Hixon, L., 1993, *Mother of the Buddhas*, p. 9.

25. Ray, R., 1994, *Buddhist Saints in India*, p. 407; Williams, P., 2000, *Buddhist Thought*, p. 107.

26. Ray, R., 1994, *Buddhist Saints in India*, p. 252.

27. Ibid.

28. Schafer, E., 1967, *The Vermilion Bird*, p. 90.

29. Fa-hsien, 1968, *Travels of Fa-hian and Sung-yun*.

30. Gombrich, R., 1996, *How Buddhism Began*; Kulke, H. & Rothermund, D., 1986, *History of India*, p. 244.

31. Gernet, J., 1995, *Buddhism in Chinese Society*, pp. 4, 248.

32. Ibid.

33. Porter, B., 1993, *Road to Heaven*, p. 88.

34. Heine, S., 2002, *Opening a Mountain*, p. 56.

35. Zürcher, E., 1972, *The Buddhist Conquest of China*, p. 145. One Yu Fa-la mentions *dhyana* as the source of his ascetic abilities.

36. Matsunaga, A. & Matsunaga, D., 1976, *Foundation of Japanese Buddhism*. T'ien T'ai meditation formulated by Chih-I (538–597).

37. Heine, S., 2002, *Opening a Mountain*.

38. McRae, J., 1986, *The Northern School and the Formation of Early Ch'an Buddhism*, p. 19.

39. Dumoulin, H., 1963, *A History of Zen Buddhism*, p. 67.

40. Chung-Yuan, C., 1969, *Original Teachings of Ch'an Buddhism*.

41. There is more on this theme in my *Dismantling Discontent*.

42. Henricks, R., 1990, *The Poetry of Han-Shan*, p. 355.

43. Lewis Lancaster at the Harvard Conference on Buddhism and Ecology. April 2, 1996, referring to Jorgensen, J.A., 1979, *The Earliest Text of Ch'an Buddhism: The Long Scroll*.

44. Henricks, R., 1990, *The Poetry of Han-Shan*.

45. Han Shan, 1983, *The Collected Songs of Cold Mountain*, from

the introduction by J. Blofeld.

46. Han Shan, 1969, *Cold Mountain*, no. 7.

47. Ibid., no 17.

48. Han-Shan, 1970, *Cold Mountain*, no. 50, p. 62.

49. Han Shan, 1983, *The Collected Songs of Cold Mountain*, no. 290.

50. Han Shan, 1969, *Cold Mountain*, no. 6.

51. Han Shan, 1983, *The Collected Songs of Cold Mountain*, no. 9.

52. Han Shan, 1969, *Cold Mountain*, no. 7.

53. Sanford, JH, & Seaton, JP (1988). Echoes Down a Frozen Mountain, Poems in the Cold Mountain Tradition by Shih-te, Feng-kan, and Shih-shu. p. 150, unpublished manuscript quoted by LaFleur, W., 1988. *Buddhism*, p. 69

54. His famous essay entitled "Walking."

55. Seaton J. & Maloney, D. (Eds.), 1994, *A Drifting Boat*, pp. 33–34.

56. Han-Shan, 1970, *Cold Mountain*, no. 61 p. 79.

57. Feng-kan, 1984, *From Temple Walls, the Collected Poems of Big Shield and Pickup*, no. 49.

58. Han Shan, 1983, *The Collected Songs of Cold Mountain*, no. 133, p. 134.

59. Ibid., no. 70.

60. Han Shan, 1969, *Cold Mountain*, no. 9.

61. Han Shan, 1983, *The Collected Songs of Cold Mountain*, no. 72.

62. Chung-Yuan, C., 1969, *Original Teachings of Ch'an Buddhism*, pp. 62–63.

63. Hansen, P., 1980, *Before Ten Thousand Peaks: Poems from the Chinese*, p. 35.

64. Ibid., p. 38.

65. Ibid., p. 77.

66. Cf., references to Zen Master Soen Sa Nim in *Dismantling Discontent* or Suzuki Roshi's *Zen Mind, Beginner's Mind* (Suzuki, S., 1970).

67. Shigematsu, S., 1981, *A Zen Forest*. Although these are Chinese koans the translator uses Japanese expressions.

68. Ibid., p. 12.
69. Ibid., p. 55.
70. Ibid., pp. 35, 155.
71. Ibid., p. 87.
72. Stonehouse, 1986, *The Mountain Poems of Stonehouse.*
73. Ibid., no. 24.
74. Ibid., nos. 11, 10.
75. Ibid., no. 36.
76. Ibid., no. 58.
77. Ibid., no. 3.
78. Ibid., nos. 53, 54.
79. Stonehouse, 1999, *The Zen Works of Stonehouse*, p. 5.
80. Stonehouse, 1986, *The Mountain Poems of Stonehouse*, no. 60.
81. Ibid., no. 84.
82. Ibid., no. 101.
83. Ibid., no. 90.
84. Ibid., no. 80.
85. Ibid., no. 94.
86. Stonehouse, 1999, *The Zen Works of Stonehouse*, p. xiii.
87. Stonehouse, 1986, *The Mountain Poems of Stonehouse*, no. 151.
88. Hsu Yun, 1974, *Empty Cloud*, p. 4. The following excerpts from Empty Cloud are found on pp. 7, 8, 15, 20, 23, 31.
89. Porter, B. 1993, *Road to Heaven*, p. 135.
90. Ibid., p. 152, and the following quotes: pp. 137–138, 142.
91. Ibid., 172.
92. Pinkerton, L., 1981, *Resilience on the Margin*; Heinrich, B., 1991, *In a Patch of Fireweed.*
93. Ji, Z., 1990, *The Natural History of China*, p. 45.
94. Tuan Y.F., 1970, *China*, pp. 4–6.
95. Quoted in McLuhan, T., 1994, *The Way of the Earth*, p. 171.
96. Sesshu, 1959, *Sesshu's Long Scroll*, pp. 33–34.
97. Tung, W., 1997, *Tales from the Land of the Dragon*, p. 157.
98. Needham, J. (Ed.), 1996, *Science and Civilisation in China: Volume 6, Biology and Biological Technology, Part 3, Agro-*

Industries and Forestry.

99. Frodsham, J., 1960, "The Origin of Chinese Nature Poetry," p. 91.

100. Ibid., p. 84.

101. Ibid., p. 86.

102. Ibid.

103. Ibid., p. 98.

104. Ibid.

105. Ibid., pp. 98–99.

106. Mather, R., 1958, "The Landscape Buddhism of the Fifth Century Poet Hsieh Ling-yün," pp. 71, 73.

107. Bodde, D., 1978, "Marshes in Mencius and Elsewhere," pp. 163, 165.

108. Mather, R., 1958, "The Landscape Buddhism of the Fifth Century Poet Hsieh Ling-yün," p. 75.

109. Wang, W., 1991, *Laughing Lost in the Mountains*, pp. xxxi, xxxii, lx, 5, 9, 14.

110. Ibid., p. 154.

111. Ibid., p. 143.

112. T'ao Ch'ien, 1953, *Poems of Tao Ch'ien*, p. 29.

113. Ibid., p. 21.

114. T'ao Ch'ien, 1993, *The Selected Poems Tao Ch'ien*, pp. 34–35.

115. T'ao Ch'ien, 1953, *Poems of Tao Ch'ien*, p. 70.

116. T'ao Ch'ien, 1993, *The Selected Poems Tao Ch'ien*, p. 34.

117. T'ao Ch'ien, 1953, *Poems of Tao Ch'ien*, p. 82.

118. Shih, FY, 1983, *li po*, pp. ii–iii.

119. Seaton, JP & Maloney, D. (Eds.), 1994, *A Drifting Boat*, p. 47.

120. Tu Fu, 1988, *Facing the Snow*, p. 18.

121. Seaton, JP & Maloney, D. (Eds.), 1994, *A Drifting Boat*, p. 157.

122. Marks, R., 1997, *Tigers, Rice, Silk, and Silt*, p. 326.

123. Coggins, C., 2003, *The Tiger and the Pangolin*.

124. Cook, FD, 1978, *How to Raise an Ox*, p. 60.

125. Yu, C., 1981, *The Renewal of Buddhism in China*, p. 20.

126. Goldstein, M., 1996, *Mahayana Buddhism*.

Chapter 4

1. Harukio, K. & Kanda C., 1976, *Shinto Arts*, pp. 14–15.
2. Herbert, J., 1967, *Shinto*, pp. 465, 469, for evidence of inconsistency.
3. Hori, I., 1968, *Folk Religion in Japan*, p. 21.
4. Ibid., p. 8.
5. Morris, DR, 1980, *Peasant Economy in Early Japan, 650–950*.
6. Totman, C., 1989, *The Green Archipelago*, pp. 17, 26.
7. *New York Times*, January 17, 1995.
8. Kerr, A., 2001, *Dogs and Demons*.
9. Hori, I., 1968, *Folk Religion in Japan*, p. 37.
10. Keene, D., 1989, *Travelers of a Hundred Ages*, p. 177.
11. Hori, I., 1968, *Folk Religion in Japan*, pp. 161–162.
12. Hakeda, Y., 1972, *Kūkai: Major Works, Translated, With an Account of His Life and a Study of His Thought*, pp. 22–23.
13. Ibid., pp. 49, 47.
14. Ibid., p. 50.
15. Ibid., p. 52.
16. Ibid., p. 51.
17. Ibid., p. 100.
18. Yamasaki, T., 1988, *Shingon*, p. 52.
19. Ebersole, G., 1981, *Matsuo Basho and the Way of Poetry*, p. 433.
20. Saigyo, 1978, *Mirror for the Moon*, p. 54.
21. Ibid., p. 20.
22. Ibid., p. 14.
23. Tokue, M., 1985, "Aesthete-Recluses During the Transition from Ancient to Medieval Japan," p. 173.
24. Ibid., p. 32.
25. Ibid., p. 5.
26. Ibid., pp. 172–173.
27. Saigyo, 1978, *Mirror for the Moon*, p. ix.
28. Ibid., p. 12.
29. Ibid., p. 61.
30. Snyder, G., 1993, "Crawling."

31. Saigyo, 1978, *Mirror for the Moon*, p. 26.
32. Saigyo, 1991, *Poems of a Mountain Home*, p. 19.
33. Ibid., pp. 19, 60.
34. Ibid., pp. 59, 143.
35. Ibid., p. 144.
36. For a contemporary exploration of this see Mountain, M., 1982, *The Zen Environment*, on "being at home where there is no home."
37. Saigyo, 1978, *Mirror for the Moon*, pp. 28, 50.
38. Watanabe, M., 1987, "Religious Symbolism in Saigyo's Verses," p. 398.
39. Saigyo, 1978, *Mirror for the Moon*, p. 25.
40. Cf., *Dismantling Discontent*, p. 46.
41. Saigyo, 1978, *Mirror for the Moon*, p. 89.
42. Saigyo, 1991, *Poems of a Mountain Home*, p. 64.
43. Saigyo, 1991, *Poems of a Mountain Home*, p. 205.
44. Saigyo, 1978, *Mirror for the Moon*, p. 77. *Satori* is a momentary clear realization.
45. Saigyo, 1978, *Mirror for the Moon*, p. 24.
46. Ibid., p. 213.
47. Ibid., p. 56.
48. Tokue, M., 1985, "Aesthete-Recluses During the Transition from Ancient to Medieval Japan," p. 177.
49. Watson, B., 1994, *Four Huts*, p. 91.
50. Ibid., pp. 93, 95, 97, 101–102, 103.
51. Ibid., p. 105.
52. Dogen, 1985, *Moon in a Dewdrop*, p. 216.
53. *Shobogenzo*, quoted in Matthiessen, P., 1985, *Nine-Headed Dragon River*, p. v.
54. Kodera, TJ, 1980, *Dogen's Formative Years in China*, pp. 77–78.
55. Cf., *Dismantling Discontent*.
56. Williams, P., 1989, *Mahayana Buddhism*, pp. 114–115.
57. Dogen, 1985, *Moon in a Dewdrop*, p. 13.
58. Ibid., p. 217.

59. Ibid., p. 105.
60. Kim, H., 1975, *Dogen Kigen—Mystical Realist*, pp. 257–258 (emphasis added).
61. Ibid., p. 254.
62. Dogen, 1985, *Moon in a Dewdrop*, p. 102.
63. Cleary, T., 1993, *Rational Zen*, p. 43.
64. Ibid.
65. Dogen, 1985, *Moon in a Dewdrop*, p. 75.
66. Soseki, M., 1989, *Sun at Midnight*, nos. 6, 7, 8.
67. Ibid., no. 77.
68. Ibid., no. 9.
69. Pollack, D., 1985, *Zen Poems of the Five Mountains*, p. 64.
70. Soseki, M., 1989, *Sun at Midnight*, pp. 149–150.
71. Soseki, M., 1994, *Dream Conversations on Zen Buddhism*, "Landscaping," pp. 111 ff.
72. Pollack, D., 1985, *Zen Poems of the Five Mountains*, pp. 5 ff.
73. Ibid., p. 12.
74. Dumoulin, H., 1990, *Zen Buddhism*.
75. Bassui, 1989, *Mud and Water*.
76. Pollack, D., 1985, *Zen Poems of the Five Mountains*, p. 65.
77. Ibid., pp. 100, 36, 101, 101.
78. Lines from scattered poems.
79. Ikkyu, 1986, *Ikkyu and the Crazy Cloud Anthology*, nos. 89, 93.
80. Covell, J., 1980, *Unraveling Zen's Red Thread*, p. 41.
81. Zuiho, M. & Haskel, P., 2001, *Letting Go: The Story of Zen Master Tosui*, p. 102.
82. Addiss, S., 1986, "The Life and Art of Fugai Ekun (1568–1654)," p. 63.
83. Hoover, T., 1977, *Zen Culture*, p. 208.
84. Blyth, R., 1949–1952, *Haiku*.
85. Dumoulin, H., 1990, *Zen Buddhism*, p. 348.
86. Ibid., p. 350.
87. Ebersole, G., 1981, *Matsuo Basho and the Way of Poetry*.
88. Basho, M., 1986, *Back Roads to Far Towns*.

89. Saigyo, 1978, *Mirror for the Moon*, p. 88.

90. Basho, M., 1986, *Back Roads to Far Towns*.

91. Ueda, M., 1991, *Basho and His Interpreters*, pp. 153, 160.

92. Pollack, D., 1986, *The Fracture of Meaning*.

93. Ibid., p. 270.

94. Ueda, M., 1991, *Basho and His Interpreters*, p. 271.

95. Ibid., p. 275.

96. Ibid., p. 300.

97. Cf., *Dismantling Discontent*.

98. Ueda, M., 1991, *Basho and His Interpreters*, p. 308.

99. Ebersole G., 1981, *Matsuo Basho and the Way of Poetry*, pp. 449–450.

100. Basho, M., 1966, *The Narrow Road to the Deep North*, p. 52.

101. Aitken, R., 1978, *A Zen Wave*, p. 18.

102. Ibid., p. 19.

103. Ibid., p, 49.

104. Ibid., pp. 50, 52.

105. Ibid., p. 53.

106. Ibid., p. 64.

107. Ibid., p. 64.

108. Ibid., pp. 108, 145.

109. Ibid., p. 146.

110. Ibid., p. 162.

111. Ibid., pp. 146, 162–163.

112. Yampolsky, P. (Trans), 1971, *The Zen Master Hakuin*.

113. Issa, 1991, *The Dumpling Field*, p. xv.

114. Ibid., p. xv.

115. Ibid., Introduction.

116. Ibid., p. xii.

117. Ibid., no. 24.

118. Ryokan, 1981, *The Zen Poems of Ryokan*, pp. 29–30.

119. Ibid., p. 28.

120. Ibid., p. 50.

121. Stevens, J., 1993, *Three Zen Masters*, p. 114.

122. See Chapter 5 on the evolution of mind in *Dismantling Discontent*.
123. Stevens, J., 1993, *Three Zen Masters*, p. 152.
124. Ryokan, 1977, *Ryokan: Zen Monk-Poet of Japan*.
125. Ryokan, 1981, *The Zen Poems of Ryokan*, p. 51.
126. Stevens, J., 1993, *Three Zen Masters*, pp. 115, 121.
127. Ibid., p. 119.
128. Ryokan, 1981, *The Zen Poems of Ryokan*, p. 57.
129. Ibid., p. 76.
130. Ryokan, 1977, *One Robe, One Bowl*, p. 16.
131. This is a mantra Zen Master Soen sa Nim recommends to confront the mind's reaction to life. See *Dismantling Discontent*, p. 231.
132. Ryokan, 1981, *The Zen Poems of Ryokan*, pp. 164–165.
133. Stevens, J., 1993, *Three Zen Masters*, p. 115.
134. Ryokan, 1981, *The Zen Poems of Ryokan*, p. 139.
135. Ibid., p. 51.
136. Ibid., p. 50.
137. Ryokan, 1977, *Ryokan: Zen Monk-Poet of Japan*, no. 142, p. 81.
138. Ryokan, 1992, *Between the Floating Mist*.
139. Ryokan, 1981, *The Zen Poems of Ryokan*, p. 144.
140. Ibid., p. 146.
141. Ibid., pp. 146, 147.
142. See *Dismantling Discontent*, Chapter 6.
143. Ryokan, 1981, *The Zen Poems of Ryokan*, p. 52.
144. Stevens, J., 1993, *Three Zen Masters*, p. 132.
145. Ibid. p. 137.

Chapter 5

1. Pendleton, R., 1962, *Thailand, Aspects of Landscape and Life*, p. 109.
2. Tate, A., 1993, *The Autobiography of a Forest Monk*, pp. 29–30.
3. Taylor, J., 1993, *Forest Monks and the Nation-State*, p. 81.
4. The form of address *Ajaan* in Thailand is an honorific title

derived from the Sanskrit *Acharya*, meaning honored teacher.

5. Taylor, J., 1993, *Forest Monks and the Nation-State*, p. 79.

6. Ibid., p. 35.

7. Quoted in Tiyavanich, K., 1993, *The Wandering Forest Monks in Thailand 1900–1992*, p. 455.

8. Tate, A., 1993, *The Autobiography of a Forest Monk*, p. 63; subsequent quotes: pp. 74, 85, 97, 99.

9. Boowa ÑāAasampanno, AM, 1982, *The Venerable Phra Acharn Mun Bhuridatta Thera*, p. 43.

10. Tiyavanich, K., 1993, *The Wandering Forest Monks in Thailand 1900–1992*, p. 188.

11. Boowa ÑāAasampanno, AM, 1982, *The Venerable Phra Acharn Mun Bhuridatta Thera*, p. 45; subsequent quotes: pp. 105, 240.

12. Interview with Ajaan Jumnien, July 10, 1996.

13. Lee Dhammadharo, P., 1991, *The Autobiography of Phra Ajaan Lee*, pp. 156–160.

14. Allan, M., 1977, *Darwin and His Flowers*.

15. Lee Dhammadharo, P., 1991, *The Autobiography of Phra Ajaan Lee*, pp. 156–160.

16. Boowa ÑāAasampanno, AM,1980, *Amata Dhamma*, pp. 101–103.

17. Taylor, JL, 1991, "Living on the Rim: Ecology and Forest Monks in Northeast Thailand," p. 110.

18. It also touches on the neurophysiology of mind. His experiences are embedded in mind chemistry, whatever their origin. As he says, he later learned to sniff borneol crystals as a way of helping to balance the energies that arose in meditation. Cf., *Dismantling Discontent*, pp. 249 ff.

19. Many books repeat as a truism that mediaeval Europeans feared the wastelands as abodes of diabolical forces. As we will see, this is too simple a picture.

20. Tate, A., 1993, *The Autobiography of a Forest Monk*, p. 74.

21. Ibid., pp. 144–147.

22. Tiyavanich, K., 1993, *The Wandering Forest Monks in Thailand 1900–1992*, p. 206.

23. Ibid., p. 208.

24. Pendleton, R., 1962, *Thailand, Aspects of Landscape and Life*, p. 102.

25. Tate, A., 1993, *The Autobiography of a Forest Monk*, pp. 144–147.

26. Tiyavanich, K., 1993, *The Wandering Forest Monks in Thailand 1900–1992*.

27. Ibid., p. 83.

28. Ibid., p. 99.

29. Ibid., p. 114.

30. Boowa ÑāÄasampanno, AM, 1982, *The Venerable Phra Acharn Mun Bhuridatta Thera*, p. 258.

31. Lee Dhammadharo, P., 1991, *The Autobiography of Phra Ajaan Lee*, p. 19.

32. Tate, A., 1993, *The Autobiography of a Forest Monk*, pp. 170–171 (emphasis added).

33. For more on this subject see *Dismantling Discontent*, Chapter 5.

34. Tiyavanich, K., 1993, *The Wandering Forest Monks in Thailand 1900–1992*, p. 158.

35. Tambiah, S., 1984, *The Buddhist Saints of the Forest*.

36. Boowa ÑāÄasampanno, AM, 1982, *The Venerable Phra Acharn Mun Bhuridatta Thera*, p. 25.

37. Carrithers, M., 1983, *The Forest Monks of Sri Lanka*, p. 291.

38. Boowa ÑāÄasampanno, AM, 1982, *The Venerable Phra Acharn Mun Bhuridatta Thera*, p. 67.

39. Carrithers, M., 1983, *The Forest Monks of Sri Lanka*, p. 238, and the following quotes pp. 85, 284.

40. An elaboration of this point is found in *Dismantling Discontent*; cf., Obeyesekere, G., 2002, *Imagining Karma*. He makes an analogous point that Buddhism adds a universal ethical dimension to the idea of reincarnation which has its

origins in earlier tribal societies.

41. Boowa Ñāṇasampanno, AM, 1982, *The Venerable Phra Acharn Mun Bhuridatta Thera*, p. 35.

42. Tate, A., 1993, *The Autobiography of a Forest Monk*, p. 75.

43. McNeely, J. & Wachtel, P., 1988, *Soul of the Tiger*.

44. See later comments on folk knowledge. Introduction to, Boowa Ñāṇasampanno, AM, 2003, *Venerable Acariya Mun Bhuridatta Thera*.

45. Taylor, J., 1993, *Forest Monks and the Nation-State*, p. 114.

46. Boowa Ñāṇasampanno, AM, 2006, *Venerable Ajaan Khao Analayo*, pp. 38 ff.

47. Ibid.

48. Tate, A., 1993, *The Autobiography of a Forest Monk*, p. 175.

49. Breiter, P., 1993, *Venerable Father*, p. 34.

50. Lee Dhammadharo, P., 1991, *The Autobiography of Phra Ajaan Lee*, pp. 39–40.

51. Tambiah, S., 1984, *The Buddhist Saints of the Forest*, p. 270.

52. Compare Davis, W., 1985, *The Serpent and the Rainbow* and Davis, 1988, *Passage of Darkness*.

53. More on this and what follows can be found in *Dismantling Discontent*.

54. Tiyavanich, K., 1993. *The Wandering Forest Monks in Thailand 1900–1992*.

55. Boowa Ñāṇasampanno, AM, 1982, *The Venerable Phra Acharn Mun Bhuridatta Thera*.

56. Ibid., p. 130.

57. Ibid., p. 155.

58. Tate, A., 1993, *The Autobiography of a Forest Monk*, pp. 155–156. This and the following quote.

59. Siam Society, 1989, *Culture and Environment in Thailand*, pp. 127 ff.

60. Tate, A., 1993, *The Autobiography of a Forest Monk*, pp. 166–167.

61. Boowa Ñāṇasampanno, AM, 1982, *The Venerable Phra Acharn*

Mun Bhuridatta Thera, p. 51.
62. Ibid., p. 238.
63. Tiyavanich, K., 1993, *The Wandering Forest Monks in Thailand 1900–1992*, pp. 431–433.
64. Taylor, J., 1993, *Forest Monks and the Nation-State*, p. 18.
65. Tiyavanich, K., 1993, *The Wandering Forest Monks in Thailand 1900–1992*, p. 484.
66. Ibid., p. 489.
67. The information which follows is based on an interview with Ajaan Jumnien, Merced, CA, July 10, 1996, conducted in the California home of a Thai woman, a schoolteacher, who married a professional American soldier during the Vietnam War. The conditions of the interview were far from ideal. Because the translator was not familiar with either meditation or natural history the accuracy of her translations is not certain.
68. Ajaan Jumnien mentioned a biography in Thai of Long Por Buddha, who died at age 103.
69. Personal communication from Harry Greene author of, 1997, *Snakes: The Evolution of Mystery in Nature*.
70. Boowa Ñāṇasampanno, AM, 1982, *The Venerable Phra Acharn Mun Bhuridatta Thera*, p. 106.
71. Klein, G. & Klein, M. (n.d.), *A Future Beyond the Sun*.
72. Breiter, P., 1993, *Venerable Father*, p. 144.

Chapter 6
1. Tiyavanich, K., 1993, *The Wandering Forest Monks in Thailand 1900–1992*, p. 552.
2. See Chapter 3 on the natural history of death in *Dismantling Discontent*.

Epilogue
1. *Dismantling Discontent*.
2. Bob Stewart, 2925 Evergreen, Arcata CA 95521

3. Her website is http://www.bloomofthepresent.com
4. http://www.impermanentsangha.com
5. This topic is explored in more detail in *Dismantling Discontent*.
6. http://www.shastaflowingwaters.com
7. Cf., *Dismantling Discontent* for some explanation; or many books on the *Jhanas*.

Appendix

1. Tae Heng Se Nim, 1990, *The Teachings of the Heart*.
2. McGovern, W., 1924, *To Lhasa in Disguise*, p. 293; Davis, W., 2011, *Into the Silence* has an excellent description of the Tibetan landscape and wildlife encountered by climbers of Mt. Everest in the 1920s.
3. Kapstein, M., 2000, *The Tibetan Assimilation of Buddhism*.
4. McGovern, W., 1924, *To Lhasa in Disguise*, and Schaller, G., 2012, *Tibet Wild*.
5. Dodin, T. & Rather, H., 2001, *Imagining Tibet: Perceptions, Projections, and Fantasies*.
6. Samuel, G., 1993, *Civilized Shamans*, p. 220.
7. Ibid.
8. Personal communication, Wade Davis. For more on the encounter see Davis, W., 2011, *Into the Silence*, pp. 405–406, 616.
9. Longchenpa, 1976, *Kindly Bent to Ease Us*, pp. 46 ff.
10. Ibid.
11. Tulku Thondup, 1989, *Buddha Mind: An Anthology of Longchen Rabjam's Writings on Dzogpa Chenpo*, pp. 168 ff.

Bibliography

Addiss, S. (1986). "The Life and Art of Fugai Ekun (1568–1654)." *Eastern Buddhist, 19*, 59–75.

Aitken, R. (1978). *A Zen Wave*. New York: Weatherhill.

Allan, M. (1977). *Darwin and His Flowers*. New York: Taplinger.

Auboyer, J. (1961). *Daily Life in Ancient India: From 200 BC to 700 AD*. New York: Macmillan.

Bapat, P. (1937). *Vimuttimagga and Visuddhimagga*. Poona: Author.

Basham, A. (1980). "The Background to the Rise of Buddhism." In A. Narain (Ed.), *Studies in History of Buddhism* (pp. 13–31). Delhi: BR Publishing.

Basho, M. (1966). *The Narrow Road to the Deep North* (N. Yuasa, Trans). Middlesex, UK: Penguin.

Basho, M. (1986). *Back Roads to Far Towns* (C. Corman, Trans). Fredonia, NY: White Pines.

Bassui (1989). *Mud and Water*. San Francisco: North Point.

Bloom, A. (1972). "Buddhism, Nature and the Environment." *The Eastern Buddhist, NS05-1*, 115–129.

Blyth, R. (1949–1952). *Haiku*. Tokyo: Hokuseido.

Bodde, D. (1978). "Marshes in Mencius and Elsewhere." In D. Roy (Ed.), *Ancient China* (pp. 158–166). Hong Kong: Chinese University Press.

Boowa ÑāAasampanno, AM (1980). *Amata Dhamma*. Udon Thani, Thailand: Wat Pa Baan Taad.

Boowa Ñāṇasampanno, AM (1982). *The Venerable Phra Acharn Mun Bhuridatta Thera*. Udon Thani, Thailand: Wat Pa Baan Taad.

Boowa Ñāṇasampanno, AM (2003). *Venerable Acariya Mun Bhuridatta Thera* (D. Silaratano, Trans). Ampher Meuang, Thailand: Wat Pa Baan Taad.

Boowa Ñāṇasampanno, AM (2006). *Venerable Ajaan Khao Analayo*. Vienna, VA: Forest Dhamma.

Breiter, P. (1993). *Venerable Father*. Brighton Beach: Author.

Buddha, G. (1995). *The Middle Length Discourses of the Buddha*. Boston: Wisdom Publications.

Buddhaghosa (1976). *Visuddhimagga*. San Francisco: Shambhala.

Bynner, W. (1944). *The Way of Life According to Lao Tzu*. New York: Capricorn.

Caras, R. (1975). *Dangerous to Man*. New York: Holt, Rinehart and Winston.

Carrithers, M. (1983). *The Forest Monks of Sri Lanka*. Delhi: Oxford University Press.

Chalmers, L. (1932). *Suttanipata*. Cambridge, MA: Harvard University Press.

Chowdhury, KA (1978). *Ancient Agriculture and Forestry in North India*. London: Asia Publishing House.

Chuang Tzu. (1968). *The Complete Works of Chuang Tzu* (B. Watson, Trans). New York: Columbia University Press.

Chung-Yuan, C. (1969). *Original Teachings of Ch'an Buddhism*. New York: Random House.

Cleary, T. (1993). *Rational Zen*. Boston: Shambhala.

Coggins, C. (2003). *The Tiger and the Pangolin*. Honolulu: University of Hawaii.

Collins, S. (1990). "On the Very Idea of the Pali Canon." *Journal of the Pali Text Society*, XV, 89–126.

Cone, M. & Gombrich, R. (1977). *The Perfect Generosity of Prince Vessantara*. Oxford: Oxford University Press.

Cook, FD (1978). *How to Raise an Ox*. Los Angeles: Center Publications.

Covell, J. (1980). *Unraveling Zen's Red Thread*. Elizabeth, NJ: Hollym.

Davis, W. (1985). *The Serpent and the Rainbow*. New York: Simon & Schuster.

Davis, W. (1988). *Passage of Darkness*. Chapel Hill, NC: University of North Carolina Press.

Davis, W. (2011). *Into the Silence*. New York: Knopf.

Dhirasekara, J. (1982). *Buddhist Monastic Discipline*. Colombo, Sri Lanka: Ministry of Higher Education.

Dodin, T. & Rather, H. (2001). *Imagining Tibet: Perceptions, Projections, and Fantasies*. Boston: Wisdom.

Dogen (1985). *Moon in a Dewdrop*. San Francisco: North Point Press.

Dumoulin, H. (1963). *A History of Zen Buddhism*. New York: Pantheon.

Dumoulin, H. (1990). *Zen Buddhism*, Vol. 1. New York: Macmillan.

Dutt, S. (1960). *Early Buddhist Monachism*. Bombay: Asia Publishing.

Ebersole G. (1981). *Matsuo Basho and the Way of Poetry*. Unpublished doctoral dissertation, University of Chicago.

Fa-hsien (1968). *Travels of Fah-Hian and Sung-Yun*. New York: Kelley.

Feng-kan (1984). *From Temple Walls, the Collected Poems of Big Shield and Pickup* (Red Pine, Trans). Port Townsend, WA: Empty Bowl.

Fisher, C. (2007). *Dismantling Discontent: Buddha's Way Through Darwin's World*. Santa Rosa, CA: Elite Books.

Freeman, C. (2003). *The Closing of the Western Mind*. New York: Knopf.

Gadgil, M. & Guha, R. (1992). *This Fissured Land*. Berkeley: University of California Press.

Geertz, C. (1940). *Agricultural Involution*. Berkeley: University of California Press.

Gernet, J. (1995). *Buddhism in Chinese Society*. New York: Columbia University Press.

Gokhale, B. (1980). "Early Buddhism and the Brahmanas." In A. Narain (Ed.), *Studies in History of Buddhism* (pp. 71 ff). Delhi: BR Publishing.

Goldstein, M. (1996). *Mahayana Buddhism*. Unpublished senior thesis, Brandeis University.

Gombrich, R. (1988). *Theravada Buddhism.* London: Routledge Kegan.

Gombrich, R. (1996). *How Buddhism Began.* London: Athlone.

Greene, H. (1997). *Snakes: The Evolution of Mystery in Nature.* Berkeley: University of California Press.

Grover, U. (1987). *Symbolism in the Aranyakas and Their Impact on the Upanisads.* New Delhi: Guruvar.

Hakeda, Y. (1972). *Kūkai: Major Works, Translated, With an Account of His Life and a Study of His Thought.* New York: Columbia University Press.

Hanh, TN (1991). *Old Path, White Clouds.* Berkeley: Parallax.

Hansen, P. (1980). *Before Ten Thousand Peaks.* Port Townsend, WA: Copper Canyon Press.

Han Shan (1969). *Cold Mountain* (G. Snyder, Trans). San Francisco: Four Seasons.

Han-shan (1970). *Cold Mountain* (B. Watson, Trans). New York: Columbia University Press.

Han Shan (1983). *The Collected Songs of Cold Mountain* (Red Pine, Trans). Port Townsend WA: Copper Canyon Press.

Harukio, K. & Kanda, C. (1976). *Shinto Arts.* Seattle, WA: Japan Society.

Harza, K. (1994). *Pali Language and Literature.* New Delhi: Printworld.

Heine, S. (2002). *Opening a Mountain.* Oxford: Oxford University Press.

Heinrich, B. (1991). *In a Patch of Fireweed.* Cambridge, MA: Harvard University Press.

Heinrich, C. (2002). *Magic Mushrooms in Religion and Alchemy.* Rochester, NY: Park Street Press.

Henricks, R. (1990). *The Poetry of Han-Shan.* Albany, NY: SUNY Press.

Herbert, J. (1967). *Shinto.* New York: Stein and Day.

Hixon, L. (1993). *Mother of the Buddhas.* Wheaton, IL: Quest Books.

Hoover, T. (1977). *Zen Culture.* London: Routledge.

Hori, I. (1968). *Folk Religion in Japan*. Chicago: University of Chicago Press.

Hsu Yun (1974). *Empty Cloud*. Rochester, NY: Empty Cloud Press.

Ikkyu (1986). *Ikkyu and the Crazy Cloud Anthology* (S. Arntzen, Trans). Tokyo: University of Tokyo.

Issa (1991). *The Dumpling Field* (L. Stryk, Trans). Athens, OH: Ohio University Press.

Ji, Z. (1990). *The Natural History of China*. New York: McGraw-Hill.

Jorgensen, JA (1979). *The Earliest Text of Ch'an Buddhism: The Long Scroll*. Unpublished master's dissertation, Australian National University.

Kapstein, M. (2000). *The Tibetan Assimilation of Buddhism*. Oxford: Oxford University Press.

Keene, D. (1989). *Travelers of a Hundred Ages*. New York: Henry Holt.

Kerr, A. (2001). *Dogs and Demons*. New York: Hill & Wang.

Khantipalo, B. (n.d.). *The Splendour of Enlightenment: A Life of the Buddha*. Bangkok: Mahamut Rajavidyalaya.

Kim, H. (1975). *Dogen Kigen—Mystical Realist*. Tucson, AZ: University of Arizona Press.

Klein, G. & Klein M. (n.d.). *A Future Beyond the Sun*. Unpublished manuscript.

Kodera, TJ (1980). *Dogen's Formative Years in China*. London: Routledge & Kegan Paul.

Kosambi, D. (1965). *Ancient India*. London: Routledge & Kegan Paul.

Kulke, H. & Rothermund, D. (1986). *History of India*. London: Routledge & Kegan Paul.

Lee, J. (1978). "Migration and Expansion in Chinese History." In W. McNeill, (Ed.), *Human Migration* (pp. 20–47). Bloomington, IN: Indiana University Press.

Lee Dhammadharo, P. (1991). *The Autobiography of Phra Ajaan Lee* (G. DeGraff, Trans). No publisher indicated.

Ling, T. (1973). *The Buddha*. London: Temple Smith.

Lipner, J. (1994). *Hindus*. London: Routledge & Kegan Paul.

Loewe, M. (1982). *Chinese Ideas of Life and Death*. London: Allen & Unwin.

Longchenpa (1976). *Kindly Bent to Ease Us*. Berkeley: Dharma.

Mahasi Sayadaw (1981). *The Wheel of Dhamma*. Rangoon: Buddha Sasana Nuggaha Organization.

Marks, R. (1997). *Tigers, Rice, Silk, and Silt*. Cambridge, UK: Cambridge University Press.

Martin, C. (1992). *In the Spirit of the Earth*. Baltimore, MD: Johns Hopkins.

Mather, R. (1958). "The Landscape Buddhism of the Fifth Century Poet Hsieh Ling-yün." *Journal of Asian Studies, 18,* 67–79.

Matsunaga, A. & Matsunaga, D. (1976). *Foundation of Japanese Buddhism*, Vol. 2. Los Angeles: Buddhist Books.

Matthiessen, P. (1985). *Nine-Headed Dragon River*. Boston: Shambhala.

McGovern, W. (1924). *To Lhasa in Disguise*. New York: The Century Co.

McLuhan, T. (1994). *The Way of the Earth*. New York: Simon & Schuster.

McNeely, J. & Wachtel, P. (1988). *Soul of the Tiger*. New York: Doubleday.

McRae, J. (1986). *The Northern School and the Formation of Early Ch'an Buddhism*. Honolulu: University of Hawaii Press.

Menzies, N. (1996). "Forestry." In J. Needham, *Science and Civilisation in China, Vol. 6, Part 3, Agro-Industries and Forestry* (pp. 540a–668). Cambridge, UK: Cambridge University Press.

Mitchell, R. (1989). *The Buddha*. New York: Paragon House.

Mitchell, S. (1988). *Tao te Ching*. New York: Harper.

Morris, DR (1980). *Peasant Economy in Early Japan, 650–950.* Unpublished doctoral dissertation, University of California, Berkeley.

Mountain, M. (1982). *The Zen Environment*. New York: Morrow.

Murcott, S. (1991). *The First Buddhist Women*. Berkeley: Parallax Press.

Needham, J. (Ed.) (1996). *Science and Civilisation in China*. Cambridge, UK: Cambridge University Press.

Norman, KR (1969–1971). *The Elders' Verses*. London: Pali Text Society.

Norman, KR (1983). "The Pratyeka-Buddha in Buddhism and Jainism." In P. Denwood (Ed.), *Buddhist Studies* (pp. 92–106). London: Curzon Press.

Norman, KR (1985). *The Rhinoceros Horn*. London: Pali Text Society.

Norman, KR (1997). *A Philological Approach to Buddhism*. London: School of Oriental and African Studies.

Obeyesekere, G. (2002). *Imagining Karma*. Berkeley: University of California.

Olivelle, P. (1996). *Upanisads*. Oxford: Oxford University Press.

Pendleton, R. (1962). *Thailand, Aspects of Landscape and Life*. New York: Duell, Sloan and Pearce.

Penner, H. (2009). *Rediscovering the Buddha*. New York: Oxford University Press.

Phongphit, S. & Hewison, K. (1991). *Thai Village Life*. Bangkok: Village Foundation Press.

Pinkerton, L. (1981). *Resilience on the Margin*. Unpublished doctoral dissertation, Brandeis University.

Pollack, D. (1985). *Zen Poems of the Five Mountains*. New York: Crossroad.

Pollack, D. (1986). *The Fracture of Meaning*. Princeton, NJ: Princeton University Press.

Porter, B. (1993). *Road to Heaven*. San Francisco: Mercury House.

Puri, B. (1987). *Buddhism in Central Asia*. Delhi: Banarsidass.

Randhawa, M. (1980). *A History of Agriculture in India*, Vol. 1. New Delhi: Indian Council of Agriculture.

Rathje, W. (1992). *Rubbish!* New York: HarperCollins.

Rawat, A. (Ed.) (1991). *History of Forestry in India*. New Delhi:

Indus Publishing.

Ray, R. (1994). *Buddhist Saints in India*. New York: Oxford University Press.

Rhys-Davids, C. (1941). *Poems of Cloister and Jungle: A Buddhist Anthology*. London: J. Murray.

Rhys-Davids, C. (1979). *The Book of the Kindred Sayings*, part 1. London: Pali Text Society.

Ryokan (1977). *One Robe, One Bowl* (J. Stevens, Trans). New York: Weatherhill.

Ryokan (1977). *Ryokan: Zen Monk-Poet of Japan* (B. Watson, Trans). New York: Columbia University Press.

Ryokan (1981). *The Zen Poems of Ryokan* (N. Yuasa, Trans). Princeton, NJ: Princeton University Press.

Ryokan (1992). *Between the Floating Mist* (D. Maloney & H. Oshiro, Trans). Buffalo, NY: Springhouse Editions.

Saigyo (1978). *Mirror for the Moon* (W. LaFleur, Trans). New York: New Directions.

Saigyo (1991). *Poems of a Mountain Home* (B. Watson, Trans). New York: Columbia University Press.

Samuel, G. (1993). *Civilized Shamans*. Washington, DC: Smithsonian.

Sangharakshita (1993). *A Survey of Buddhism*. Glasgow: Windhorse.

Sarao, K. (1990). *Urban Centres and Urbanisation as Reflected in the Pali Vinaya and Sutta Pitakas*. Delhi: Vidyanidhi.

Schafer, E. (1967). *The Vermilion Bird*. Berkeley: University of California Press.

Schaller, G. (2012). *Tibet Wild*. Washington: Island Press.

Schmithausen, L. (1991). "Buddhism and Nature." *Studia philologica Buddhica*, Occasional paper series VII Tokyo Institute for Buddhist Studies.

Seaton, JP & Maloney, D. (Eds.) (1994). *A Drifting Boat*. Fredonia, NY: White Pine.

Sesshu (1959). *Sesshu's Long Scroll*. Rutland, VT: Tuttle.

Sharma, R. (1983). *Perspectives in Social and Economic History of Early India*. New Delhi: Munshiram Manoharlal Publishers.

Shaw, M. (1988). "Buddhist and Taoist Influences on Chinese Landscape Painting." *Journal of the History of Ideas, 49*(2), 183–206.

Shigematsu, S. (1981). *A Zen Forest*. New York: Weatherhill.

Shih, FY (1983). *li po*. Unpublished doctoral dissertation, University of British Columbia.

Schultes, R. (1976). *Hallucinogenic Plants*. New York: Golden Press.

Siam Society (1989). *Culture and Environment in Thailand*. Bangkok: Author.

Snyder, G. (1993). "Crawling." *Wild Earth, 3*(3), p.6ff.

Soseki, M. (1989). *Sun at Midnight: Poems and Sermons* (WS Merwin, & S. Shigematsu, Trans). San Francisco: North Point Press.

Soseki, M. (1994). *Dream Conversations on Zen Buddhism* (T. Cleary, Trans & Ed.). Boston: Shambhala.

Stevens, J. (1993). *Three Zen Masters*. Tokyo: Kodansha.

Stonehouse (1986). *The Mountain Poems of Stonehouse* (Red Pine, Trans). Port Townsend, WA: Copper Canyon.

Stonehouse (1999). *The Zen Works of Stonehouse* (B. Porter [Red Pine], Trans). San Francisco: Mercury House.

Strong, J. (1992). *The Legend and Cult of Upagupta*. Princeton, NJ: Princeton University Press.

Suzuki, S. (1970). *Zen Mind, Beginner's Mind*. New York: Weatherhill.

Tae Heng Se Nim (1990). *The Teachings of the Heart*. Occidental, CA: Dai Shin Press.

Tambiah, S. (1984). *The Buddhist Saints of the Forest*. Cambridge, UK: Cambridge University Press.

T'ao Ch'ien (1953). *Poems of T'ao Ch'ien* (L. Chang, & M. Sinclair, Trans). Honolulu: University of Hawaii Press.

T'ao Ch'ien (1993). *The Selected Poems of T'ao Ch'ien* (D. Hinton,

Trans). Port Townsend, WA: Copper Canyon Press.

Tate, A. (1993). *The Autobiography of a Forest Monk.* Chengmai, Thailand: Wat Hin Mak Peng.

Taylor, J. (1993). *Forest Monks and the Nation-State.* Singapore: ISAS.

Taylor, JL (1991, February). "Living on the Rim: Ecology and Forest Monks in Northeast Thailand." *Sojourn: Journal of Social Issues in Southeast Asia,* 6(1), 106–125.

Tiyavanich, K. (1993). *The Wandering Forest Monks in Thailand 1900–1992.* Unpublished doctoral dissertation, Cornell University.

Tokue, M. (1985). "Aesthete-Recluses During the Transition from Ancient to Medieval Japan." In E. Miner (Ed.), *Principles of Classical Japanese Literature* (pp. 150–180). Princeton, NJ: Princeton University Press.

Totman, C. (1989). *The Green Archipelago.* Berkeley: University of California Press.

Tu Fu (1988). *Facing the Snow* (S. Hamill, Trans). Fredonia, NY: White Pine Press.

Tuan, YF (1970). *China.* London: Longmans.

Tulku Thondup (1989). *Buddha Mind: An Anthology of Longchen Rabjam's Writings on Dzogpa Chempo.* Ithaca: Snow Lion

Tung, W. (1997). *Tales from the Land of the Dragon.* Boston: Museum of Fine Arts.

Ueda, M. (1991). *Basho and His Interpreters.* Palo Alto, CA: Stanford University Press.

Upatissa (1961). *Vimuttimagga.* Colombo, Sri Lanka: Balcombe House.

Wagle, N. (1966). *Society at the Time of the Buddha.* Bombay: Popular Prakashan.

Wang, CW (1961). *The Forests of China.* Cabot Foundation Publication No. 5. Cambridge, MA: Harvard University.

Wang, W. (1991). *Laughing Lost in the Mountains* (T. Barnstone,

Trans). Hanover, NH: University Press of New England.

Watanabe, M. (1987, May). "Religious Symbolism in Saigyo's Verses." *History of Religions, 27*, 382–399.

Watson, B. (1994). *Four Huts.* Boston: Shambhala.

Williams, P. (1989). *Mahayana Buddhism.* London: Routledge.

Williams, P. (2000). *Buddhist Thought.* London: Routledge.

Yamasaki, T. (1988). *Shingon.* Boston: Shambhala.

Yampolsky, P. (Trans) (1971). *The Zen Master Hakuin.* New York: Columbia University Press.

Yu, C. (1981). *The Renewal of Buddhism in China.* New York: Columbia University Press.

Zuiho, M. & Haskel, P. (2001). *Letting Go: The Story of Zen Master Tosui.* Honolulu: University of Hawaii Press.

Zürcher, E. (1972). *The Buddhist Conquest of China.* Leiden, the Netherlands: Brill.

Zysk, K. (1991). *Asceticism and Healing in Ancient India.* New York: Oxford University Press.

Further Reading

Amaro, B. (1984). *Tudong.* Petersfield, UK: Chithurst Forest Monastery.

Anderson, EF (1993). *Plants and People of the Golden Triangle.* Portland, OR: Dioscorides.

Ang, A. (1989, March). "Taoist-Buddhist Elements in Wang Wei's Poetry." *Chinese Culture* 30(1), 79–89.

Badiner, A. (Ed.) (1990). *Dharma Gaia.* Berkeley: Parallax.

Batchelor, M. & Brown, K. (Eds.) (1992). *Buddhism and Ecology.* London: Cassell.

Besserman, P. & Steger, M. (1991). *Crazy Clouds.* Boston: Shambhala.

Bhasin, V. (1987). *Ecology, Culture, and Change.* New Delhi: Inter-India Publications.

Bodiford, W. (1993). *Soto Zen in Medieval Japan.* Honolulu: University of Hawaii.

Brewster, E. (1975). *The Life of Gotama the Buddha.* Varanasi: Bhartiya Publishing House.

Buddha, G. (1967). *The Middle Length Sayings.* London: Pali Text Society.

Buddha, G. (1987). *Thus I Have Heard: The Long Discourses of the Buddha Digha Nikaya* (M. Walshe, Trans). London: Wisdom Publications.

Buswell, R. (1992). *The Zen Monastic Experience.* Princeton, NJ: Princeton University Press.

Chah, A. (1985). *A Still Forest Pool.* Wheaton, IL: Theosophical Society.

Chakravarti, U. (1987). *The Social Dimensions of Early Buddhism.* Delhi: Oxford University Press.

Ch'en, K. (1964). *Buddhism in China.* Princeton, NJ: Princeton University Press.

Collcut, T. (1981). *Five Mountains.* Cambridge, MA: Harvard

University Press.

Cubitt, G. & Stewart-Cox, B. (1995). *Wild Thailand*. Cambridge, MA: MIT Press.

Dutt, S. (1962). *Buddhist Monks and Monasteries of India*. London: Allen & Unwin.

Dutt, S. (1978). *The Buddha and Five After-Centuries*. Calcutta: Sahitya Samsad.

Fairservis, W. (1971). *The Roots of Ancient India*. New York: Macmillan.

Futrakul, P. (1989). *The Environmental History of Pre-modern Provincial Towns in Siam to 1910*. Unpublished doctoral dissertation, Cornell University.

Hart, W. (1987). *The Art of Living*. San Francisco: Harper & Row.

Haskel, P. (1984). *Bankei Zen*. New York: Grove Press.

Hung Ju, Bhikshu, & Hung Yo, Bhikshu (1977). *Three Steps, One Bow*. San Francisco: Ten Thousand Buddhas Press.

Ikeda, D. (1986). *The Flower of Chinese Buddhism*. New York: Weatherhill.

Ikemoto, T. & Stryk, L. (Eds. & Trans) (1981). *The Penguin Book of Zen Poetry*. London: Penguin.

Jayatilleke, K. (1974). *The Message of the Buddha*. New York: The Free Press.

Keyes, C. (1977). *Golden Peninsula*. New York: Macmillan.

Khantipalo, B. (1981). *Calm and Insight*. London: Curzon Press.

Kornfield, J. (1993). *A Path with Heart*. New York: Bantam Books.

Kyaw Min, U. (1987). *Buddhist Abhidhamma*. Union City, CA: Heian.

LaFleur, W. (1988). *Buddhism*. Englewood Cliffs: Prentice Hall.

Law, B. (Ed.) (1973). *Geography of Early Buddhism*. Varanasi: Bhartiya Publishing House.

Lin, P. (1993). *Lin He-jing: Recluse-poet of Orphan Mountain* (P. Hansen, Trans). Waldron Island, WA: Brooding Heron Press.

Lutkins, P. (1990). *Aspects of the Aesthete-Recluse Tradition in Japanese Culture*. Unpublished master's thesis, Columbia

University.

Maharaj, SN (1973). *I Am That*, Vol. 1. Bombay: Chetana.

Majupuria, T. (1989). *Wildlife Wealth of India*. Bangkok: Craftsman.

McKinnon, J. (Ed.) (1983). *Highlanders of Thailand*. Oxford: Oxford University Press.

Mendelson, E. (1975). *Sangha and State in Burma*. Ithaca, NY: Cornell University Press.

Menzies, N. (1988). *Trees, Fields, and People: The Forests of China from the Seventeenth to the Nineteenth Centuries*. Unpublished doctoral dissertation, University of California, Berkeley.

Minato, M. (Ed.) (1977). *Japan and Its Nature*. Tokyo: Heibonsha.

Nakamura, T. (1957). *Sesshu Toyo 1420–1506*. Rutland, VT: Tuttle.

Ñāṇamoli, B. (1972). *The Life of the Buddha*. Kandy, Sri Lanka: Buddhist Publication Society.

Nyaṇatiloka, Bhikku (1971). *Guide through the Abhidhamma-Pitaka*. Kandy, Sri Lanka: Buddhist Publication Society.

Odin, S. (1991). "The Japanese Concept of Nature in Relation to the Environmental Ethics and Conservation Aesthetics of Aldo Leopold." *Environmental Ethics, 13*, 345–360.

Pali Text Society (1989). *Poems of Early Buddhist Nuns*. London: Author.

Parker, J. (1989). *Playful Nonduality*. Unpublished doctoral dissertation, Harvard University.

Plutschow, H. & Fukuda, H. (1981). *Four Japanese Travel Diaries of the Middle Ages*. Ithaca, NY: China-Japan Program, Cornell University.

Rahula, W. (1959). *What the Buddha Taught*. New York: Grove.

Rodzinski, W. (1984). *The Walled Kingdom*. New York: The Free Press.

Sakaki, N. (1987). *Break the Mirror*. San Francisco: North Point.

Satomi, M. (1987). *Passionate Journey*. Boston: Shambhala.

Shaner, D. (1989). "The Japanese Experience of Nature." In J. Callicott & R. Ames, *Nature in Asian Traditions of Thought* (pp. 163–182). Albany, NY: SUNY Press.

Stryk, L. et al (Trans) (1973). *Zen Poems of China and Japan*. Garden City, NY: Doubleday.

Suzuki, DT (1959). *Zen and Japanese Culture*. New York: Bollingen.

T'ao Ch'ien (1952). *Tao the Hermit* (W. Acker, Trans). London: Thames & Hudson.

Than Tun (1988). *Essays on the History and Buddhism of Burma*. Whiting Bay, UK: Kiscadale. Thomas, E. (1927). *The Life of Buddha as Legend and History*. New York: Knopf.

Totman, C. (1985). *The Origins of Japan's Modern Forests*. Honolulu: University of Hawaii Press.

Trungpa, C. (1978). *Glimpses of Abhidharma*. Boulder, CO: Prajna Press.

Ury, M. (1992). *Poems of the Five Mountains*. Ann Arbor, MI: University of Michigan Press.

Wagner, M. (1981). *Wang Wei*. Boston: Twayne.

Watson, B. (1990). *Kanshi: The Poetry of Ishikawa Jōzan and Other Edo-Period Poets*. San Francisco: North Point.

Watson, B. (1990). *The Rainbow World*. Seattle, WA: Broken Moon.

Watts, A. (1989). *Zen*. New York: Random House.

Wiltshire, M. (1990). *Ascetic Figures Before and in Early Buddhism*. Berlin: Mouton de Gruyter.

Yamahata, DH (n.d.). *Falling Leaves, A Shooting Sprout*. Unpublished manuscript.

Index

CHANGE
MAKERS
BOOKS

Changemakers publishes books for individuals committed to
transforming their lives and transforming the world. Our
readers seek to become positive, powerful agents of change.
Changemakers books inform, inspire, and provide practical
wisdom and skills to empower us to create the next chapter of
humanity's future.
Please visit our website at www.changemakers-books.com

Printed and bound by CPI Group (UK) Ltd, Croydon, CR0 4YY